PLEASE REFER TO PRINTED
RECEIPT FOR DATE DUE

RURAL BANK STAFF LIBRARY

GENERAL SECTION

1. The library, which is available to officers of the Bank only, will be open during the hours mentioned on the Library Notice Board.
2. Subscriptions are payable in advance on the 1st September each year.
3. Each member may borrow four books, which may be changed as often as desired.
4. Each book may be held for a period up to fourteen days. Any book may be held for a further period on application, if it is not reserved. The Committee may, however, determine a shorter period for books in popular demand.
5. Any book lost or destroyed by the holder must be replaced or paid for at a price assessed by the Committee.
6. The Committee may, in its discretion, require borrowers to make good any damage caused to books while in their possession.

REFERENCE SECTION

1. Reference books may be borrowed on the same conditions as those set out above, except that they shall be subject to recall for official use.
2. Special consideration will be given to students borrowing books from this section.

THE PITCAIRNERS

THE PITCAIRNERS

by

ROBERT B. NICOLSON

With the assistance of

BRIAN F. DAVIES

ANGUS AND ROBERTSON

996
Nic

First published in 1965 by
ANGUS & ROBERTSON LTD
89 Castlereagh Street, Sydney
54 Bartholomew Close, London
107 Elizabeth Street, Melbourne

LIBRARY OF CONGRESS CATALOGUE CARD NO. 65-25531

Registered in Australia for transmission by post as a book
PRINTED IN AUSTRALIA BY HALSTEAD PRESS, SYDNEY

To

THE PEOPLE

of

PITCAIRN ISLAND

and

NORFOLK ISLAND

ACKNOWLEDGMENTS

My warmest thanks to Brian Davies for his help in presenting the results of my researches.

Thanks are also due to the following:

Dr Mackaness, author of *The Life of Vice-Admiral William Bligh*, for his help in the initial stages of research for this work; the Mitchell Library, the Dixson Library, and the Public Library of New South Wales for help in checking through records, manuscripts, and books on the subject; Robert Langdon, author of *Island of Love*, for his help with the Bonwick Transcripts at the Mitchell Library; the Norfolk Island Administration for help with the genealogical section of the book.

Valuable help was given by people on Norfolk—Leslie Quintal, Billy Pat Quintal, Mrs Merval Hoare, Mrs Hagar Blucher, Karl Davies—and others too many to name; and I should like also to mention the following persons and institutions with gratitude:

John Christian, Chief Magistrate of Pitcairn Island; the Royal Society in Sydney; the Bishop Museum in Honolulu; the Polynesian Society in Wellington; the Nantucket Whaling Museum; the Auckland Institute and Museum; the Australian Museum in Sydney; Qantas Empire Airways in Sydney; United Press International in Sydney; the Embassy of the U.S.S.R. in Canberra; E. C. R. Raine, of Edgecliff, Sydney; the *Honolulu Chronicle*; the Archives in Honolulu; A. J. Grey of the Royal Australian Historical Society; the Society of Australian Genealogists in Sydney; Bernard Christian-Bailey of Sydney; Parkin Christian of Pitcairn Island; Charles Noack, formerly of the German Navy.

R. B. N.

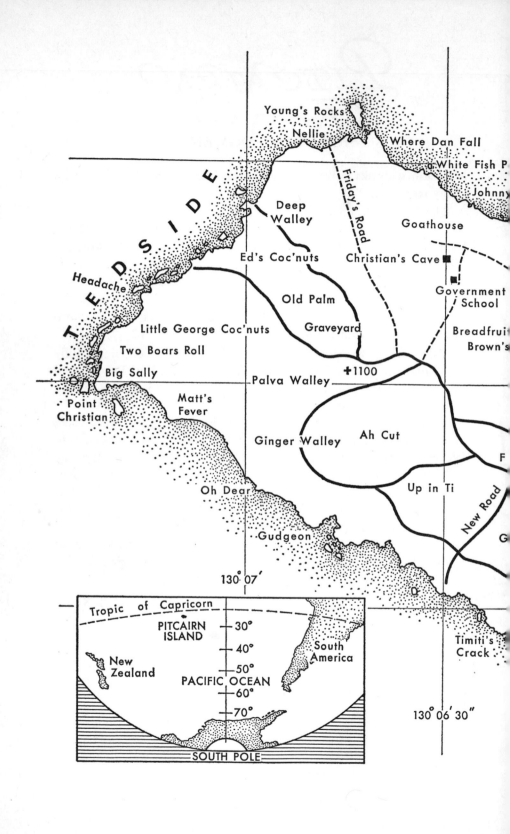

Young's Rocks

Nellie

Where Dan Fall

White Fish P

Johnny

T E D S I D E

Deep Walley

Goathouse

Friday's Road

Ed's Coc'nuts

Christian's Cave

Headache

Old Palm

Government School

Little George Coc'nuts

Graveyard

Breadfrui
Brown's

Two Boars Roll

Big Sally

+1100

Palva Walley

Point Christian

Matt's Fever

Ginger Walley

Ah Cut

F

Up in Ti

New Road

Oh Dear

G

Gudgeon

130° 07'

Timiti's Crack

Tropic of Capricorn

PITCAIRN ISLAND

30°

New Zealand

40°

South America

50°

PACIFIC OCEAN

60°

70°

130° 06' 30"

SOUTH POLE

CONTENTS

ILLUSTRATIONS

It was now the depth of winter in these parts, and we had hard gales and high seas that frequently brought us under our courses and low sails: the winds were also variable, and though we were near the tropic, the weather was dark, hazey, and cold, with frequent thunder and lightning, sleet and rain. The sun was above the horizon about ten hours in the four and twenty, but we frequently passed many days together without seeing him; and the weather was so thick, that when he was below the horizon the darkness was dreadful: the gloominess of the weather was indeed not only disagreeable but a most dangerous circumstance, as we were often long without being able to make an observation, and were, notwithstanding, obliged to carry all the sail we could spread, day and night, our ship being so bad a sailor, and our voyage so long, to prevent our perishing by hunger, which, with all its concomitant horrors, would otherwise be inevitable.

We estimated our course westward till the evening of Thursday the 2d of July, when we discovered land to the northward of us. Upon approaching it the next day, it appeared like a great rock rising out of the sea: it was not more than five miles in circumference, and seemed to be uninhabited; it was, however, covered with trees, and we saw a small stream of fresh water running down one side of it, I would have landed upon it, but the surf, which at this season broke upon it with great violence, rendered it impossible. I got soundings on the west side of it, at somewhat less than a mile from the shore, in twenty-five fathom, with a bottom of coral and sand; and it is probable that in fine summer weather landing here may not only be practicable but easy. We saw a greater number of sea birds hovering about it, at somewhat less than a mile from the shore, and the sea here seemed to have fish. It lies in latitude 20°2' S., longitude 133°21' W. and about a thousand leagues to the westward of the continent of America. It is so high that we saw it at the distance of more than fifteen leagues, and it having been discovered by a young gentleman, son to Major Pitcairn of the marines, who was unfortunately lost in the Aurora, we called it Pitcairn's Island.

—CAPTAIN PHILIP CARTERET,
Account of a Voyage Round the World

INTRODUCTION

Pitcairn Island is a small volcanic island situated in the South Pacific Ocean at latitude 25°04′ south and longitude 130°06′ west. It is roughly 1350 miles east-south-east of Tahiti; 1910 miles east by south of Raratonga in the Cook Islands; 3320 miles east by south of its administrative head-quarters in Fiji; some 3300 miles east-north-east of Auckland, New Zealand, the southern terminal of its main line of communications; and just over 4100 miles from the Panama Canal, the gateway to the United Kingdom, the United States, and the north-east.

It is of irregular shape, about two miles long by a mile wide and, from the best available map, its area is 1120 acres (only one and three-quarter square miles). Flat or flattish land forms only 88 acres (8 per cent) of the total surface of Pitcairn; rolling land covers 352 acres; steeply sloping land 385 acres; and cliffs the remaining 295 acres.

It is a rugged island of formidable cliffs of reddish-brown and black volcanic rock, nowhere giving easy access from the sea.

From Hulianda Ridge just above the landing at Bounty Bay, round the south-east corner where St Paul's Point rises lofty and bristling, through Down Rope, with its tiny beach, past Gudgeon to Christian's Point at the western extremity, the cliffs are sheer and inhospitable, capped by volcanic ash and tuff. Many of the land slopes, too, on the western side are very steep, the highest point on Pawala Valley Ridge, only a few hundred yards from the coast, being 1100 feet above sea level. In the north, from cliffs over two hundred feet high, the land rises a little less precipitously to about nine hundred feet; and the slopes of Flatland, which nestles in the centre, run comparatively gently downwards to the north-east and the settlement of Adamstown.

In local parlance there are a number of "walleys", though many are only minor depressions in rock caused by normal weathering. For most of the year they carry no water, but just west of Adamstown "Brown's Water" is a spring of intermittent flow. The lower slopes and floors of the valleys have soil of colluvial origin and are usually heavily covered with fruit-trees.

Geographically, Pitcairn is comparable with other Pacific islands such as Hawaii, Tahiti, and Samoa. It appears to have been formed by progressive volcanic activity and to be the top of a volcano, the base of which is far below the sea. The rock structure is dominated by basalts with later additions of andesites, trachytes, and pyroclastics and minor intrusions of obsidians and pitchstones.

The population at the beginning of 1964 was 85—a considerable drop from the maximum number of 233 reached in the 1930s.

Much has been written about this romantic island—but much of it has been romance. This account of the island and its people has been compiled, where possible, from original material, printed work only being used where it is substantiated by diaries, letters, Admiralty reports and suchlike material.

The present Chief Magistrate of Pitcairn Island, Mr John Christian, told me, during his round-the-world tour in 1962, that his main concern was that the truth should be told about Pitcairn. This I have endeavoured to do.

PART ONE

MEN OF THE *BOUNTY*

CHAPTER I

MUTINY OF THE *BOUNTY*

MESSRS Boardman and Pope's ship *Topaz* was 140 days out from Boston. The spring gales of the Atlantic five thousand odd miles astern, master and crew had fetched up round the Cape of Good Hope, though many miles south of a landfall, into the southern latitudes of the Indian Ocean. Kerguelen Island, half-way between Africa and the new continent of New Holland, was in the offing. Their quest was seals. Kerguelen would supply them with fresh water and wood for the galley stoves, so that thus re-victualled, the *Topaz* could run south for the Antarctic regions and the fortune in sealskins that was Boardman and Pope's business. The Boston firm's commission was entrusted to the *Topaz* and her master, a Nantucket skipper, Mayhew Folger.

Folger had beaten out of Boston Harbour on a spring Sunday, 5th April 1807.

His journal and log record the progress of his voyage: procuring salt at the Cape Verde Islands, calling at Trinidad, unsuccessfully seeking two scantily recorded islands in the South Atlantic, and finally giving up to steer east "in a high Southern Latitude, for the Coast of New Holland [keeping] to a track quite unfrequented by former navigators, in hopes of falling in with some new islands".

Four months after leaving Trinidad, the *Topaz* was in sight of Kerguelen. But the island was hung with storm-clouds; and the ship's barometer foretold gales even as Folger tried to work his ship to the entrance of a harbour. The weather closed in fast. "There came a violent snow-storm and violent gale of wind which forced me from the land, and thinking I should save time by running for Vandeman's Land, concluded to stear for that place, where I arrived the Middle of October and procured a supply of wood and water in Adventure Bay."

First contact with the strange ship sighted riding at anchor in the bay was made for the infant British colony by the armed vessel *Porpoise*. Signals being made between the two ships, the *Porpoise* escorted the weather-beaten *Topaz* up the Derwent River to Hobart Town. There Folger went ashore and paid his respects to the Lieutenant-Governor, Colonel David Collins. The Yankee skipper also took the opportunity of transacting some business, landing a supply of "rum and Gin". In addition, he took on board "several natives to see the ship and landed them again".

It is interesting to note what happened to the supply of rum and gin. In a dispatch to Viscount Castlereagh on 30th June 1808, William Bligh, Governor of New South Wales, reporting on his arrest, included the following report by Robert Campbell on the "Spirit Traffic":

That the officers of the Porpoise when at the Derwent, commanded by Lieutenant Symons, received from the American Ship Topaz, belonging to the same merchants as Captain Dorr [of the *Jenny*], upwards of Eight hundred gallons of Rum, and one hundred and fifty of Gin, that about three hundred was only on account of the Ship, for which Bills were drawn on the Victualling Board, and the remainder was purchased by the Officers on their own private account, and afterwards Sold by them at two and three pounds per gallon.

The visit to Hobart Town was a welcome break in the long voyage, but the sojourn ended on 3rd November, when Folger set sail once more on the search for seals. Now he set his course for the Chatham Islands, 536 miles east of New Zealand, the southernmost tip of which he passed on his port side as the *Topaz* tacked out into the Pacific. He took his first seals seven months after leaving Boston, his crew slaughtering scores of the hapless creatures on the rocks off Pitt Island, one of the Chatham group.

The *Topaz's* next call was on the Antipodes Islands, 458 miles south-east of New Zealand. There, Captain Folger found "two sealing companies from Port Jackson—but not one Seal".

Fruitless weeks followed, the days becoming colder, and only the heaving swell to meet the eyes of Folger's look-outs as he took the *Topaz* farther and farther south. There were no seal islands on his random course, and no seals to be had. Early in the new year of 1808, therefore, Folger decided to abandon the search in southern latitudes and sail north again in quest not only of seals but of warmer seas and fresh water.

With masts and rigging straining, the sturdy *Topaz* came about and stood to the north while her master consulted his charts. One by one the points of his dividers moved from South Sea island to South Sea island, settling at last on Pitcairn's Island.

Pitcairn's Island had been discovered—a lonely, uninhabited outcrop—

by Captain Philip Carteret in 1767 when cruising in the Pacific in H.M.S. *Swallow*. Recording that there was water there, Carteret described the island as "a great rock rising out of the sea"—just the type of island where untold numbers of seals might be found. But Carteret had made an error in his calculation of the position of the island, and it was not until 6th February 1808 that the island was sighted by Folger:

At $\frac{1}{2}$ past 1 P.M. saw land bearing SW by W$\frac{1}{2}$ steared for the land. . . . at 2 A.M. the Isle bore South 2 leagues dis. Lay off & on till daylight. at 6 A.M. put off in two boats to Explore the land and look for seals. On approaching the Shore saw a Smoke on the land at which I was very much surprised it being represented by Captain Carteret as destitute of Inhabitants, on approaching Still more the land—I discovered a boat paddling towards me with three men in her.

It was a canoe built in Tahitian style, containing three young men, as dark as the crew of the *Topaz* would expect islanders to be, and almost naked. Yet something about their general appearance seemed different. The ship's boat hove to, and Mayhew Folger waited, puzzled, not only at finding the island inhabited but at the appearance of the natives. The canoe pulled up a short distance away, and one of the "natives" called out in strangely accented English, asking Folger who he was and what ship it was.

Folger answered, "It is the ship *Topaz* of the United States of America. I am Mayhew Folger, her master, an American."

This, in turn seemed to puzzle the islanders. "You are an American? You come from America?" one of them asked. "Where is America? Is it in Ireland?"

To this strange question Folger asked in reply, "Who are you?"

One of the "natives" replied that they were Englishmen, and that they were born on the island he could see.

"How then are you Englishmen, if you were born on that island, which the English do not own, and never possessed?" asked Folger.

"We are Englishmen because our father was an Englishman."

"Who is your father?"

In his strange English accent back came the simple answer, "Aleck."

"Who is Aleck?" was the captain's next question.

"Don't you know Aleck?"

"How should I know Aleck?" asked the bewildered Folger.

"Well then, do you know Captain Bligh of the *Bounty*?"

At this, the answer to the riddle of the island burst upon the mind of Mayhew Folger.

For nearly twenty years the world had speculated on the fate of the *Bounty* and the whereabouts of the mutineers, but hope of finding her had been abandoned. The world was tantalized and the mutineers were "sighted" in many different ports, but the *Bounty* and mutineers had vanished into the wastes of the Pacific. Despite hopes and sanguine theories, there was never a trace of her.

Now Mayhew Folger was on the verge of the mystery's solution.

A little more than twenty years before, H.M.S. *Bounty*, "an armed transport" of 215 tons, had sailed from Spithead for Tahiti to get bread-fruit plants to be shipped to the West Indies. The plantation owners there considered the breadfruit would be a cheap food for their slaves.

Through the influence of Sir Joseph Banks, the British Government had bought the merchant vessel *Berthia* and refitted her for the voyage to the South Seas. Renamed *Bounty*, she was placed under the command of Lieutenant William Bligh. Bligh had previously sailed to the Pacific as Captain Cook's sailing master on H.M.S. *Resolution*.

After many delays, the *Bounty* finally set sail on 23rd December 1787, with a crew of 46, including two gardeners to tend the breadfruit plants. For the first two weeks they experienced nothing but fierce gales. After leaving Santa Cruz Bligh split the watch into three, "giving the charge of the third watch to a Mr Fletcher Christian, one of the mates". The captain considered three watches to be more beneficial to the health of his crew than the usual two—and a healthy crew meant a more efficient ship.

On 2nd March 1788 Bligh gave Fletcher Christian "a written order to act as lieutenant". Fletcher Christian had joined the *Bounty* as master's mate on 7th September 1787. In the muster book of the ship his birthplace was recorded as Whitehaven and his age as 21. Whitehaven was the sea-port in Cumberland used for communication with the Isle of Man, where the Christian (or McChristian) family was well known in the history of the island. Actually, Fletcher Christian was born several miles from White-haven, at Moorland Close. The exact date is unknown, but he was privately baptized on 25th September 1764, probably within a day or so of his birth because of the illness that was sweeping Cumberland at the time. There-fore, he had joined the *Bounty* less than three weeks before his twenty-third birthday.

He was the tenth son of Charles Christian, an attorney-at-law. His mother was Anne Dixon, daughter and co-heir of Jacob Dixon. Anne's mother had been a Miss Fletcher, and it was after this well-known and respected Cumberland family that Fletcher Christian had been named. Fletcher's brother Edward, a barrister-at-law, was later to write that "Fletcher Christian was an excellent scholar, having remained at school longer than young men generally did, when they proposed entering the Navy".

One of Christian's first voyages was on board H.M.S. *Cambridge*, when he was eighteen. William Bligh was a lieutenant on the same vessel. After qualifying as a midshipman, Fletcher Christian was given the charge of a watch from the East Indies to England aboard H.M.S. *Eurydice*, under Captain Courtney.

On their return to England, Captain Taubman, a relation of Christian's, suggested that the young man should serve under William Bligh, who was already an experienced navigator. Taubman made the application on Christian's behalf to Bligh, Taubman and Bligh both being from the Isle of Man and personally acquainted. When told that the complement of officers was already filled, Christian offered to serve before the mast until a vacancy should occur among the officers. To this Bligh agreed, and Christian served twice under Bligh aboard the *Britannia*, a merchant vessel trading to the West Indies.

On the second voyage to Jamaica, Christian was signed on as a gunner, but Bligh ordered him to be treated as an officer. The captain spent some time teaching his protégé the use of charts and navigational instruments. When Bligh was chosen to command the *Bounty* after leaving the *Britannia*, it was he who recommended to the Admiralty that Fletcher Christian be signed on as master's mate. So it is quite obvious that before the *Bounty* sailed for Tahiti, William Bligh and Fletcher Christian were well acquainted.

On 11th March, three weeks after Bligh had written that "what has given me much pleasure is that I have not yet been obliged to punish any one", one of the seamen, Matthew Quintal, was given "two dozen lashes for insolence and contempt to the Master".

Matthew Quintal had volunteered to serve aboard the *Bounty*, and with another future mutineer, William Mickoy, had transferred from H.M.S. *Triumph*. Both these men were unsavoury characters. Quintal was only twenty-one, and his companion, Mickoy, was about twenty-five. The latter had been involved in several brawls, as evidenced by the scars on his body and face. They were the last two of the crew that finally sailed on the *Bounty* to actually join the ship.

From 24th March, the *Bounty* encountered thirty days of storms and tempests, with hail, rain, and snow. A superstitious sailor might have said it was a bad omen for the voyage ahead. Many of the crew became ill, and two suffered broken ribs. Showing as much sail as he dared, reefing it when his seamanship counselled, Bligh drove the ship into the teeth of the gales.

Dwarfed by gigantic waves, her crew slipping and scrambling through precarious footholds on rolling, storm-drenched decks, the *Bounty* shuddered her way southward for Cape Horn. The men drew breath between cascading seas to curse the elements for their near-mortal savagery, Bligh for his single-minded resoluteness, and breadfruit, as a fine exercise in Admiralty stupidity to which they had fallen victim.

But more often during those days there was no time to think, beyond making the next stay fast, slackening sheets and shortening them, furling, unfurling, until their numbed minds could not discern night from storm-blackened day, in the struggle to keep *Bounty* on top of the rollers, and not below.

And all this time, one of Bligh's key men was his master's mate, Fletcher Christian: seeing the watch out, driving the men on, driving himself.

Finally, when the *Bounty* was beginning to halt in her tracks at each successive, crashing sea, Bligh—to the intense relief of his crew—turned his back on Cape Horn and set a fresh course, through the still turbulent seas, for the Cape of Good Hope.

The *Bounty* moored at Simon's Bay, Cape Town, on 24th May. The same day Bligh recorded in his log, "Punished John Williams with 6 lashes for neglect of duty in heaving the lead." John Williams came from Stepney in London, and at the age of twenty-six joined the crew the same day as Fletcher Christian. He had apparently been born on the island of Guernsey.

The *Bounty* was refitted at Simon's Bay, repairing the storm damage, and, supplies and water once more aboard, she set sail on 1st July. The next stop was at Van Diemen's Land. Here they spent a fortnight anchored in Adventure Bay on Bruny Island, a little more than thirty miles south of present-day Hobart. Then, more or less on the course Folger was to follow some twenty years later, *Bounty* sailed south of New Zealand, discovering and naming the Bounty Rocks on the way.

Ship's routine progressed normally. The Pacific was calm and gentle. Then, through the neglect of the alcoholic surgeon on board, one of the seamen died. And ten days later, on 19th October, Bligh recorded that "John Mills and William Brown refusing to dance this evening, I ordered their grog to be stop't with a promise of further punishment on a second refusal". Before leaving England, Bligh had signed on as an A.B. a partially-blind fiddler for the express purpose of supplying music so the crew could spend a couple of hours each day dancing on deck—a compulsory recreation conducive to the health of the crew, in the captain's opinion.

John Mills, the gunner's mate, was the oldest of the crew who were to become mutineers. In the *Bounty's* muster book he is shown as coming from Aberdeen, and being aged thirty-nine. William Brown was signed on as a supernumerary "borne for Wages and Victuals" to assist the botanist, David Nelson. The two incurred their punishment exactly a week before landfall at Tahiti.

On 26th October 1788, forty-four weeks out from England, H.M.S. *Bounty* came to anchor in Matavai Bay. With the ship secured, and a tent erected ashore near Point Venus for the botanist and his assistant to store their plants in, the sum of the voyage so far could be expressed in many different ways, and least of the components, by eighteenth-century standards, was the punishment administered by Bligh to his crew *en route*: very minor affairs.

The factor that concerned the choleric captain most was the delays he had suffered—the tedious fitting-out by stops and starts in England, the consequent lateness of his unsuccessful attempt to round Cape Horn, failure of which therefore he could attribute to the Admiralty as much as to the weather—and now, he found, all had combined to bring his ship to Tahiti at the wrong time of year. The breadfruit could not, at this stage, be moved.

Bligh, *Bounty*, and crew would have to stay at Tahiti for another five months—a disastrous delay.

The days began to pass.

As lazily as her off-duty seamen might stretch themselves under the South Sea sun, the *Bounty* rode at anchor, shifting easily with tides and swell, now this way, now that; the island water lapping her hull played a siren song; her shadow grew tall on the bay's sparkling waters; and as to which was the pleasanter time to be ashore—the velvet dusks and whispering nights of moonlight or the noon-hot days—her men were

undecided. The Tahitian women were not over-concerned with the problem. They made love to the Englishmen, willingly and casually, at any
time of day.

Indeed, few sailors anywhere can have had such a reception ashore.
They spent the days and the nights making love, the women passing from
hand to hand, enamoured of each and all of the fair-skinned visitors.

There was only Captain Bligh to introduce a note of reality. (And he,
as far as records attest, celibate, to set his men an example!)

On 3rd November 1788 he noted: "Several petty thefts having been
committed by the natives owing to the negligence and inattention of the
Petty Officers and men, which has always more or less a tendency to
alarm the chiefs, I was under the necessity this afternoon to punish Alex^r
Smith 12 lashes for suffering the gudgeon of the larger cutter to be drawn
out without knowing it." This punishment was given despite the pleas
of the natives, whose lack of Western principles was compensated for by
sympathetic generosity. Their humanity notwithstanding, Smith received
his lashes at the masthead. He is recorded in the muster book as being
twenty years of age when he signed on the *Bounty*, with London as his
home town.

Soon it was Christmas, and on Christmas Day Bligh had the *Bounty*
moved a few miles away to another bay, called Oparre, for safer anchorage
from storms.

January 1789: the breadfruit grows, the *Bounty* continues to wait.
Bligh again sees the chiefs, with whom he is on good terms, and again
he explains to them the service he will be doing them by carrying the
plants as a present for King George. They are deeply honoured that the
great king, so far distant, thus recognizes them. The off-duty watches
from the *Bounty* continue to conduct their "affairs" with certain of the
chiefs' peoples with unabated ardour.

Then three of the crew desert. Bligh hurries ashore again to see the
chiefs. The men must be brought back. The King will be angry that any
of his subjects are disobedient.

Two and a half weeks later, with the help of the natives, the three
absconders are captured and returned to their ship.

On 22nd January Bligh "read the articles of War to the ship's company and punished the deserters as follows: Chas Churchill with 12 lashes
and Wm Muspratt and Jno Millward with two dozen each and remanded
them back into irons for further punishment." Again, on 14th February,
"Punished Chas Churchill with 12 lashes and Wm Muspratt and Jno Mill-

ward with two dozen each as their remaining part of their punishment for desertion and I directed them to be released from confinement."

For the men, assembled to "witness punishment", the reading of the Articles of War was a sobering moment; for the watching natives the whole episode was something of a Roman holiday; but, by the standards of the day, once again Bligh had shown more mercy than retribution to the offenders, and erred on the side of restraint. The officer of the watch, Thomas Hayward, who was asleep on duty when the desertion took place, was put in irons for eleven weeks.

A few days later: "this afternoon I punished Isaac Martin with 19 lashes for striking an Indian". Two dozen had been ordered, but at the request of the native chief of Matavia, Martin was given less. Aged thirty, and a native of Philadelphia, Martin, bearded and bad-tempered, seems to have been of the same breed as the aggressive Quintal and Mickoy.

The heaviest punishment ordered by Bligh was one hundred lashes "severely given" to one of the natives caught stealing from the ship. Tinah, the chief who had interceded on Isaac Martin's behalf, brought the thief on board the *Bounty* with the request that Bligh should kill him. However, the considerate captain was willing to deal no more severely, proportionately, with the native than with his own men. The punishment was, however, a salutary lesson to the rest of the Tahitians.

One thing is clear: Bligh emerges as a just man and a moderate one; the welfare of his ship was his first consideration, and the health and disposition of his crew were implied in this.

Work finally intruded on the crew's idyll. By March 1789 the bread-fruit was ready for transplantation and shipping, and the men fell to, potting and stowing the plants on board. By 1st April 1015 breadfruit plants, and a number of other species suggested to Bligh by Sir Joseph Banks, were safely aboard.

Three days later, 4th April, the *Bounty* was ready for sea. With due ceremony and dignity Bligh paid his respect to the Tahitian chiefs. The crew's farewells to their sweethearts were touching.

On the point of departure, Bligh's relationship with Fletcher Christian warrants examination. In the months after giving his first mate a "written order to act as Lieutenant", Bligh's journal suggests a growing dissatisfaction with Christian's attitude. There was no record of an open breach or quarrel, but Christian does not appear in Bligh's log as a strong right-hand man. Nor, for that matter, was Bligh really satisfied with any of his officers.

From Christian's subsequent relationship with the men, after the mutiny, one could almost deduce that he was too ready to fraternize with them, for the sake of being liked. Certainly, inasmuch as he was as "passionately involved" with the Tahitian girls as any of the crew, it is probable that during the Tahitian sojourn he formed close relations with at least a number of the crew—closer probably than Bligh or any other Royal Navy captain of the day would have considered desirable between one of his lieutenants and the men.

Or perhaps, being a young man, Christian just found it hard to knuckle down to sea-duty again, after such a spell of shore-leave.

Whatever the thoughts in each man's mind, there was no hint of trouble when the *Bounty* finally came to sail, after twenty-three weeks among the easy-going natives—longer than any ship previously had stayed among the Tahitians. Ahead was the prospect of a twelve-month cruise back to England.

One week later they discovered the island of Aitutaki. The next day Bligh "punished J^{no} Sumner with 12 lashes for neglect of duty".

Since the *Bounty* had sailed from England almost sixteen months before, eight of the crew had felt the lash for various reasons—Matthew Quintal, John Williams, Alexander Smith, Isaac Martin and Charles Churchill, William Muspratt, John Millward, and now John Sumner.

On 23rd April the *Bounty* anchored off the island of Annamooka, nineteen days out from Tahiti. For the first time, there was a serious clash between Bligh and Christian.

Parties were sent ashore for water and wood, but the natives became threatening. According to the bos'n's mate, James Morrison, whose journal has survived, so troublesome were the natives "that Mr. Christian, who had command of the watering party, found it difficult to carry out his duty; he informed Lieut. Bligh of this, who damn'd him for a cowardly rascal, asking him if he was afraid of a set of naked savages while he had arms; to which Mr. Christian answer'd 'the arms are no use while your orders prevent them from being used.'"

"Cowardly rascal"—and there is no reason to doubt Morrison—is strong abuse, and one wonders how deeply Christian resented it. It shows up Bligh's bitter tongue—and there is little doubt that many of the crew preferred the lash to Bligh's tongue. Probably Bligh could have flogged them all twice over, and they would have accepted it as part of life at sea with the King's Navy, but his scathing tongue they detested.

The clash between Christian and Bligh went no further, and on 26th

April the *Bounty* cleared Annamooka and pursued her course steadily westward.

On 28th April 1789, south of the island of Tofua, "just before sunrise, Mr. Fletcher Christian, officer of the watch, Charles Churchill, master at arms and ship's corporal and several others came into my Cabbin while I was fast asleep". Thus, simply, did Bligh begin his description of the mutiny aboard His Majesty's Ship *Bounty*.

At pistol point, Bligh and eighteen loyal members of the crew were set adrift in one of the *Bounty's* launches: an open boat 23 feet long, 2 feet 9 inches deep, and 6 feet 9 inches wide. When it left the ship's side the launch was loaded to within seven inches of the gunwale.

As the two vessels drew apart, cries of "Huzzah for Otaheite!" rang out from the *Bounty*. Bligh and his men were left to their fate in the open sea.

In fact, it is now one of the great stories of the sea that iron-willed William Bligh took his tiny, overcrowded boat 3618 miles over almost uncharted seas to reach Timor in forty-one days: a period in which the men on board lived on starvation rations and endured enormous suffering. Only one man died before they reached Timor—a victim of the natives of Tofua. The credit for saving the lives of the other seventeen crew members must rest with Bligh.

The mutiny itself seems to have been carried out without a great deal of planning, and was over before most of the crew—and not all remaining on board were active mutineers—quite realized what was happening.

In another way, the mutiny of the *Bounty* still had to run its course.

CHAPTER II

CAPTAIN CHRISTIAN

The story is now taken up by James Morrison, the bos'n's mate, who kept a rough diary in the form of notes during the voyage and later amplified them into his Journal, now in the Mitchell Library, Sydney.

Morrison wrote: "Mr. Christian now finding himself master of the Ship ordered the Plants thrown overboard to Clear the great Cabbin which was finished by the 1st or 2nd of May and the Effects of the Officers were Collected into it with the Taheite & Friendly Island Cloth & Curiositys, Mr. Christian Himself took possession of Mr. Bligh's Cabbin."

It was not Christian's intention to replace Royal Navy order with anarchy, or to turn to piracy. The well-educated, olive-skinned young man realized that, for him, the mutiny had to be more of a *coup d'état* in that he was taking over from Bligh. How clearly he saw that a mere change of leadership would not be sufficient for the men's plans, or when awareness of the full extent of their power broke through the men's reasoning, conditioned by years of navy discipline is open to conjecture.

For the time being the likable Christian was acknowledged master. Under him, the men saw the half-spoken thoughts and unexplored dreams of their long stay in Tahiti coming to fruition. Now they could satiate themselves in long tropical days, and luxuriate in idleness and sensuousness, enfolded by the warm South Seas and the warmer brown arms of the supple native women.

That the "easy life" and women of Tahiti were at the core of the mutiny cannot be doubted. The spur-of-the-moment act of mutiny triggered off by Bligh's actions had its origins in the liaison between a British sailor, too long at sea, and a Tahitian beauty hidden from sight on the island.

Fletcher Christian planned swiftly. For fear of discovery, the mutineers would find an island and establish themselves ashore. Houses would be built and cultivation undertaken. As to women, the men could make their own arrangements.

However, some of the crew who had not been actively involved in the mutiny, were not in agreement. Morrison's Journal describes how a plan to retake the ship was discovered. The keys of the arms chest were taken and entrusted to Churchill, one of the active mutineers, who, from then on, made his bed on the chest, while "each of Mr. Christian's party were armed with a Brace of Pistols Mr. Christian himself never going without a Pistol in his pocket the same which Lieutenant Bligh formerly used, and a sharp look out was kept by his party one of which took care to make a third when they saw any two in Conversation".

Apart from Bligh's "Cabbin" and pistol, not to mention his command, Christian also acquired his old master's books. These included an account of the discovery by Captain Cook in 1777 of the island of Tubuai, in the Austral group. The next step followed: to go to Tubuai and investigate it themselves as a possible asylum, as Cook had made no landing there.

With the crew divided by Christian into fresh watches, the *Bounty* accordingly got under way for Tubuai, arriving there on 28th May 1789.

During the passage "Christian Cut up the old Studding sails to make uniforms for all hands, taking his own for edging, observing that nothing had more effect on the mind of the Indians than uniformity of Dress".

"When we got in with the Island the Small Cutter was sent with Geo Stuart to examine the reef, and find the Opening described by Captain Cook."

Stewart gingerly took the cutter in towards the reef, tiller in hand, eyes straining for first sign of a break in the churn of surf, feeling the inshore currents snatch at the little boat and envious that, because of its shallow draught, the native canoe approaching could handle the surf and currents so much easier. The *Bounty* men rested on their oars, backing water sufficiently to hold the cutter true, waiting.

Not until the canoe ranged alongside was the natives' intention clear. It was a boarding party!

In the boat-to-boat scuffle that followed, the quick-fingered natives took several items of equipment from the cutter, and were not finally driven off until, terrified by a pistol shot, they fled back to land. But they had at least shown the way through the reef.

The following day, the twenty-ninth, the *Bounty* entered the lagoon and anchored, and the "next Morning weighed and Warped in to a Sandy Bay, mooring with one bower & the Kedje in 3½ fathom two Cables length from the Shore"—no doubt, in view of the previous day's incident, uneasy of its welcome.

In stilted language, Morrison describes the scene: natives fiercely daubed with Polynesian ochres flocking round the ship in canoes, and blowing conch shells, their brown skins clothed in woven reds and whites; on the shore more natives armed with clubs and spears of a "shining" black wood; more conch shells blowing and smoke rising from the villages in the interior of the island.

Tubuai was reserving judgment on its visitors. But the following day, when the natives once more encircled the *Bounty* with their canoes, an old man went on board. He was ceremoniously received by Christian and given presents. Morrison's verdict was that the old man seemed to be of "quite a friendly nature".

At noon, there were more canoes seen coming out to the ship, including a double canoe "full of weomen neatly dressed and their heads & necks decorated with flowers & Pearl Shells".

Now the whole bay resounded to the screech of the conch shells, more and more canoes followed; at least fifty canoes, with fifteen or twenty men manning the paddles in each, surrounded the *Bounty*, with the double canoe carrying the women in the van. One, whom Morrison later found to be a chief's daughter, stood up and began to sing to those on board. Her companions—"young and handsom having fine long hair which reached their waists in waving ringlets", says Morrison—stood swaying and undulating, beating time to her song.

But the *Bounty's* men were wary of a trap. In Morrison's words: "This we supposed that the weomen had been Sent as a Snare as they came so readily on board".

Altogether eighteen women went on board, accompanied by five men. The crew of the *Bounty* were very doubtful of the women, but treated them with civility and gave them all presents. No sooner were the five men on board, however, than they began to steal everything they could lay hands on. This time, Christian acted before the more hastily-tempered of his men could.

When one of the natives stole the compass card, the mutineers' leader sprang at the man and, throwing a grip on him, took the card back. After further scuffling, Christian gave him "two or three stripes with a rope's end".

The whole native party took to their heels, sliding down the ship's sides to the canoes. The last to go leapt overboard. Immediately the other natives flourished weapons they had concealed in their canoes and drove the vessels at the *Bounty*.

Replica of H.M.S. *Bounty*, built for the M.G.M. film *Mutiny on the Bounty*

ON THIS SITE STOOD
THE GRAMMAR SCHOOL WHICH
WILLIAM WORDSWORTH, POET LAUREATE,
ATTENDED AS A BOY.
TO THIS SCHOOL ALSO CAME
FLETCHER CHRISTIAN,
LEADER OF THE MUTINY OF THE BOUNTY
APRIL 28TH 1788

Plaque on the site of Cockermouth Grammar School commemorating
Wordsworth and Fletcher Christian. The date of the mutiny should
read 1789

A ragged cannonade of pistol and musket shot met them. Christian took long enough to aim and fire at natives making off with the ship's buoy, and then mustered a gun party at the double. A shower of spears and stones landed on deck as the gun crew hastily loaded the four-pounder with grape-shot.

Conch shells sounding, the canoes drove again at the *Bounty*.

The four-pounder poured grape-shot into the leading canoes.

Wounded and panic-stricken, the Tubuaians fled, several of their canoes holed and leaking badly. Their blood up, the mutineers lowered the ship's boats and set off in pursuit. And before Christian's last "Lower away!" had sounded, the excited seamen were pulling strongly away. And if those still on board watching the chase needed any proof that the hollow cracking from across the bay was small-arms fire, that the tiny puffs of smoke, white against the lagoon's blue waters, were musket shot, it was there in the natives' dying.

They made a stand on the beach, driving the *Bounty's* boats back with a hail of stones, but when more of their numbers fell, they fled.

Christian learnt later that twelve natives, including one woman, had been killed in the encounter. But there and then the mutineers named it "Bloody Bay".

Despite the bad beginning, the majority of the mutineers were satisfied that Tubuai was an ideal place to settle. The next step, then, was to try to win the Tubuaians over. But the following day there was no sign of the natives, although two of the *Bounty's* boats were sent to the eastern end of the island, and Christian landed at several places, leaving hatchets as presents.

In the morning, the watch on board saw several natives appear on the beach, going to haul up their canoes. Christian immediately dispatched a boat with a young goat and two pigs as presents, but the natives ran away before the presents could be landed.

Not discouraged, Christian, confident in his new-found command, decided to return to Tahiti to procure hogs, goats, and poultry with which to stock Tubuai, or, as Alexander Smith later put it, "to procure stock and some women". This latter requirement seems to suggest the mutineers were not quite so confident of the charms of the Tubuaian girls.

Soon the *Bounty* was ready for sea. She slipped safely through the reef, and once more her destination was Tahiti.

The crew were ordered by Christian to make no mention of the mutiny to the Tahitians, but to tell them that Captain Bligh had met Captain

c

Cook, and that a settlement was to be made on an island. (The news of Cook's death had been expressly withheld from the Tahitians on the strict order of Bligh.) The mutineers' story was to be that they were returning under their captain's orders to obtain livestock.

The crew were also warned by Fletcher Christian that anyone who deserted would be shot, presumably as an insurance against a lone absconder ultimately causing the mutineers to be discovered by searching ships.

And so, seven weeks after leaving Tahiti, the *Bounty* once again came to anchor at Matavai Bay on 6th June 1789. The natives accepted the explanation for the return of the *Bounty* without question.

Morrison recorded that "By the 16th we had mustered about 460 hogs, Mostly breeders 50 goats and a quantity of Fowles a few dogs & Cats, and for a few red feathers we got the Bull & Cow. . . ."

"We prepared for sea Having on board 9 men 8 boys 10 women & one female child, some of whom hid themselves below till we were at sea", but none appeared unduly worried, when told by Christian that they would never again see Tahiti.

The return journey to Tubuai was a very rough passage, and, to set the mutineers' shrewd bargaining with red feathers at nought, the bull died.

Seven days after leaving Matavai Bay, the *Bounty* came to anchor again in Bloody Bay. This time their reception by the Tubuaians was very different. "We now found the natives quite Friendly, and they appeared a different people, coming on board in a peaceable manner without weapons, or conch shells, or the least appearance of hostility."

In fact, many of them were wearing spent bullets from the *Bounty's* previous visit round their necks as decorations! Even more surprising, the *Bounty* men found the natives little afraid at the sight of firearms, whereas when the hogs were landed, the Tubuaians were clearly terrified of the beasts.

The explanation lay in the political division of the island. These natives were not those who had fought Christian and his men on their first visit. They were from a different tribe and under a chieftain called Tummotoa, whose domain included the region of Bloody Bay. The hostile natives were from a tribe led by another chieftain, Tinnarow. The third island chieftain was Taroatehoa, whose territory covered the north-eastern quarter of the island.

All this was explained by Tummotoa when he went on board the

Bounty. He and Christian pledged their friendship and the island prince was given presents of hatchets, highly prized red feathers, and cloth and matting from Tahiti. Since his domain covered a good half of Tubuai, Tummotoa found the news that the whites were going to settle quite acceptable, and the idea of their living amongst his people quite exciting.

To cement their friendship, Tummotoa stayed the night on board as Christian's guest.

The following day, Christian posted a skeleton watch, made sure this time the four-pounder cannon was already loaded with grape-shot, and led the rest of his crew off to explore the island, with the reservation that, for the sake of harmony, Tinnarow's domain would be given wide berth until good relations were restored.

Passing through the lush growth of Tummotoa's lands, with the quick-glimpsed flash of colour as a parrot skimmed the palm fronds before their eyes, Christian's sunburnt sailors felt that the misty green mountains and black sands of these islands were more a part of their life and blood than England's fields and moors. The South Seas were in their blood. And country girls and gin-palace doxies seemed poor rivals for raven-haired beauties as generous with their favours as nature had been with its endowment of their charms.

With such thoughts to occupy their minds, Christian's party crossed from Tummotoa's region, dissatisfied with what it had to offer, into the territory of the third chieftain, Taroatehoa.

Here an even more friendly greeting awaited them, Taroatehoa welcoming his strange white visitors with open hands and heart. A feast was prepared and mats laid for the guests. Fishing parties went off the reef, and the women prepared to sing and dance.

Thus, hours later, garlanded and fêted, Christian exchanged names with Taroatehoa, the custom for very special friends. Moreover, Christian had decided that Taroatehoa's domain, despite its smallness, offered the best site for a settlement. Unfortunately, Christian had blundered.

When Tummotoa learnt that Christian was to settle in another part of the island he became very angry. The mutineers' declaration that they wished to continue their friendship with him was rebuffed, and the offended Tummotoa joined forces with Tinnarow, sending Christian a warning that he and his men, since they had made a choice contrary to his wishes, should never again show themselves in his or in Tinnarow's part of the island. Christian's request for even a talk with Tummotoa went unheeded.

The breach between the two was further complicated by the need to rely on Tummotoa for supplies to supplement the meagre products of his Taroatehoa's small domain.

Undeterred, however, Christian pressed ahead with his plans for the settlement, confident of the superiority of his powder and shot if trouble did occur. At the same time he was mindful of the need to keep firm control over his men. With the island already divided into three factions, Christian must surely have been aware of the dangers of desertion by any of the men or frictions between them.

Perhaps for the first time since the mutiny, Christian was wagering with a false hand, and, as though he was provoking fate, the first open affront to his authority was not long in coming.

With the site of the settlement selected, at a spot on the north-eastern shore of Tubuai where four creeks emptied into the sea, Christian decided the first building, their residence, would be constructed as a fort. One day not long after the clash with Tummotoa, Christian returned to the *Bounty* to find that John Sumner and Matthew Quintal had slipped overboard and gone ashore, despite Christian's order that no one was to leave the ship without his permission.

The two absconders were away all night. In the morning, Christian called them to account.

"We are now our own masters," the two replied.

Christian's response was to pull out Bligh's old pistol and cock it.

"I'll let you know who is master," he snapped, and had both of them clapped in irons.

But it was a hollow display of force on his part. He had not the necessary brutality to punish the two men, and he had not a vested authority behind him to enforce a penalty.

Quintal and Sumner were released the next morning, on a promise not to disobey orders again. To save further trouble, Christian was forced to relax the rule, and the mutineers accepted a new ruling that two men would be permitted ashore each night, and anyone who wished would be given shore leave on Sundays.

The chink had been found; the mutineers', not so much Christian's armour, had they realized it fully, had been pierced. More and more the order drilled into them by years of discipline would slowly disintegrate. Christian might still be in command, but of their own momentum the parts of the body corporate would acquire an independent life.

For the time being, however, this process was stayed by circumstance.

Armed clashes with the natives forced the mutineers back into unity.

It had been decided to call their residence Fort George. The site was purchased from Taroatehoa with some of the red feathers brought from Tahiti. These feathers, Christian had discovered, were more highly prized by the natives than hatchets, nails, or other European tools.

On 18th July work on the project was started. All the men were engaged in it, except a small party set to clearing ground for planting yams. A week later a party of natives ambushed a group of the mutineers out collecting coconuts.

Outnumbered, the men fought their way back to the fort construction. A few days later Alexander Smith was captured. He had been following one of the island girls. He was dragged across the island to Tinnarow's house and made prisoner. A rescue party set out to free him. Word of their advance preceded the vengeful sailors, and they found Smith, in the bush, clad in only his shirt. The only comfort in the incident for Smith was that the girl whose allurements he had pursued had taken no part in the tormenting of the captive, as was the case when other members of *Bounty's* crew were enticed into unfriendly sections of the island. She even followed Smith back to the ship.

Christian now decided to take the initiative. Word was sent to Tinnarow that Christian and his men still wished to be friends, but first the chief would have to return certain articles stolen from working parties.

Tinnarow refused, and Christian sent out a raiding party which drove the natives from the village and burnt Tinnarow's house to the ground, after confiscating his "household gods".

There was a temporary peace, enabling the mutineers to get on with the job of building Fort George. Christian's plans were ambitious.

It called for walls 18 feet thick at the base, surrounded by a moat 18 feet wide and 20 feet deep. A drawbridge was to cross the moat, and four-pounders were to be set up at each corner and swivel guns along the sides. Including the moat, the whole area would have measured one hundred square yards.

The dimensions of this grand design suggest that Christian was something of a dreamer. That his hopes foundered on subsequent events are still visible. Even in 1902 a visitor to Tubuai, Alvin Seale, described the unfinished fort as it then was: "The fort consists of the ordinary military square of earth work thrown up to the heights of perhaps 6-7 feet. Its open side faces the sea, about 300 feet distant; the size of the fort is 125 feet by 120 feet. It is now overgrown with trees and brush and a native house is in the open side."

Today, grass has filled the shallow moat and the wind bowls sand across the square. Seabirds shriek where Christian scolded, and parrots glint and the timeless surf still surges up the beach, unchanging from the *Bounty's* days; South Sea magic seduces just as subtly and impartially those who follow, and the sojourn of the mutineers in Tubuai, for all their noise and bustle, seems only a brief encounter disturbing momentarily a South Sea dream.

But the *Bounty's* men dreamed their own dreams, and so they worked to build Fort George, made love with their women, quarrelled among themselves, fought together against the natives, and laughed, and fished, and joked aloud about where Bligh was, and privately wondered—some of them—whether they had his blood on their hands. All of them speculated on how safe from discovery they were. And each new day began with such a sunrise, they swore they had never seen one to match it before.

About this time they had a remarkable escape.

Unknown to the mutineers, the brig *Mercury*, under Captain John Henry Cox, was in the vicinity. He had been too long at sea to know the story of the mutiny, disclosed at the end of Bligh's astonishing voyage across the Pacific to Timor in the open boat in which the mutineers had set him adrift; but in retrospect Cox reread his log with some chagrin at having obviously come so close to the wanted men without knowing it. "August 9, 1789, In the afternoon, we saw the Island of Toobouai, bearing North East by East half East, distant about eleven league; and at eight at night passed within two miles of it. We perceived several lights on shore, and fired two guns to draw the attention of the inhabitants; but night prevented us from seeing them."

When the *Mercury* reached Tahiti they were quite mystified at talk of Titreano, the Tahitian name for Christian. The natives told Cox that Titreano had returned in his ship, leaving Bligh at Tootate (Aitutaki), which was the story the mutineers had been told to use in explanation of Bligh's absence and the *Bounty's* return. "This story was corroborated by Otoo and several chiefs; who further informed us that Captain Titreano had sailed by fifteen days before our arrival, and had carried several Otaheitan families with him to Tootate. Where Tootate could be, and who they meant by Titreano, we could not then conjecture."

Back on Tubuai the mutineers, unaware of their narrow escape, were beset with problems—thefts by the natives, fights between the women, and Christian's faltering hold on the men. The work of building the fort, begun so readily, was becoming an increasing burden. Better to tend to fo'c'sle duty than sweat away in the sun; after all, had they mutinied only to change one taskmaster for another, and he without the authority of King or Navy to command their obedience? This was not freedom, working and at all times in danger from the savage "Indians".

Two more incidents decided the mutineers to quit Tubuai, and convinced the more superstitious of the seamen that fortune had deliberately evaded them since the first bloodshed in Bloody Bay, if not since the mutiny itself.

On 2nd September, Tinnarow and a group of followers arrived in the half-built fort bearing presents and asking for peace, and the return of their household gods. But they had come like Greeks, and the mutineers were not unprepared.

From the account Morrison has left of how the natives' plot was uncovered, it would appear the mutineers were lying in wait for Tinnarow. An undisclosed number of natives were killed in the first volley, and a short, fierce skirmish drove off the rest.

Apparently Tinnarow had plotted with one of the Tahitians in Christian's party to murder the mutineers and to seize and loot the ship and the men's possessions. In turn the Tahitian was betrayed by Christian's woman, Mauatua, who had time to warn her lover before Tinnarow arrived. The Tubuaians also seemed to have the idea that the moat being dug around the fort was to bury them in after the Europeans had exterminated them!

Their disengaged allies, Taroatehoa's people, viewed these encounters with equanimity. They were still on the friendliest terms with Christian's men, and their hospitality included their women. Their only condition seems a quite reasonable one, that none of the women should go aboard the *Bounty*. Otherwise there was no objection to any of them sleeping with the crew ashore.

But this, it seems, was not good enough for some of the mutineers, and according to Morrison's Journal, they

. . . began to Murmer, and Insisted that Mr. Christian would lead them, and bring the Weomen in to live with them by force and refused to do any more work till evry man had a wife, and as Mr. Christian's desire was to perswade rather than force them, He positively refused to have any thing to do with such an absurd demand. Three days were Spent in debate, and having nothing to employ themselves in, they demanded more Grog this he also refused, when they broke the lock of the Spirit room and took it by force.

Christian's armour was torn away; his hand forced at last.

He was overthrown by the men's demand—so absurd, as Morrison saw —to abuse the kindness of their remaining friends on the island. His leadership and moderation were melted, as Bligh's had been, in the cauldron of the men's passions. One wonders what helpless thoughts he had as the recalcitrant mutineers locked themselves and the grog in debate for three days. Bitter, perhaps, with the knowledge that obviously it would be the last such jointly shared council of war, and held to such fruitless purpose.

Grog and women—as bluntly as that—had finished the mutiny!

Chapter III

IN SEARCH OF A HOME

FLETCHER CHRISTIAN called a general meeting of the crew remaining on the *Bounty* on 10th September 1789. In Bligh's old "Cabbin" heated arguments and discussions took place deciding the future of the twenty-five men.

Christian, according to his brother Edward's account, asked that whatever happened he should be allowed to remain in command of the *Bounty*, as "I have done such an act that I cannot stay at Otaheite". He said he intended to land upon the first island the ship should reach after running before the wind. "I will never live where I may be carried home to be a disgrace to my family," Christian told the meeting.

Although not an active participant in the mutiny, Midshipman Edward Young was the first to agree to follow Christian, and was soon followed by seven others.

It was agreed that the *Bounty* should return to Tahiti and that sixteen of the men would land there, receiving a share of everything on board, including arms and ammunition. Christian, however, was to take the ship "in a proper Condition to go to Sea, with Her Sails Tackle and furniture".

A week later, on 17th September, the *Bounty* sailed from Tubuai. Until the day of departure, Taroatehoa and his people had always treated Christian and his men with great respect, and fear of repercussions from Tinnarow and Tummotoa caused Taroatehoa's younger brother, Taroamiva, and two other natives to join the *Bounty*.

Once again the island of Tahiti emerged from beyond the horizon, growing bigger as the *Bounty* kept her course for Matavai Bay. Two days before, under the lee of the island of Mehetia, the mutineers had divided arms, ammunition, trade goods, wine, and clothing into two shares—one for those going ashore at Tahiti, and the other for those remaining on board.

For the third time, the *Bounty* slid to anchorage in Matavai Bay. The shore party's belongings were shifted ashore by nightfall, and Christian went ashore to make what farewells he thought valid in view of the changed relationship between the landed mutineers and their leader. Heywood and Stewart he advised to give themselves up as being blameless when a warship came looking for the mutineers, as he was convinced it would. To Heywood, Christian entrusted messages to his family. Then he rowed back to the *Bounty*.

It was 23rd September 1789.

There were thirty-five on board: nine mutineers, six Polynesian men, nineteen women, and a baby. The mutineers were Christian, Edward Young, John Mills, Isaac Martin, William Mickoy, Matthew Quintal, Alexander Smith, John Williams, and William Brown.

The majority of the women, with the probable exceptions of Christian's wife and Jenny, Isaac Martin's wife, had been tricked into going aboard, thinking that the *Bounty* would be staying at least overnight. Thus they went readily below to supper and to bed.

And when Christian came back on board they were thus too occupied to notice that the anchor cable was quietly cut and the ship was got under way. The *Bounty* was a mile outside the reefs before the ocean swell caught her and the women realized they had been tricked. In desperation one woman jumped overboard and set out to swim for shore. Probably most of the remainder would have followed her, had they dared.

Having realized the extent of the native women's reluctance to leave their families, Christian took good care to ensure that when the *Bounty* passed the atoll of Tetriaro, twenty-six miles north of Tahiti, the atoll was far enough away to discourage any of the other women from trying to swim to shore. However, once female partners were selected—one each for the mutineers and three in all for the six Polynesian men—the *Bounty* turned round for Moorea, a small island only nine miles from Tahiti, and there put ashore the six women whom nobody had chosen, and who, said Jenny later, were "rather ancient".

The *Bounty* now sailed north by east, while Christian's first choice for a possible home, the Marquesas, came under debate.

There remained on board the nine mutineers, six native men, twelve women, and the young baby, Sully or Sarah. Sully's mother, Teio, or Mary, had formed a liaison with Mickoy, although the baby was not his, as several accounts claim. This made a total of twenty-eight souls setting out, albeit some unwillingly, in search of a home.

When Captain Bligh arrived at Timor he issued the following description of the *Bounty* men, "made out from the recollection of the persons with me, who were best acquainted with their private marks".

Fletcher Christian, master's mate, aged 24 years, 5 feet 9 inches high, blackish, or very dark complexion, dark brown hair, strong made; a star tatowed on his left breast, tatowed on his backside; his knees stand a little out, and he may be called rather bow legged. He is subject to violent perspirations, and particularly in his hands, so that he soils any thing he handles.

Edward Young, midshipman, aged 27 years, 5 feet eight inches high, dark complexion, and rather a bad look; dark brown hair, strong made, has lost several of his fore teeth, and those that remain are all rotten; a small mole on the left side of his throat, and on the right arm is tatowed a heart and dart through it, with E.Y. underneath, and the date of the year 1788 or 1789.

John Mills, gunner's mate, aged 40 years, 5 feet 10 inches high, fair complexion, light brown hair, strong made, and raw boned; a scar in his right arm-pit, occasioned by an abscess.

William Brown, assistant botanist, aged 27 years, 5 feet 8 inches high, fair complexion, dark brown hair, strong made; a remarkable scar on one of his cheeks, which contracts the eye-lid, and runs down to his throat, occasioned by the king's evil; is tatowed.

John Williams, seaman, aged 25 years, 5 feet 5 inches high, dark complexion, black hair, slender made; has a scar on the back part of his head; is tatowed, and a native of Guernsey; speaks French.

Alexander Smith, seaman, aged 27 years, 5 feet 5 inches high, brown complexion, brown hair, strong made; very much pitted with the small-pox, and very much tatowed on his body, legs, arms, and feet. He has a scar on his right foot, where it has been cut with a wood axe.

Matthew Quintal, seaman, aged 21 years, 5 feet 5 inches high, fair complexion, light brown hair, strong made; very much tatowed on the back-side, and several other places.

William Mickoy, seaman, aged 25 years, 5 feet 6 inches high, fair complexion, light brown hair, strong made; a scar where he has been stabbed in the belly, and a small scar under his chin; is tatowed in different parts of his body.

Isaac Martin, seaman, aged 30 years, 5 feet 6 inches high, dark complexion, brown hair, slender made; a very strong black beard, with scars under his chin, is tatowed in several places of his body.

Fletcher Christian's "wife" was Mauatua (or Maimiti), whom Christian preferred to call Isabella. She had accompanied Christian to Tubuai when the attempt to settle there had been made.

Edward (Neddy) Young, chose a young girl called Teraura for his wife, and renamed her Susannah.

John Mills, the gunner's mate, changed his wife's name from Vahineatua to Prudence. The assistant botanist, William (Billy) Brown, had a

Tahitian called Teatuahitea for his wife. No English name has been recorded for her.

The most tragic liaison, as events were to prove, took place when John Williams took Faahotu as his wife.

On the trip to Tubuai, Alexander Smith had sailed with Teehutea-tuaonoa or Jenny. However, this time his wife was Obuarei, and Jenny lived with the American, Isaac Martin. As a memento of her liaison with Smith, Jenny had A.S./1789 tattooed on her arm; tattooing was quite the vogue on Tahiti, and many of the crew had taken advantage of the native tattooists to have various parts of their anatomy decorated. Later, on her return to Tahiti, Jenny gave two accounts of this voyage, which were published.*

Matthew Quintal called his wife Sarah instead of her own name of Tevarua. His friend William McCoy† lived with Teio, or Mary, Sully's mother.

Of the three native men who had sailed on the *Bounty* from Tubuai, one had remained at Tahiti. The two still on the ship were Taroamiva, who had "changed his name" with a Tahitian and was now called Teta-hiti, and Ohoo. Tetahiti's wife was Tinafornea, but after the custom of the islands, he shared her with his fellow-countryman Ohoo.

The three Tahitian men were Minarii (or Menalee), Teimua, and a youngster called Niau. Minarii shared his wife Mareva with the other two Tahitians.

The last of the native men to accompany the mutineers was Tararo (or Talaloo), who came from Raiatea, one of the islands in the western part of the Society Islands. Like the mutineers, Tararo had a wife to himself. Her name was Toofaiti.

The Pitcairn Islanders to this day have a tendency to use the letter "l" instead of "r", which accounts for the variation in the spelling of some of the native names.

One speculates on their lives on board the *Bounty*, for there is no record of their daily routine. But one can readily imagine their days passing in such idleness and sensuousness as sailors can rarely have enjoyed at sea, before or since—decks strewn with Tahitian sleeping mats, the women preparing meals, the men having the run of the ship, and the

---

* One in the *Sydney Gazette*, 17th July 1819, the other in the *Bengal Hurkaru*, 2nd October 1826.

† As "Mickoy" came to be spelt "McCoy", the latter spelling will be used from this point.

Bounty heeling on, sweeping from tack to tack, with the wind now astern, now abeam.

Watch-keeping on the helm and look-outs would still have been conducted with the utmost seriousness, for not only must the fugitives find a home, they must also escape detection. How well the rest of the ship's sea routine was maintained is hard to say, though the starch and discipline duties—those more trifling than necessary—would no doubt have been as quickly flung overboard as much of the breadfruit was.

And if Christian's authority as the mutineers' leader had waned, his role of ship's captain and navigator was undisputed—and respected. Bligh's pupil had learnt well. Moreover, at his disposal were all the master navigator's books and charts. The mutineer crew conceded that Christian had every right to Bligh's old cabin.

And frequently Christian was to be found in the "great Cabbin" poring through Bligh's books seeking a description of an island that would exactly fill his requirements: uninhabited, isolated, and without a harbour for shipping.

So far he had considered many, but sighted none.

Soon they were hundreds of miles to the west of Tahiti.

In retrospect from the present, Christian's voyage on the *Bounty* ranks as an epic of Pacific exploration: a voyage whose findings could never be reported.

Shortly, the *Bounty* fell in with what must have been the southernmost group of the Cook Islands. Jenny said that after many days a small island was discovered, called by the natives Purutea. There is confusion as to whether "Purutea" was Rarotonga or one of the outlying Cook Islands from which the *Bounty* moved to Rarotonga. "A canoe came off bringing a pig and cocoanuts with them."

The missionary John Williams, who visited the Cook Islands in 1823, found that information of Captain Cook's voyage had been made known in the islands. In his *Narrative of Missionary Enterprise in the South Sea Islands* he recorded:

Not very long after this, a large ship did actually arrive; and from the description the natives gave me of her, I have no doubt but that it was the Bounty, after she had been taken by the mutineers. This vessel did not anchor, but one of the natives took his little canoe, and, summoning all his courage, ventured to go on board. On returning to the shore, he told his astonished countrymen that it was a floating island; that there were two rivers of water flowing on it; that two large *taro* plantations, with sugar-cane, bread-fruit, and other trees, were growing there, that the keel scraped the bottom of the sea; for he dived as deep as man could go, and could not see its termination. I account for these singular statements, by supposing that the pumps were at work while the man was on board, which he mistook for rivers, or streams, and that the two plantations, bread-fruit trees, etc., were the large boxes which were fitted up throughout this vessel for those exotics, which it was the specific object of the Bounty to convey from Tahiti to the West Indies. From this vessel was obtained a pointed piece of iron, about two feet six inches in length, which the natives immediately dedicated to the gods. . . .

Although the mutineers had thrown many of the breadfruit plants overboard after setting Bligh adrift, they had kept some for possible replanting at Tubuai or at whatever island they should chance to settle upon, as well as orange seeds, taros, and other plants.

Further indication of the apparent visit of *Bounty* to the Cook Islands was later given by Maretu, a local authority on the early history of the island, to Dr Wyatt Gill. Maretu claimed that Goodenough, who called at Rarotonga during the year 1814, was not its discoverer, since before him,

There came here a very large ship, but the people did not land. Two canoes went off to that ship, and bartered some goods from the white people, amongst them the *Anae*; they purchased these things with fowls, coconuts, and bananas. As they left, a man named Maia stole a large box from the ship, and in it was found the orange and the *motini*. Makare was the name of the captain. One of the chiefs who went on board, named Tamarua, reported that they had *taro* swamps and young banana trees, besides young bread-fruit trees and many packages of *anae,* with stones also. They were wild with astonishment at that ship. It was from thence we obtained the first oranges, whilst Kaputini procured a *mautini* from there.*

The Rarotongan scholar and translator of Maretu's statement, Stephen Savage, affirms that Makere is the Maori transliteration of McCoy. Maude states that "McCoy was presumably the man with whom the informant spoke; was quite possibly in charge of the watch at the time; and may well have conveyed the impression that he was in charge of the vessel". Savage does not give any translation of *Anae* and *motini* (or *mautini*).

Maude points out that "an exhaustive search has established that only two vessels reported sighting Rarotonga before Goodenough's visit, and both passed the island within a few months of the event. Of these, one

---

* Quoted by H. E. Maude, "In Search of a Home", *Journal of the Polynesian Society*, vol. lxvii, No. 2, June 1958.

had no contact with the shore, while the other was known to be short of provisions and would certainly not have given the appearance of a floating horticultural exhibition."

From Morrison we learn that when the *Bounty* sailed from Tahiti she was full of livestock and various plants common to the islands. And from Jenny we learn that the ship carried yams, taro, bananas, and *aute*. Alexander Smith affirms the fact that some of the breadfruit plants were kept on board. Therefore the unusual description of the "trees" growing on the ship is readily explained. It would seem then that Fletcher Christian was the discoverer of Rarotonga.

Jenny's account of the visit states that

One of the natives ventured on board and was much delighted by the pearl-shell buttons on Captain Christian's Jacket. The Captain in a very friendly manner gave the man the Jacket. He stood on the ship's gunwale showing the present to his countrymen, when one of the mutineers shot him dead. He fell into the Sea. Christian was highly indignant at this. He could do nothing more, having lost all authority, than reprimand the murderer severely: the other natives in the canoe immediately picked up their murdered companion, placed the body in the canoe and paddled towards the shore with loud lamentations.

There is no other check on this statement, which does not appear to be recorded elsewhere, but as there is no reason to doubt the rest of her account, her report of bloodshed is no doubt true. Clearly Christian's disciplinary control of the men was ineffectual. One could perhaps profitably speculate on whether the wanton murderer was someone of the temper of Quintal or McCoy, and more on the temper of the ship's company generally. What personal strains and clashes were developing as the weeks of the voyage passed? What jealousies and rivalries between the Polynesian women occurred to set the men quarrelling among each other, now that the order established aboard by methodically imposed service discipline had vanished and passions and emotions had free rein and unregulated time to gather heat and intensity?

Yet Christian must still have imposed some sort of restraint on his charges or the little party must surely have disintegrated. His "written order to act as Lieutenant" was not entirely valueless, although clearly the man's personal authority and undoubted dignity, which in waters other than the South Seas would have rendered mutiny an act beyond his moral capability, commanded a certain respect and loyalty. At all events, while Christian was still plotting the *Bounty's* course he was master. But each blow at his authority, such as the murder of the native, was to prepare the day when anarchy would be the rule on Pitcairn, and Christian's a hollow voice.

For the time being, however, Pitcairn and the brooding shadow of their future had not entered their reckoning. Christian set a fresh course for the *Bounty*, taking her out of "Purutea", and west again on their restless search. The ship rolled in the open sea again, and there was only the salt spray of the sea winds for company as the land breezes and their nostalgic fragrances faded astern.

Jenny continued: "After several days more [we] saw one of the Tongataboo or Friendly Islands. . . ." At this island the mutineers stayed two days and traded with the natives for pigs, chickens, and yams.

The natives told the visitors that Captain Cook had left them horned cattle which were still living. Captain Cook himself recorded that "there were no such animals within many months sail of their island", when he left cattle at the island of Tongatabu itself. From Tongatabu Christian again continued westward. He was now less than one hundred miles from Tofua, the island off which the mutiny had taken place seven months before.

A few days' sailing from Tongatabu, the watch on deck sighted a small, low island in the west.

One can estimate that they were probably about eight weeks out of Tahiti, and it appears that Christian was ready to call a halt to their wanderings, though he can hardly have been satisfied that he was off the "beaten track", or that the island itself met all the mutineers' requirements for a hide-away. But, according to Jenny, "Here Christian proposed to stop".

The boat was sent on shore to ascertain whether the island was inhabited or not. Before they had time to land people were seen on the beach. After landing and remaining awhile on shore the boat returned to the ship with the news. Had this been an uninhabited island, Christian would have destroyed the ship and stayed there. Finding the inhabitants were numerous they sailed away that night to windward.

Doubtless all agreed that attempting to settle when there were all the risks of another fiasco such as they experienced on Tubuai was just not worth their while.

It was a "low, lagoon island, which they call Vivini, where they got birds, eggs and cocoa nuts"—perhaps the island of Ono-i-Lau, in the Fijian

Thursday October Christian

John Adams

group. The island lies on the latitude of 20°39′ S., and Christian seems to have roughly followed the parallel of 21° S. after he left Rarotonga. Another possibility is that the island visited was Vatoa, which is only 209 feet above sea level, compared to 370 feet for Ono-i-Lau. The entrance to the lagoon on Vatoa is also less intricate that that of Ono-i-Lau.

At sea again, Christian turned again to Bligh's books and scanned his charts, looking this time to the east.

Among the books was an edition of *Hawkesworth's Voyages*, published in 1773, which contained a brief description by Captain Carteret of the discovery and naming of Pitcairn's Island.*

Carteret's description of the island seemed ideal to Christian, and, probably not long after leaving "Vivini", the *Bounty* turned east for Pitcairn Island. For some days after leaving "Vivini" the ship had still sailed to the west, while Christian considered the Solomon Islands—or Islands of Solomon as they were then called—but decided their location was too uncertain to warrant a search.

The *Bounty* now had hard sailing, into the teeth of the south-east trades which had hitherto favoured their westward passage. It is likely that the pumps seen working at Rarotonga (Purutea), if that is what the "rivers" on board were, now would be working all the time; for the new course pitted her against the sea, and the jarring ocean beat remorselessly against her planking, straining caulking and seams into a never-ending creaking and worrying of wood against wood. Timbers shuddered and masts strained into the whip of the wind.

It was a long, weary period of tacking to keep the *Bounty* sweeping up and down the latitude of 25° S., on which, according to Carteret, Pitcairn was to be found.

At least once they passed land not many days after turning to the east. From Jenny's description of passing between two mountainous islands, it was probably the northern portion of the Tongan Archipelago. But the wind was too strong for them to attempt a landing, and most were now eager to try Pitcairn.

Yet two months were to pass without sight of Pitcairn, and before very long, Jenny wrote, "all on board were much discouraged; they therefore thought of returning to Tahiti".

---

* Quoted at the beginning of this book. An interesting sidelight appears in a notebook that belonged to Captain Carteret and is now in the Dixson Library in Sydney. The island was named after Robert Pitcairn, the midshipman who first sighted the island. But if it had been discovered by one of the crew, he would have received a bottle of rum!

D

Carteret, in positioning Pitcairn, had erred, setting it two hundred miles to the east of its actual location. At the time of Carteret's discovery, H.M.S. *Swallow* was sailing through heavy storms, and had illness on board, and his navigational equipment was faulty.

But Christian had only to continue running along the line of latitude, which proved to be correct, to encounter Pitcairn.

It was sighted on 12th January 1790, in the evening.

From Tahiti, the *Bounty* had voyaged almost three thousand miles in four months, until now before them lay Pitcairn, "like a great rock rising out of the sea". The sun was just going down. But there was light enough to see the green, wooded slopes, to discern coconut palms and breadfruit-trees—there would be no need of those they had brought along! But if the island looked green and inviting, the coastline was hostile. Rock-bound and set with forbidding cliffs, it was difficult to see where to make a landing. And, in fact, the seas were so rough no landing could be attempted for three whole days.

The *Bounty* circumnavigated the island several times, finally standing off within sight of a small beach on the western side of the island. "One can readily picture the tense expectancy of those last days off the island," Maude writes, "as the little group of Europeans and Polynesians stood at the rail of the *Bounty*, speculating on its suitability for permanent settlement".

And who could doubt that the "little group" was more than weary of days at sea and aching to stretch their legs on shore again? Moreover, if Pitcairn was not suitable they could only look forward to more days at sea again. But, judging from the picturesque island's appearance, only hostile inhabitants could cause them to leave.

Accordingly, when on the fifteenth, the seas had moderated sufficiently to allow a boat to be lowered, Christian led a well-armed scouting party ashore to explore.

With the *Bounty* standing out to sea, Christian, William Brown, John Williams, William McCoy, Minarii, Teimua, and Niau rowed through the surf on the western coast and landed.

The first mutineers were ashore on Pitcairn Island.

Two days later Christian and his party were back on board. He returned, says Adams, "With a joyful expression such as we had not seen on him for a long time past. The island had, in fact, exceeded his most sanguine hopes: in its fertility, its beauty, its temperate climate and, above all, in its now demonstrated inaccessibility, Pitcairn was ideal for his purpose. And in addition, the race which had planted it ready for their use had apparently died out or departed."

The long search was ended. The mutineers, nine months after seizing the *Bounty*, had found a hiding-place and a home. As Maude puts it:

... Christian and his followers had seen much and done much; they had attempted the colonization venture at Tubuai, which even if a failure had given them invaluable experience and a knowledge of the necessary conditions for future success; they had criss-crossed the Pacific three times, visiting the Society, Austral, Cook, Tonga and Fiji Groups; they had discovered the important island of Rarotonga; they had searched in vain for the lost islands of Mendana and Quiros; they had acquired wives and an entourage; and now, after sailing over 7,800 miles from the day they left Bligh and Tofua, the mutineers had found their future home and the *Bounty* her last resting-place.

Chapter IV

PITCAIRN'S ISLAND

Fletcher Christian took his party ashore to make a first-hand inspection of the island. Clambering up the steep rocks, they found water, wood, good volcanic soil, and various kinds of fruit in abundance sufficient for their needs. Alexander Smith (Adams) reported many years later that "We found on the Island, Cocao Nut trees—Plantains, Yams, Bread fruit, Taro, Sweet Potatores, Appai root".

When he returned to the ship Christian informed the rest of the crew that the island was ideal. It had sufficient resources to maintain them, good soil for planting the yams and bananas they had brought with them, and a difficult approach from the sea to deter passing ships. Moreover, there were plenty of hiding-places should any ship chance to send ashore a landing party.

With a sense of homecoming, the mutineers made ready to land.

The *Bounty* was moved to the northern side of the island, to a little bay where she could be taken in close enough to be made fast to a tree ashore. This spot they called the "Landing Place".

Not until thirty-five years later was the name changed to "Bounty Bay".

While the *Bounty's* hawser fretted against the tree bark, the men and women were busy moving everything that might prove useful onto the island. Young Sully, now more than a year old, was taken ashore in a barrel for safety.

The livestock—pigs, fowls, goats, dogs, and cats—were also taken ashore, and the excited squealing and barking might have been heard a league away to sea.

The *Bounty's* sails were set up as tents until more permanent living quarters could be built, and the stores were carried up the 200-foot ascent to the top of the cliff, which they came to call "The Edge". For protection the more perishable goods were placed in caves.

One question remained: what to do with the ship? There was more or less common agreement between the mutineers that she must be destroyed. The problem was how—whether to burn her or run her ashore —and when. Christian was for running her aground.

While the women fussed with stores, preparing a meal, the men argued which was the better course. Matthew Quintal took the matter into his own hands, setting fire to the carpenter's storeroom.

Flames burst through the ship's caulking seams, feeding on the boiling tar. Her ropework spread spidery fingers of flame through the rigging. Fire flared through the open portholes. Those that were closed blew open. Bulkheads first glowed red with heat and then burst into flames. Bit by bit the blazing upper deck began to fall through to the mess decks below. The for'ard mast exploded and, dropping, crashed into Bligh's old "Cabbin". One by one, the other masts blew up. The gilt scrolling on the ship's stern, fanciful but long-since weather-beaten, grew misshapen and grotesque, twisting and charring before vanishing in flames.

Fire now burned cruelly the length of the ship. The hands of the arsonist, Matthew Quintal, trembled. The entire band gathered to watch, the smoke stinging their eyes, the crackling fire an ominous furnace in which any who wished could see strange shapes and portents.

The *Bounty* burned. Stricken, with the flame dying at last, but fire eating still to the water's edge, she drifted sluggishly onto rocks. Thus, "berthed" for the last time, the *Bounty* burned out. The ship that had come thousands of miles across the world to gather breadfruit was dead.

And, in dying, the luckless *Bounty* sealed up for eighteen years the last trace of the mutineers.

Her destroyer, Matthew Quintal, would not explain his impulsive action beyond declaring his fear that they would all be discovered. He gave no other reason for the sudden assumption of decision and action which caused him to go aboard and set fire to the vessel while the others were still talking.

Perhaps he preferred action to Christian's willingness to talk; perhaps he was alarmed that if the discussion on the *Bounty's* fate lasted too long they might in fact be betrayed to some passing ship by her presence; perhaps it was an act of violence against their final committal to land, a gesture against the world from which they were outcasts, a world of whose existence the *Bounty* was a constant reminder and a mockery.

So Quintal burned her—not as the others might have done, to remove dispassionately evidence of their whereabouts, but as a man might commit murder.

The burning of the *Bounty* is said to have occurred on 23rd January 1790.

With their fate now settled, the new inhabitants of Pitcairn Island began seeking sites for permanent dwellings.

A flat area not far from The Edge was selected and cleared. Care was taken to ensure that a line of trees should remain between the "village" and the sea, so that the houses would not be visible to passing ships.

A hut was built on top of a mountain where each couple took it in turn to reside for one week, keeping a look-out for possible ships. This site is still known today as Lookout Ridge.

The safety of the community was uppermost in their minds at this stage. After some discussion it was decided that the dogs were a danger to their concealment. Their barking might be heard at sea by some ship. Not altogether without compunction, they killed the dogs.

Not long after the arrival of the mutineers, signs of an earlier occupation of the island were found. The ruins of several huts were discovered, and near The Edge were three or four rudely carved images, as well as morais. Stone hatchets and fish-bones were found when they began to dig their garden plots, and on top of the mountain were burying places.

Who these previous inhabitants were has not been discovered. It is possible they were from the Gambier Islands—losers in some intertribal war, set adrift on rafts without means of propulsion or steering. After being carried by the ocean currents to Pitcairn Island, they would have lived out the rest of their lives without hope of rescue.

At first it was feared that the island might still be inhabited, and the new-comers were alert for sudden attack. But as time passed their fears subsided.

Gradually a village took shape. Houses were built, the ground was tilled and fenced. Paths and animal pads began to cleave the bush. The native women helped by making roofs from pandanus leaves—a Tahitian skill.

With the grandeur of conquerors, the mutineers divided their little world into nine parts, one for each of themselves—and none for the native men!

Under Christian, life on Pitcairn fell into an easy pace. The village sheltered behind the line of trees hiding it from the sea; once a week a couple went up to Lookout Ridge to keep watch on the sea while, once their fear of attack wore off, the rest gradually explored the island, coming to know it intimately. Duties were allotted on a roster basis. Apart from individual plantings, there was a communal cultivation area in which were planted yams, taro, plantain, and *aute*. The stock, mainly pigs, was divided among the mutineers.

And so they prospered, waxing fat with the seasons in which they "were fortunate in reaping good crops and everything went on in a prosperous way for about two years".

That there was no major rift between them in that time was all the more remarkable after an incident which occurred only a few months after their arrival on Pitcairn.

Jack Williams's wife, Faahotu, died of scrofula, leaving the mutineer as much put out as he was bereaved, at being the only white man on the island without a woman. To Williams the solution of his problem was simple—take one of the women of the native men. However, with more foresight than they had shown when dividing the island, the others persuaded him that this would only cause trouble and that he should wait until Sully, Bill McCoy's stepdaughter, came of age. By Tahitian standards that would be about another eleven years. For a while this had to satisfy the disgruntled Williams.

Fletcher Christian, still nominally the head of the little group, continued to hold sway on the island, despite minor disagreements. He was always referred to as "Mr Christian", whereas the midshipman, Edward Young, was known to all and sundry as "Neddy".

Christian's status is underlined by an incident involving Alexander Smith. Smith refused to repair the fence allotted to his care, thus allowing his hogs to break into the area under cultivation. Christian warned Smith that he would shoot any hogs he saw going through the fence.

"Then," replied Smith, "I will shoot you."

Hearing this, the others immediately seized Smith and would have set him adrift on the open sea but for the intercession of Christian himself.

How easily forgotten such clashes were, as well as the inevitable day-to-day animosities of nine aggressive seamen confined to a small island, can only be conjectured. Only their daily routine is certain: farming and fishing, the weekly look-out duty, long spells of idleness, sudden bursts of activity—Smith finally repaired the fence—and even tailoring. For when the sails were no longer used for tents they were put aside to make clothing for the men. The women made their own clothing, the paren and tibuta, for themselves, and the maro and tibuta for the native men, from tapa cloth. As for the native men, they were employed by the mutineers to gather birds' eggs and to till the ground, and "from being their friends, in the course of time became their slaves".

In October 1790 the first child was born on the island. He was the son of Fletcher Christian and Mauatua. As if to assert his rejection of the outside world, Christian called his son by the strange name of Thursday October, the day and month of the child's birth.

This birth was followed by those of Matthew Quintal, Daniel McCoy, and Elizabeth Mills; the last-named lived to the age of about ninety-three.

Meanwhile, the native men's discontent was not far from revolt, and it needed only Jack Williams's impatience for another woman to trigger bloodshed. As time went on he became increasingly discontented, until he finally threatened to leave the island in one of the *Bounty's* boats unless he had another wife.

By now, so contemptuous of the native men had the mutineers grown, that it was decided—supposedly by lot—that the Raiatean, Tararo (or Talaloo), should give up his wife, Toofaiti. She was apparently quite agreeable to move in with Williams, and did so, changing her name to Nancy.

Tararo fled into the wilds of the island. In secret, with the rest of the native men, he plotted revenge. They would kill all the whites.

But the women betrayed them. Out of loyalty they revealed the murder plan to their white lovers.

As leader, Christian, armed with a musket, went alone seeking the conspirators. The first he chanced upon—the circumstances are not recorded—was Ohoo. Taxed with the plot, the Tahitian fled and joined Tararo in hiding in the mountainous area of Pitcairn.

Confronted with their discovery—presumably at musket point—the rest of the native men promised to kill their fellow conspirators if they themselves were pardoned.

So the first blood was shed.

Tetahiti, the biggest and strongest of the natives on Pitcairn, found and murdered Ohoo. Both were Tubuaians of the same tribe. Another native, Minarii, went after Tararo. Nancy, who seems to have continued visiting her former husband in hiding, led Minarii to him. At their rendezvous an attempt was made to poison Tararo. When this failed the two men began fighting. With Nancy's help, Minarii overcame Tararo and killed him. The spot where the murder took place is still known today as Talaloo's Ridge.

The first native revolt was over, and two had died. The remaining four native men continued to be treated badly, the more so, they realized too late, because of the revolt.

But crops continued to prosper and babies to be born. Christian's wife gave birth to another son, whom he called Charles, apparently after his own father. Then in 1793 Mary Anne Christian and John Mills were born. Apart from young Sully, the eldest child on the island—Christian's first-born, Thursday October—was now nearly three. With his playmates —little Matt Quintal, Daniel McCoy, and Betsy Mills—the first native-born Pitcairn Islanders were growing up sturdy, dark-complexioned, black-haired youngsters, thriving on a healthy diet and the open air. Their Polynesian mothers lavished affection on them. By their presence, if at times the men had to grope for reality, the children gave a greater sense of permanence to the island venture.

But reality was something Matthew Quintal and his friend Billy McCoy had difficulty in grasping. Nearly three years on the island had not improved either's temper, and had only seasoned their violence. Consequently, they were becoming notorious for their treatment of the native men. It has been reported that on occasions Quintal would beat his "servant" and then rub salt water into the wounds.

Towards the end of 1793 the native men were again plotting murder.

Chapter V

MASSACRE ON PITCAIRN

OUTNUMBERED by the whites by more than two to one, the four men were careful this time not to let word of their plot leak out to any of the women. The assassins were Teimua, Niau, Minarii, and Tetahiti.

The drama begins in the morning.

It must be a fine day, for most of the women are busy on the other side of the island, swimming and gathering birds' eggs. They have taken the children with them. There is nothing to suggest the day will be different from any other.

Fletcher Christian, thickened out since his days on the *Bounty*, is working in his garden, digging yams. He wants to remain near his house, because Isabella is inside, awaiting the birth of their third child. His spade bites rhythmically. Now and again, he stoops to loosen the earth around a yam.

Jack Williams, too, is working. He also saw the women and children go off. For company now, until they return, there is only the distant, monotonous surging of the surf. Occasionally he hears the noises of wild pigs rooting through the undergrowth. After three years, the hogs are numerous and running wild.

Accordingly, Williams's neighbour, Isaac Martin, is not surprised this morning when the big Tubuaian, Tetahiti, borrows a musket from him to shoot, so he claims, a hog. Handing the weapon over, Martin goes back to his garden.

Quintal and McCoy are out. McCoy is visiting the ex-gunner's mate, John Mills, to help him. Mills, although now approaching fifty, has carried his years well. His well-kept garden is as fruitful as any on the island. The two men relax in the sun talking. Quintal may join them later. Working for them is Minarii.

Mr Midshipman Young, Neddy, swarthier still these days from his years in the sun, with his dark curls now thickened and grown almost to his shoulders, is on look-out duty for passing ships. But never once has a sail been sighted, and his gaze wanders. The duty has now become more or less a holiday from the day-to-day business of making a living from the soil of Pitcairn, and the keen vigilance of the earlier days is forgotten.

The botanist, Bill Brown, is another working in his garden. Brown, who is on friendly terms with the natives, wonders why he has not seen Tetahiti this morning.

Still another industrious gardener this day, although cheerfully waiting for the sun to grow too hot for work to be done, is Alex Smith. Hoeing yams, he plans to add them to the tidy store he is building up.

The women and children are chattering and swimming. The nine white men go their separate ways.

One thing occupies McCoy and Mills. They know that Teimua and Niau have disappeared. McCoy in particular savours the punishment the two will receive when they return. He does not know that Teimua and Niau have muskets.

The two natives have stolen the muskets and slipped off to hide in the bush. Gliding elusively from cover to cover, unseen by the whites, they have managed to contact Minarii and Tetahiti. And now Tetahiti has borrowed the musket from Isaac Martin.

Forces joined, the three men, Teimua, Niau, and Tetahiti, make their way through the bush to Jack Williams's place.

Nothing is said. He is shot dead.

Isaac Martin, close enough to hear the shot, passes it off as Tetahiti shooting the hog he mentioned. But Williams is dead among his yams.

Now the three assassins go to John Mills's place to get Minarii. With the two "runaways" hiding out of sight, Tetahiti approaches Mills and McCoy and asks if the former will let Minarii help him bring in a hog he has shot. Mills, with McCoy nodding approval at the thought of fresh pork, readily agrees.

The four now continue on their way.

They appear next out of the bush at Fletcher Christian's. That well-educated young man, whose ambitions evaporated in the headiness of the South Seas, and who yet commanded the respect, when Bligh's had vanished, of mutineers and natives alike, turns to face his assassins. Suddenly he realizes their purpose.

Again, without a word, the assassins fire.

Fletcher Christian falls, mortally wounded, and shortly afterwards dies.

There now are seven whites to four natives. The murderers still need stealth.

Teimua and Niau therefore hide in Bill McCoy's house, while Tetahiti goes to tell McCoy, who is still talking to Mills, that the two runaways are ransacking his house. In a murderous fury, McCoy rushes home, Tetahiti at his heels. From inside the hut a shot is fired, but goes wild. Now McCoy is alert to the trap. He dashes back to John Mills. But Mills, on friendly terms with Minarii, refuses to believe there is any danger. He shrugs sceptically and stays working at his chores. Panic-stricken, McCoy races on, this time to Fletcher Christian's. He is the first to learn that Christian is dead.

In headlong flight now, McCoy blunders into an equally terrified Matthew Quintal, who by now has learnt of the natives' revolt. The two friends take to the bush.

Mills continues to work placidly in his garden. Teimua and Niau fire at him from ambush, but only wound him. They cut off his head with a hatchet.

The American, Isaac Martin, is next. Once again, their aim is poor; Minarii finishes the job with a wooden hammer, beating Martin to death. Their next victim, Brown, might have survived. One report says Tetahiti had warned Brown, his friend, of what was happening and had fired to miss him when the attack on his house came. But whether Brown is dead, wounded, or only feigning as he lies in his garden after the shooting, Minarii's dreadful hammer claims another European life, dashing Brown's brains out.

There is only one left now still at work, gardening—Alex Smith. Sarah Quintal comes to warn him—of what, Smith can't fathom, for her English is as poor as his grasp of Tahitian is, but, seeing her excited state of mind, he follows her from his plantation, only to run straight into the armed natives.

Smith turns on his heels and flees. The natives' musketry is again wild.

Events have moved swiftly. The dead have fallen within an hour. Quintal, McCoy, and Smith are in hiding. The natives are in full possession of their former masters' domains. Edward Young is still at the lookout, oblivious—intentionally or otherwise—of the massacre that has just taken place below.

Of the men in the bush, Smith is the first to make a move. As stealthily as his attackers would have come, he returns to his house for supplies.

This time he is caught. The natives surprise him as he desperately stuffs yams into a bag. He is hit by a musket ball, which passes through his right shoulder and out through his throat. He falls, but struggles half to his feet to defend himself against the butt end of a musket. One of his fingers is broken and he falls again. Quickly, Tetahiti steps to deliver the *coup de grâce*; placing his musket at Smith's side, he pulls the trigger. The musket misses fire!

Smith breaks free and runs again. But at a call to surrender, with a promise of mercy, Smith, badly wounded and weak from loss of blood, surrenders. His captors hold to their word and he is taken to Fletcher Christian's house without further injury. As they go in, wordlessly, they pass Christian's dead body.

CHAPTER VI

REBELS FALL OUT

LATER that day Edward Young was brought in to join Smith. Apparently, while the murders were in progress, he had been hidden by the women, all of whom had a great liking for him.

There is, however, some doubt about the so-called protection given to Neddy Young. Alexander Smith himself suspected that Young was aware the massacre was to take place, but had been promised immunity. Smith's suspicion arose when one of the natives remarked on the way to Christian's house that they had forgotten that Young had told them not to hurt Smith.

At the time of the massacre, Young was ill with asthma (or possibly consumption) and he should have proved an easy mark for the killers. To add to this is the fact that when Teimua and Niau first went into hiding they would sometimes visit Young and help him in his garden.

The party of men settled down in Fletcher Christian's house with the women and children spread out among various other houses. McCoy and Quintal remained in hiding in the mountainous area of Pitcairn.

But the troubles that beset the island were not yet over.

The native men now began to quarrel among themselves as to who would have first choice of the women whose husbands had been killed. Although Susannah was the wife of Neddy Young, she was also a great favourite of both Minarii and Teimua. Teimua was accompanying a song by Susannah on his nose flute (one week after the murders!) when Minarii came in, and out of jealousy shot his fellow-countryman. When the shot failed to kill Teimua, Minarii calmly reloaded and fired again, this time killing him.

Later, Tetahiti was consoling Susannah over the loss of Teimua when Minarii came in again and, seeing the two together, attacked Tetahiti. Another murder would have been committed but for the intervention of the women.

Afraid to remain any longer in the village, Minarii fled to the mountains. There he joined Bill McCoy and Mat Quintal. The two whites naturally treated him with suspicion until he handed over his musket. Then they allowed him to remain, and to show defiance the two appeared on a ridge overlooking the village and fired a volley.

To strike a truce, Tetahiti and Niau sent Alex Smith with a message to McCoy and Quintal that if they killed Minarii they would both be free to rejoin the community in the village. The two renegades agreed to this and killed Minarii. Fear of treachery, however, was still uppermost in their minds, and they refused to return while Tetahiti and Niau were still in command.

It was now the turn of the women to take a hand in the murders. The widows of the murdered men entered into a plan with Neddy Young to kill the last two natives.

It was well known that Bill Brown's widow, Teatuahitea, was one of the women wanted by Tetahiti. She allowed the big Tubuaian to go to bed with her without arousing his suspicions. No sooner had he fallen asleep than in came Susannah. This girl—still only about eighteen years of age—hit the sleeping man across the throat with an axe. But she did not hit him hard enough, and when he began struggling to his feet she split his skull open with another blow of the axe.

Susannah gave a signal to Neddy Young, who was not far away. He was showing Niau the correct way to load and fire a musket. On receiving the signal from his wife, Young fired at the unsuspecting native at point-blank range and killed him.

Thus, of the fifteen men who had landed on the island from the *Bounty* in 1790, eleven had been murdered—so far!

Treachery and murder had been so rife on the island that when McCoy and Quintal were told that the last two natives were dead they refused to believe it. Alex Smith, returning to the village, told Neddy Young that the two friends in hiding wanted proof of the deaths. So the scalp of one of the latest victims and the arm of the other were cut off and sent to McCoy and Quintal in their mountain hide-out. With this evidence they were satisfied, and returned to rejoin the remainder of the settlement.

This has been recorded as occurring on 3rd October 1793, almost four years after the mutineers had arrived at Pitcairn to spend the rest of their lives in peace and security!

With the four men on the island, there were now eleven women remaining. The only other original arrival from the *Bounty* was, of course, young Sully, by then aged about five.

The women were taken over by the four ex-mutineers. Neddy Young took in Nancy Williams and Isabella Christian. He also now had a family of three children, Thursday October, Charles, and Mary Christian, the oldest being three and the youngest only a very young baby.

Alexander Smith took over Prudence Mills and her two children, Elizabeth and John. Mareva, the widow of the Tahitians, and Tinafornea, the widow of the Tubuaians, also joined his household.

Teatuahitea joined Mary in the McCoy home, and Jenny teamed up with Mat Quintal and his wife, Sarah.

The community now seemed to live in reasonable peace for a while. The members spent their time fencing in and cultivating their grounds and attending to the building of their houses. Extra food was obtained by fishing and catching birds. They built pits to trap the wild hogs that were rooting up their yams.

From time to time, the women changed their abode and the number of children on the island began to increase.

Two months after the death of the last two natives, Neddy Young began a journal, which unfortunately appears to have disappeared. Parts of it were copied by Captain Beechey when he visited the island in 1825. This seems to be the only record of it.

Young recorded under 12th March 1794: "Going over to borrow a rake, to rake the dust off my ground, I saw Jenny having a skull in her hand: I asked her whose it was? and she told it was Jack Williams's." Young wanted to have the skull buried, but the women would not agree. "Accordingly when I saw M'Coy, Smith and Mat. Quintal," wrote Young, "I acquainted them with it, and said, I thought that if the girls did not agree to give up the heads of the five white men in a peaceable manner, they ought to be taken by force, and buried."

From time to time rumours have circulated that Fletcher Christian did not die on Pitcairn, but that he escaped from the island. The story that he went to South America has been discredited, but the fact that he was supposed to have been seen in England received a good deal of credence. It may be noted here that Young mentioned "the heads of the five white men", which indicates that there was no truth in the rumours. At the time the journal was written there was no reason whatsoever to mention the word "five" if it were not true. No ship had visited the island since the arrival of the *Bounty*, and as McCoy, Quintal, and Smith are mentioned by name, it is quite evident that Fletcher Christian was really **dead.**

Some of the women, especially Jenny, were not at all contented with their life on Pitcairn and, "since the massacre, it has been the desire of the greater part of them to get some conveyance, to enable them to leave the island". So it was that on 14th April the same year the men began to build them a boat. So eager was Jenny to leave that she even tore up the boards of her house to obtain the planks and nails needed.

The building of the boat seems to have been a ruse to quieten the women as it was not finished until 13th August. When it was launched two days later, "according to expectation she upset".

Mat Quintal and Bill McCoy were brutal in their treatment of their women. It is said that Quintal even bit off his wife's ear when she apparently displeased him in some way. He also proposed that the four remaining men should not "laugh, joke, or give any thing to any of the girls".

Nearly nine months after the massacre, the bones of the victims were at last buried—on 16th August 1794. And on 3rd October they celebrated the murder of the native men with a party at Mat Quintal's house.

Conspiracies on the island were not yet at an end. It was discovered that the women intended to murder the men while they were sleeping. The women were seized on 11th November, but, on their promising to behave themselves and never again to give any cause "ever to suspect their behaviour", they were released and not punished.

But, recorded Neddy Young, "We did not forget their conduct; and it was agreed among us, that the first female who misbehaved should be put to death; and this punishment was to be repeated on each offence until we could discover the real intentions of the women." Four days after the women were seized, the men hid two muskets in the bush to be used should any of them escape in the event of any future attack by the women.

The suspicions of the men were well founded. Almost three weeks later, on 30th November, the women attacked. But there were no fatalities and once more the women were forgiven.

The war of nerves continued. From time to time the women went off and hid themselves in unfrequented parts of the island, at the same time letting their menfolk know that they, too, were armed.

Ignoring their temperamental "wives", the ex-mutineers built two canoes to help them with fishing. These took only a couple of days to make and were launched on 4th May 1795.

Nothing of importance appears to have occurred on Pitcairn until 27th

E

December, when a ship was sighted close in to the island. However, because of the very heavy surf no attempt was made by the ship to land, and by midday it was out of sight.

One week later Young wrote in his journal that the sea was "smoother than they had ever recollected it since their arrival on the island". If the ship had been a week later in passing, their hiding-place would surely have been discovered.

Apparently the year 1796 passed fairly quietly, and in the following year the islanders decided to try their hand at salting meat. Then, should there be a lack of fish, or poor crops, a ready supply of food would be available.

The women appeared to have accepted their lot. The men dined at one another's homes, and they did more for the comfort and well-being of the women. Vegetables and meat were freely exchanged between families, to be repaid when stocks would permit.

Bill McCoy began experimenting with the roots of the ti-trees and sugar-cane to distil some kind of spirit. The first bottle was successfully made on 20th April 1797. Mat Quintal converted one of the *Bounty's* kettles into a still and there began a period of wild intoxication on the island. McCoy in particular became addicted to the spirits, and eventually, while under the influence of the potent brew, threw himself over a cliff and was killed. His body was found by Alex Smith's daughter, Dinah. When McCoy was buried the others resolved never to drink again. But their intention was shortlived; they were soon distilling and drinking again. The women also took to the spirits and joined their menfolk in drinking bouts.

In 1799 Sarah Quintal fell from a cliff while searching for eggs and was killed. Mat Quintal maintained that he was entitled to another wife to replace her, the object of his attention being Fletcher Christian's widow. Neddy Young would not agree. In retaliation, Quintal, no doubt inflamed with grog, threatened to kill the Christian children. Smith and Young decided to strike first. Inviting Quintal in for drinks, they waited until he was well under the influence and then killed him with an axe. In later years Elizabeth Mills told of the terror felt by the women and children at the sight of so much blood on the walls of the house. In just over nine years on Pitcairn there had now been twelve murders and one suicide. Smith's wife, Obuarei, had already been killed by a fall from one of the cliffs.

But there were now twenty children on the island: Sully, aged 10;

Thursday October Christian, 9; Charles Christian, 8; Matthew Quintal, Daniel McCoy, and Elizabeth Mills, each about 7; Mary Christian and John Mills, 6; and the following, born between 1794 and 1799: Sarah, Jane, and Arthur Quintal, Polly, Robert, George, William, Edward, Dolly, and James Young, and Alexander Smith's two daughters, Dinah and Rachel (or Rebecca). The only other child born on Pitcairn had died when only a week old. Thus, with the nine remaining women and Young and Smith, the population of the community had reached thirty-one, three more than when the *Bounty* had arrived.

With only two men left, Young spent some time improving the reading ability of Alex Smith, who had apparently had only a very elementary education. The main reading matter was the Bible from the *Bounty* and the Book of Common Prayer.

Neddy Young, who had been suffering for some time from asthma (or consumption), finally died in 1800.

Alexander Smith continued distilling spirits, and on one occasion while intoxicated thought he saw an angel about to attack him with a dart. This angel he took to be Michael the Archangel.

The combined effects of reading the Old Testament and the fright he received at this vision brought about a complete change in Smith. He now became religious, and tried, as best he knew, to give his little community some kind of religious instruction. So, after being involved in brawls, mutiny, murders, immorality and drunkenness, the last surviving *Bounty* mutineer on Pitcairn turned to religion. This undoubtedly saved the island community from complete disintegration.

When Smith read to the children from the Bible the youngsters were quite sure that what he said "came from his head". Church services were held on Sundays, and both Wednesdays and Fridays were kept as fast days—the Wednesdays because of Smith's having some confused memory of Ash Wednesday.

Smith became the virtual patriarch of the island, and the children looked upon him as their father. He kept a kind of record in which he noted down the work done by the various members of his community.

In the meantime there had been three more births on the island, Edward Quintal, Catherine McCoy, and another daughter to Smith, whom he called Hannah. After the death of McCoy, Quintal, and Young, the last child of the first generation was born. This was Alexander Smith's last child, George, who was born to Mary, the widow of McCoy.

Then in 1806 a new generation was born. Thursday October Christian married Susannah (Teraura), the widow of Edward Young. The ceremony was carried out with the use of a ring that had belonged to the dead midshipman. The first child born of the union was Joseph Christian. His father was only about sixteen and his mother, who had already borne a child to Mat Quintal about six years before, was aged about thirty-one.

In the same year James Young became ill and died; he was aged about seven years.

At the beginning of 1808 Thursday October's second son, Charles, was born.

Then, on 7th February 1808, great excitement swept through the community. A ship had been sighted lying off the island.

Thursday October and two of the other youngsters put out in one of the canoes to greet the ship. Approaching the vessel, they noticed two boats on their way from the ship towards the Landing Place.

Thursday pulled up his canoe and called out, asking the men in the boat who they were, and what ship was there.

One of the strangers in the boat answered, "It is the ship *Topaz* of the United States of America. I am Mayhew Folger, her master, an American."

The conversation that followed, as we have already seen, revealed the truth to Folger. As he stared in amazement at the three young men in the canoe, he recalled the times he had discussed the mutiny with his friend Amaso Delano, and both had wondered at the fate of Christian and his friends. While at Timor many years before, Captain Delano had copied out the journal of Captain Edwards. Captain Bligh has often been described as a tyrant—but what about Captain Edwards?

Bligh had arrived back in England in March 1790. Everywhere he was hailed as a hero. The court martial held in October to inquire into the seizure of the *Bounty* had honourably acquitted Bligh of responsibility for her loss. The British Government ordered the Admiralty to send out an armed vessel to apprehend the missing mutineers. This was done, the vessel being the 24-gun frigate *Pandora*, under the command of Captain Edward Edwards.

The *Pandora* arrived at Tahiti on 23rd March 1791, and fourteen of the sixteen crew members who had remained at Tahiti were either captured or surrendered. Without exception, Edwards considered them all guilty and confined them in irons in a "round house" built on the quarter deck—this was the infamous "Pandora's Box"—eleven feet by eighteen.

The other two mutineers were dead. One had been killed by his fellow-countryman, and the other by natives in revenge for the first murder.

The *Pandora* sailed from Tahiti on 8th May, and spent some time searching unsuccessfully for Christian and his crew on various islands.

On 28th August the *Pandora* was wrecked off the Great Barrier Reef. In spite of the danger of drowning, Captain Edwards refused to allow the prisoners to be released from their stifling box. In the confusion that followed, however, they were set free at the very last moment. Of the crew of 120, 31 were drowned. Of the fourteen prisoners, four met a similar fate.

Four of the ship's boats were used to sail to Timor, whence the remaining prisoners were taken back to England for trial. A court martial on 18th September 1791 acquitted four of the men and sentenced the other six to death. Three of these prisoners were later pardoned. Aboard H.M.S. *Brunswick*, on 29th October 1792, the other three mutineers were hanged.

The account was closed, and only Alexander Smith was left on Pitcairn to tell Christian's story to Mayhew Folger.

CHAPTER VII

EARLY CALLERS

IN HIS log book, Mayhew Folger's account of his visit to Pitcairn Island contains what can only be described as a rather confused account of the settlement—some of the confusion no doubt deliberately caused by Alexander Smith, who, being in some doubt as to his future, was at pains to present himself in the most favourable light. Folger's log relates:

I went on shore and found there an Englishman by the name of Alexander Smith, the only person remaining out of the nine that escaped on board the ship Bounty, Captain Bligh, under the command of the arch-mutineer Christian. Smith informed me that after putting Captain Bligh in the long boat and sending her adrift, their commander—Christian—proceeded to Otaheiti, then all the mutineers chose to Stop except Christian, himself and seven others; they all took wives at Otaheiti and Six men as Servants and proceeded to Pitcairn's Island where they landed all their goods and Chattles, ran the Ship Bounty on Shore and Broke her up, which took place as near as he could recollect in 1790—soon after which one of their party ran mad and drowned himself another died with a fever, and after they had remained about four years on the Island their Men Servants rose upon and killed Six of them, Leaving only Smith and he desperately wounded with a pistol Ball in the neck, however he and the widows of the deceased men arose and put all the Servants to death which left him the only Surviving man on the Island with eight or nine women and Several Small Children. . . . he Immediately went to work tilling the ground so that it now produces plenty for them all and the[re] he lives very comfortably as Commander in Chief of Pitcairn's Island, all the Children of the deceased mutineers Speak tolerable English, some of them are grown to the Size of men and women, and to do them Justice I think them a very humane and hospitable people, and whatever may have been the Errors or Crimes of Smith the Mutineer in times Back, he is at present in my opinion a worthy man and may be useful to Navigators who traverse this imense ocean, such the history of Christian and his associates.

Lieutenant William Fitzmaurice interviewed Mayhew Folger at Valparaiso on 29th September 1808. He reported that the *Bounty* chronometer was confiscated by the Governor of Juan Fernandez.

The *Nautical Magazine* in 1840 published a rather interesting account of this chronometer, contributed by R. A. Newman, who had been the captain of H.M.S. *Sparrowhawk*:

May 18th, 1840, Mr Mouat, Chronometer-maker, &c., at Valparaiso, received from Captain Herbert, of H.M.S. Calliope, the Chronometer,

> Larcum Kendall,
> London.
> A.D. 1771.

This chronometer was in H.M. late ship the Bounty, at the time of the mutiny, and has been in Chili since the time of the arrival of the American ship that first touched at Pitcairns Island, after the mutineers settled themselves there. It was stolen from the American captain on the ship's passage from Juan Fernandez to Valparaiso; and next made its appearance at Concepcion, where it was purchased for three doubloons by an old Spaniard of the name of Castillo, who kept it in his possession till his death, which happened lately at Santiago; when his family sent it to Capt. Herbert, to be conveyed to the British Museum. Capt. Herbert sent it to Mr Mouat to be put in order, and from his relation I am enabled to give these particulars.

On the chronometer being taken to pieces it was found to be in a complete state of preservation. . . .

The chronometer is six inches in diameter, with three dials on its face—one for hours, one for minutes, and one for seconds; with an outer silver case, made as the outer cases of pocket watches were sixty or seventy years ago; so that its appearance is that of a gigantic watch. . . .

On this day (23rd of June,) it was delivered to Capt. Herbert, being then fast on Greenwich mean time Oh. Om. 26.5s. and losing daily 3.5 seconds. . . .

The Calliope sailed from Valparaiso for China, on the 1st of July, 1840; and thus will this, now very interesting instrument, in all probability, return to the place of its construction. . . .

The second mate of the *Topaz* told William Fitzmaurice that it was Christian who threw himself off the rocks into the sea when he became insane shortly after their arrival at Pitcairn. The second mate also stated that "another died of a Fever before the Massacre of the whole took place". This is just one of the many conflicting reports on the early days on Pitcairn that have been repeated from time to time.

The Commander-in-Chief of the Brazil Station, Sir Sydney Smith, sent a copy of the log entries of the *Topaz* to the Admiralty in 1809.

However, the Admiralty was too busy with the troubles in Europe caused by Napoleon Bonaparte to pay any attention to the fate of a single survivor of the mutineers of the *Bounty* who had disappeared twenty years before.

In 1813 Mayhew Folger wrote to the Admiralty explaining, in greater detail than his log entry showed, his visit to Pitcairn. He wrote that when the three young men met him in their canoe, they had some fruit and a hog as presents for him. He also stated that the native men had killed all the whites six years after the landing, except Alexander Smith. The Admiralty still, however, took no action.

Bloodshed past and murder only a dark dream, Pitcairn slumbered on at last at peace.

It was to be six and a half years before the island was visited again after the departure of the *Topaz*. And so little had word of the island spread, so well disregarded had the affair been by the Admiralty, that their next visitors were to be as surprised as Folger was.

On 17th September 1814, at about half past two in the morning, the British frigates *Briton* and *Tagus* discovered an island about five or six leagues to the south-south-east. Captain Pipon of the *Tagus* reckoned their position as 24°40′ S., and 130°24′ W., and "as in all the charts in our possession there was no land laid down in or near this longitude, we were extremely puzzled to make out what island it could be."

At daylight the ships bore up and ran for the island to find out if it was inhabited. They were "surprised at beholding plantations, regularly laid out, and huts or houses, much more neatly built than those we had lately seen at the Marquesas Islands".

Captain Pipon wrote:

As Pitcairn Island was described as uninhabited, we naturally conjected this in view could not be the place, particularly when, in bringing to, two or three miles off the shore, we observed the natives bring down their canoes on their shoulders, and shortly after darting through a heavy surf and paddling off to the ships; but our astonishment may be better conceived than described on finding that the inhabitants spoke the English language perfectly well.

Thursday October Christian, from his place in one of the canoes, called out, "What, won't you heave us out a rope now?" He came aboard and was described by Pipon as

. . . about twenty five years of age, a tall fine young man about six feet high, with dark black hair, and a countenance extremely open and interesting.

He wore no clothes except a piece of cloth round his loins, a straw hat ornamented with black cock's feathers, and occasionally a peacock's, nearly similar to that worn by the Spaniards in South America, though smaller.

Lieutenant Shillibeer of the *Briton* made a sketch of Thursday October Christian, which is reproduced facing page 32.

In his account of the visit to Pitcairn Island, Shillibeer refers to Fletcher Christian's son as "Friday October Fletcher Christian", but both Captain Pipon and the captain of H.M.S. *Briton*, Sir Thomas Staines, refer to him as "Thursday October". Even today on Pitcairn there are those who maintain that his name was Friday and not Thursday, but as the account of the island given by Shillibeer is full of inaccuracies, besides those deliberately given by Alexander Smith, the considerable weight of evidence is that Thursday October is the correct name.

Continuing his narrative, Pipon stated that Thursday October "spoke English in a manner most pleasing, and he was accompanied by another young man, by the name of George Young, a very fine youth of about seventeen or eighteen years of age, who also spoke English perfectly well".

The young men gave Captain Pipon a short version of the history of the island, but referred him to "an old man" called John Adams for further details. This "old man" was Alexander Smith. It appears that on the *Bounty* he had signed up as Smith, but after the visit of the *Topaz* he had changed his name to Adams. There is some doubt as to his real name, though a letter received on Pitcairn some time later seems to indicate that his name may really have been Adams.

At this time Adams was fifty years old. To Pipon and Staines he gave his version of the mutiny of the *Bounty*, taking care to deny any personal participation in it himself, "being at the time it happened sick in bed". The records prove otherwise, and eleven years later Adams did at last admit complicity in the mutiny.

When the two captains came ashore the islanders were very much alarmed in case the warships had come to remove their leader. They were relieved to learn that the visitors had had no previous knowledge of their presence on the island. John Adams, for that is how he will be referred to now, declared himself prepared to go back to England. However, the tearful pleadings of his wife and children, as well as other islanders, decided the captains against this. His wife at this stage was Mary, the widow of McCoy and mother of Sully.

Pipon recorded, "In deed it would have been act of great cruelty and inhumanity to have taken him from his family, who would be left in the greatest misery, and the settlement in all probability annihilated." But, he adds:

... had we been inclined even to seize on old Adams, it would have been impossible to have conveyed him on board; again, to get to the boats, we had to climb such precipices as were scarcely accessible to any but goats, and the natives and we had enough to do in holding on by the different boughs and roots of trees, to keep on our feet. Besides, from the nature of the island, the inhabitants might retire to such haunts as to defy our utmost search; a measure which they would naturally have had recourse to the moment any intention of seizing any of them had been manifested.

In his report to Vice-Admiral Manley Dixon at Rio de Janeiro, dated at Valparaiso on 18th October 1814, Sir Thomas Staines, in referring to Adams, said that his "exemplary conduct and fatherly care of the whole of the little colony, would not but command admiration. The pious manner in which all those born on the island have been reared, the correct sense of religion which has been instilled into their young minds by this old man, has given him the pre-eminence over the whole of them, to whom they look up as the father of the whole and one family."

There were at this stage seven of the original Tahitian women left on the island, Brown's widow, Teatuahitea, and the widow of the two Tubuaians, Tinafornea, having died since the visit of the *Topaz*. Mareva, the widow of the Tahitian men, had also died. It seems as though Sully is included in the count of the "seven women of the original settlers".

Since the departure of the *Topaz*, Sarah, the daughter of Charles and Sully Christian, Mary, the daughter of Thursday October and Susannah Christian, William McCoy, the son of Daniel and Sarah McCoy, and John, the son of the second Matthew Quintal and Elizabeth, had been born. Sully, the daughter of Mary, who came to Pitcairn with William McCoy, had married Fletcher Christian's second son about 1810. Sully's mother, now married to John Adams, had been the midwife to the little community, but was now blind and not able to move about very much. Daniel McCoy had married Matthew Quintal's daughter Sarah about 1811, and Quintal's son Matthew had married Elizabeth (Betsy) Mills.

Not long before the arrival of the two frigates, the second Matthew Quintal had a fit while out fishing, fell from his canoe, and was drowned.

The same year his son, the third Matthew Quintal of Pitcairn, was born. Also in 1814 Daniel McCoy's second son, another Daniel, was born; Charles Christian's second child, Edward, was also born; and Susannah presented Thursday October with another daughter, whom they called Polly.

John Mills, the only son of the gunner's mate of the *Bounty*, fell from the rocks when aged about twenty-one. He died without having been married, so the name of Mills died out on Pitcairn.

Both Pipon and Staines reported that the island abounded in yams, plantains, goats, hogs, and fowls. They were fed on roasted yams and coconuts and other fruits.

Sir Thomas Staines in his report also said, "I cannot, however, refrain from offering my opinion, that it is well worthy the attention of our laudable religious societies, especially that for propagating the Christian religion; the whole of the inhabitants speaking the Otahitian tongue as well as English."

Pitcairn settled down again after the departure of their new friends, until a ship called the *Sultan* arrived from Boston. The master, Captain Reynolds, agreed to take Jenny from Pitcairn back to Tahiti. It is from Jenny that we obtained some information on the voyage of the *Bounty* after its departure from Tahiti for the last time, and for some of the information on the early days of Pitcairn. Her first account was given to a gentleman from Sydney who had gone to Tahiti to set up a sugar mill.

Eighteen months passed before another vessel visited the island, which by this time was becoming famous throughout the world. This time it was a merchant vessel, the *Hercules*, under the command of Captain James Henderson. His account of his visit was published when he returned to Calcutta in the *Calcutta Journal*, dated 20th July 1819.

He related that he arrived at Pitcairn on the morning of 18th January 1819. When within two or three miles of the island, nine of the young men of the island came out in their canoe.

On approaching us, the first thing they asked was, whether we were a man of war or a merchantman, American or English? On being answered that we were a trading ship under British colours from India, they came on board.

After breakfast I went on shore at 7 a.m. and was received on the rocks by old Mr. Adams, and all the other inhabitants of the Island; but not before the Islanders that were in the boat with me had given a shout or cry peculiar to themselves to signify my being a friend. I delivered to Adams the box of Books from the Missionary Society of London, and a Letter from Adams's brother, who is still living at Wapping in London. I read this Letter to him, giving him a description of his family, mentioning the death of one sister, and the prosperity of another. This affected him much, and he often repeated that he never expected to see this day, or indeed one of his countrymen more.

The following is a copy of the letter which Adams is reputed to have written back to his brother, and published in the Calcutta *Government Gazette* for 27th July 1820:

To Mr. Jonathan Adams, Wapping.
My Dear Brother,

I this day have the greatest pleasure in my life since I left my native country, that is of receiving your letter, dated the 13th October, 1817. I have now lived on the island 30 years, and have a wife and four children, and considering the occasion which brought me here, it is not likely I shall ever leave this place. I enjoy good health, and, except the wound which I received from one of the Otaheitans when they quarrelled with us, I have not had a days sickness. I understand it is the intention of the Missionary Society of London, to send a person here to instruct us in the Christian Religion; I can only say I have done every thing in my power to instruct them in the path to Heaven, and, thank God, we live comfortably and happy, and not a single quarrel has taken place these 18 years. Should this reach you in time, that is before the gentlemen come out which is intended by the Missionary Society, should it be in your power to send me any useful articles, they will be received with many thanks and kindness. Inform the Missionary Society I have received the box of books by the last India ship, Hercules, Captain Henderson. Wishing you every health and happiness this world can afford you, I remain, my dear brother, your very affectionate brother,

JOHN ADAMS

Pitcairn's Island,
South Seas, Jan. 18. 1819.

In his account of Pitcairn, Captain Henderson continued:

I then ascended the rocks, and was led through groves of bread-fruit, cocoanut, plantain and what they call the tea tree, till we reached their village, formed on an oblong square. Their dwellings are all of wood, and very ingeniously contrived, so as to be shifted at pleasure, and were uncommonly clean. They had also built one or two houses with second stories since the frigates were there.

The account of the mutiny given by Adams to Captain Henderson then followed. The only interesting point in it is the observation that Christian approached Quintal for help to build a raft so that he might leave the ship.

Henderson landed a ram, two ewes, and "a lamb of the South American breed", as well as potatoes, wheat, and paddy for planting. "Their greatest want was implements for agriculture, mechanical tools, and cooking utensils, of which we could only supply them with one pitch pot, one or two spades, and a saw, with a few knives and forks, some plates, a few pairs of shoes, and the reading glass of my Sextant for old Adams, whose sight was failing."

There appears to be no account of the visit of the *Stanton*, which visited Pitcairn shortly after the *Hercules* left the island. The *Stanton* was a whaler which had set out from Fairhaven in the United States for the Pacific area.

The seventh ship to call at Pitcairn since the *Bounty* days, and the third in 1819, was the English whaling vessel, the *Elizabeth*, commanded by Henry King.

After discovering and naming Elizabeth Island, the ship sighted Pitcairn on 2nd March. The barren appearance of the hill near the Landing Place made a very poor impression on the Englishman, who contrasted it to the fertile hills and dales of England.

As they arrived within half a league of the island late in the afternoon, no attempt was made to land, but a light was set up in the main rigging to attract attention.

On shore, Dorothy (Dolly) Young was working on a plantation in sight of the ship and ran to tell the rest of the islanders about the new ship. Two fires were lit in answer to the light aboard the *Elizabeth*.

Early next morning, King took his ship in close to the Landing Place, expecting that some of the islanders might come out to her. A few minutes later, King recorded:

. . . we saw a boat with nine men come out from amongst the rocks, through a tremendous surf. I now sent my boat to meet them, and tow them on board. When they came alongside, they ascended the ship's side with much good humour, and came aft on the quarter-deck where I saw, and taking me by the hand, gave it a hearty shake, and said, "How do you do Captain." They then asked the ship's name, my name, where bound, whence from, and made many other trifling inquiries, in very good English. After satisfying them respecting these matters, I invited them into the cabin, and set before them some salt-beef, grog, biscuit and porter, with which they seemed pleased. Putting their hands before them,

in the position of prayer, and saying grace, they began to refresh themselves, and were much pleased with the porter.

The practice of the Pitcairn Islanders in saying grace never failed to
impress the officers of the various vessels calling at Pitcairn.

King reported that he examined the young men closely while they
were eating and found most of them to be about six feet tall, very muscular and agile. After the meal, and having said their grace once more,
"They then went on deck, where they gave surprising proofs of their
agility, by going aloft, jumping overboard, and swimming round the
ship, while it was going through the water at a rate of two knots per
hour."

Captain King and the ship's surgeon, with five of the islanders, prepared to go ashore, the other four being quite willing to remain on
board until the captain should return.

When I got near the shore, I found the surf so violent, that I durst not
attempt with my boat to go through it. I went in theirs, when one of them
taking hold of me, bid me not fear, for should the boat upset, he would
take me safe on shore. We now entered the surf, when, to my surprise,
a number of young women and children came half way into the surf to
assist in landing the boat. These women ventured far beyond their depth,
and assisted in bearing the boat up, by swimming and sustaining it with
their hands. We landed in safety, and were immediately met by John
Adams, a hearty corpulent old man, who, like the rest, was naked, with
the exception of a piece of cloth round his middle.

Henry King accepted the invitation of Adams to visit his house. The
way led up a very steep hill and along a narrow footpath. The islanders
found it so easy, in contrast to the visitors, that they actually carried
the surgeon up the hill when he found the going too difficult.

From the top of the hill they went by road through the woods, and
after crossing valleys abounding with coconut palms, they arrived at the
village "situated in a beautiful valley". Each of the seven houses had a
fine lawn before it, and two of them were of two storeys.

They all stopped at the house of Thursday October Christian for
dinner, consisting of a sucking pig, cooked in the Tahitian style, fowls,
and plenty of yams and plantains. Bananas and "a species of apple peculiar
to the island" were served after dinner. After grace was said by Adams,
each of the islanders repeated it in order of seniority.

Apparently John Adams had not been able, even had he wanted, to
stop the distilling that had caused so much trouble ten years before, as

Captain King states that "There was an abundance of plantains and some sugar-cane, from which they extract molasses and liquor".

In the evening, after supper, they entertained us with an Otaheitean dance, which consisted of various writhings and distortions of the body, by no means obscene, yet in no respect pleasant. While some were dancing the rest sat down to look on, in company with six sailors belonging to the ship, when suddenly one of the young women jumped up and ran to her brother, saying, "she would not sit any longer near that naughty man (pointing to one of my sailors,) for he wanted her to commit fornication." I asked the man why he behaved so rude to people that had treated him so well? He told me that it was by mere accident he put his foot against hers, and that he had never spoken to her.

Next morning, after sleeping ashore, the captain prepared to return to his ship, but the sea, or "Davey", as it was called by the Pitcairners, was too rough.

We were all sitting down in conversation, when a little child ran down to go into the surf. I ran to prevent the child, and so did the wife of Charles Christian, saying at the same time to Diana, the eldest daughter of John Adams, "Diana, your child will be drowned." Adams having told me, prior to this, that his daughters were not married, I expressed my surprise to the wife of Christian. Old Adams hearing this, took me aside, and gave me the following account:
Notwithstanding his paternal care of his daughters, Edward Quintral [*sic*] and Diana had committed an offence against the laws of God, for which he supposed them worthy of death, and accordingly gave orders that they should be shot; but as no person seeming willing to execute his orders, he made the necessary preparations for executing them himself, when he was strongly opposed by Auther Quintral [*sic*], who said that though the offence was certainly a great one, and the more so as a similar one had not been committed since the death of Christian, yet he did not conceive it to be a crime worthy of death. The rest being of the same opinion, Adams changed his mind also, but forbade them to marry.

King was of the opinion that the reason for Adams's change of heart was that he wanted labour for cultivating his plantation, and would not allow any of his daughters to marry.

With "Davey" calmer the next day, the whole population accompanied King aboard the *Elizabeth*, but many of them very quickly became sea-sick.

In return for their refreshments, King gave the islanders a whale-boat, some books, razors, combs, and whatever else he could spare that he considered they might need. The books were very well received, as they expressed the wish to be able to read and write.

An example of their outlook was given by Arthur Quintal, who refused two claw-hammers from the captain. When Adams told him it was improper to refuse a gift from "their countrymen", Quintal replied that it would be much more improper to take things that were not wanted.

On board the *Elizabeth*, King had a long discussion with Adams, and at last convinced him that he should allow his daughter to marry Quintal. The wedding was scheduled for the next day. The captain gave Adams "some porter, wine, and spirits, to regale themselves with at the wedding".

The crew was so impressed by the islanders that everyone aboard gave them presents, including almost two hundred books of all kinds. And "even the sailors belonging to the ship behaved with a degree of modesty in the presence of these naked females, that would have surprised a Joseph Andrews".

Before leaving the ship, one of the young men asked to be taken to England, but his mother in tears requested that he should not go. Then two of the crew asked for permission to remain on the island, but King felt constrained to refuse this request also.

After seeing the islanders safe among the rocks, King set sail for Cape Horn on his way back to England, arriving back at Deptford on 13th July 1819.

PART TWO

FENUA MAITAI

CHAPTER VIII

THE *SURRY* AND THE *RUSSELL*

THIRTY years have passed on Pitcairn: the mutiny long over, the British Government no longer much interested in its sequel, the sole survivor of the mutineers, John Adams (previously Alexander Smith), and their descendants living in peace in one of the furthermost points, and probably one of the smallest, of European colonization—for that, in essence, is what it became. Pitcairn Island had secured its niche in history as the repository for the remains of a famous mutiny, and now could join the world with an open countenance as a respectable community.

What sort of a community had come from its founding fathers? What life did they sow on this green island, this "great rock", this tiny two-and-a-quarter-mile spit of land, those men who died so violently and hideously behind its sheltering shores?

From the men of *Bounty* and their Polynesian women there were forty descendants living on the island at the beginning of 1820—twenty children and twenty grandchildren.

And they, unknowing of their fathers' dark past and bloody endings, or protected from their influence by the vision-inspired religion of John Adams, were a people of greater innocence than was possessed by either of their parents' races, without traditions, background, or experience of either race's civilization.

They were a people in the midst of the nineteenth-century world, but not of it, their state resembling that of the Tristan Da Cunhans today. To them, Pitcairn Island embraced the limits of the knowable world. All else was really inconceivable, despite the visits of ships and the word of "their father", John Adams.

Yet it is unlikely that any other community so small and in so small a territory had such a story to share with the rest of the world—a story first taken up by two of the island's earliest visitors, Captain Thomas Raine of the merchantman *Surry* and Captain Arthur of the American whaler *Russell*.

After Folger in the *Topaz* and the two British frigates *Tagus* and

Briton, these two ships were amongst the first to spend any time at Pitcairn, and their masters took the trouble to record the island life.

A thousand leagues from the American coast, as Captain Carteret put it, Pitcairn's new era began in the colony of New South Wales, even more leagues distant.

It was the year 1820. The settlement at Sydney faced famine and starvation, the colony's old afflictions, because of drought and a dearth of vessels calling there.

When the *Surry,* a ship of 310 tons, arrived from London with a few passengers, prisoners, and merchandise, the master, Captain Thomas Raine, decided to do something about the food shortage. After revictualling, he sailed for Chile on 19th December to pick up a cargo of wheat for the young colony.

Having announced his intention of making a return Pacific crossing, Raine was given in Sydney a small cargo of books and seeds to take to the Pitcairn Islanders. His intention was to call at Pitcairn on the return journey to Sydney, and so he arrived at Valparaiso on 2nd February 1821, and began loading the wheat. Roughly six weeks later, he was ready to sail again, and cleared Valparaiso on 10th March.

Between times he had learnt of the fate of a wrecked whaling crew and decided to search for survivors *en route* to Pitcairn.

The wrecked ship had been the *Essex,* from Nantucket, and the skipper, Captain Pollard, and one of his crew arrived in Valparaiso while Raine was there. From Pollard himself Raine heard how the *Essex* had been wrecked by a whale "about eighty or ninety feet long"; how the captain with seven of his crew had eventually landed on what they thought was Ducie Island;* and how, finally, Pollard set out for Easter Island with four of his men, leaving three behind on Ducie.

On the way to Easter Island, Pollard and one other man ate their three companions, including the cabin-boy, to keep themselves alive!

Raine decided to see if he could pick up the three men left behind on Ducie, but he found there no sign of them.

On 8th April Elizabeth Island was sighted, and three men were seen on the beach. One of them swam out to the vessel, and it was learnt that they were the three *Essex* survivors left behind by their captain. A landing was made and the men rescued.

* Ducie Island had been discovered by Captain Edwards in the *Pandora* in 1791 while searching for the missing mutineers of the *Bounty.*

Three days later, the *Surry* sighted Pitcairn Island. It is to her surgeon, Dr David Ramsay, that historians are indebted for one of the most informative and interesting accounts of early Pitcairn.

Early on 11th April they were close to the island and decided to go round it. However, in the afternoon the English flag was seen on the south-east side, "and we immediately hauled up for it, we soon observed a canoe coming off and two of the inhabitants in it—they asked us how we did in a pretty good English—we hove to and they came on board —soon after other canoes came off and all came on board—they appeared highly pleased to see us and invited us on shore".

Dr Ramsay continued:

The Captain, second Mate and myself went in to the gig. On our approaching the shore the danger from landing through such a surf obliged us to lay on our oars till canoes which had got ahead of the breakers, came up to us. Then we were quite enraptured, the mountainous height of the land, the abrupt precipices, the roaring surf and the coppered natives on the black rocks, their fairy forms now seen, now hid by the dashing wave, seemed the genii in the fancied regions in Alladin. But we were afraid to land as there is no beach and the breakers running high, we waited till the men in the canoes came up with us and they should show us the way to get ashore. The channel formed by large rocks being very narrow, it requires great caution in the surf. One man, Quintal, swam out to us to watch the signal and tell us when to pull in, another stood on a high rock with a branch to wave to him, the rest stood on each side of the rocks showing the passage through which the boat must go.

The man on the rock seeing the sea smooth gave the signal and in we went. When we came to the men on the rocks they took hold of the boat and ran her slap out of the surf and then took her (all of us having got out) on their shoulders and carried her up into the shade. After this we made ready to go to their houses, which were about 100 feet above the level of the sea and about half a mile to the north of the landing place— the road was very difficult of ascent to us but we all got up safe—at an open space about half way to the houses they stopped and said prayers— they first sing a psalm then pray (on their knees) then sing a psalm again which concludes their services. I have never at any time seen a more serious manner in devotion than at this time. It is a lesson to the most austere Christian in Europe.

We were welcomed on our arrival at the village, if I may call it so, by all the people as if we were their brothers or children. In fact they did not know what to do for us. The first house we went into was where they were making a kind of rum from the root of a particular tree and sugar cane mixed—there we sat down and had a glass of grog.

Continuing with his story, Dr Ramsay recorded:

John Adams who lived a little higher up the country was sick and we went to visit him—after a little conversation about different things, and giving him a great many books (particularly those sent by Miss Thornton from England) seeds, etc. we returned to the other houses and J. Adams came along with us. The house, belonging to the family of Young we stopped there. Supper was soon put on the table, which consisted of a roast pig, plantains and yams with a kind of drink which they call tea made from the cocoanut and sugar cane with a little ginger in it which grows on the island: it is certainly much superior to our own in taste as well as nutriment. After all were seated, most of the people on the floor, the table not being large enough for all of us for every inhabitant was there, Adams said grace, to which all said Amen. And at no meal do they ever forget this Christian duty. We passed the rest of the evening in dancing and singing. The women showed us the Otahetian dance, as also the men, they liked very much to see English men dance.

At this point, Ramsay relates the story of the *Bounty*, in which Adams claimed the mutiny was caused when "the crew became infatuated with the females and disgusted with Bligh's tyranny".

Late that night, the visitors were shown to their beds, which consisted of a frame about two feet high, with posts of the same height. Many pieces of cloth were used to make up the mattress, and cloth was also folded over for use as a pillow. Several of the islanders, both men and women, made themselves makeshift beds on the floor, and slept in the same room, with apparently no thought in their minds that there was anything unusual in this.

At about eight o'clock in the morning the three visitors were given a breakfast of soup made from yams, and tea, plantains, roast fowl and yams.

While the captain was supervising the loading of the gigs with stores for the ship, Dr Ramsay remained in the village watching the women preparing dinner and making cloth, which he observed still followed the customs of Tahiti.

The Captain returned and told me that after loading the boats which was done by swimming through the surf with the fruit, they, to his great astonishment, amused themselves by taking a flat board about 3 feet long, on the upper side smooth and on the under a ridge like a keel, and went out on a rock and waited till a large breaker came and when the top of it was close on them, away they went with the piece of wood under their belly on the top of this breaker and directed themselves by their feet into the little channel formed by the rocks, so that when the surf left them they were only up to their knees in water. They were very dexterous in keeping off the rocks, which to us would be inevitable death. Their method of swimming is like the dog but inclining a little to one side. The road from the village to the beach is very steep and narrow in some places but both men and women run up and down with great ease with a load on their shoulders and were very desirous of carrying us up or down any difficult place.

In Captain Raine's own account of his visit to Pitcairn, he described the surfboard riding of the islanders by their own term of "sliding". The surfboard "somewhat resembling a butcher's tray, but round at one end and square at the other", was used with equal dexterity by both the men and the women.

Captain Cook refers to surfboard riding at the Sandwich Islands during his voyage there, but makes no mention of it at Tahiti. As there appears to be no early record of the sport in Tahiti, it seems that "sliding" was developed by the young inhabitants of Pitcairn Island themselves.

The islanders were described as being a well-made race, copper in colour, and having European features; both men and women quite stout, and their hair black and generally hanging down in ringlets, as shown by the drawing of Thursday October Christian.

An unusual practice was that both men and women had their ears pierced, and generally wore small flowers in the holes.

They go naked excepting that the men have a piece of cloth put round their middle and coming up between their legs, hangs down like a small apron. The women have a kind of petticoat which is very short and also a piece of cloth hanging over their breasts; they suckle their children sometimes for a couple of years and almost always till they are far advanced in their next pregnancy. The women wear also a long piece of cloth with a hole in the middle through which they put their heads, the ends hanging down before and behind—this they call Obidah like the Ponches of the Spaniards.

The islanders spoke both Tahitian and English, as their mothers had not learnt to speak English very well. Because of the lack of practice with adults, their speech was rather like that of children. The first record of their speech was made by Dr Ramsay. This indicates that the exchange of questions and answers between Captain Folger and three of the islanders in 1808, as given by Amaso Delano, were later put into reasonable English.

The following are examples that Ramsay copied down in his record:

I like very much hear you talk—that very good—Captain Raine very funny man—we like to do well but we know not how—no good in doing wrong—When I do wrong something in my head tell me so. Suppose one man strikes me, I no strike again, for the Book say "suppose one man strike you on one side, turn the other to him,"—suppose he bad man strike me, I no strike him, because no good that, suppose he kill me, he can't kill the soul. He no can grasp that, that he go to God much better place than here.

That their piety was authentic and deep-seated is unquestionable. As some of them explained to Dr Ramsay: "If they no pray to God they grow wicked and then God have nothing to do with the wicked."

One of the Youngs told Captain Raine, "We wish very much that person would arrive that is to teach us to read and write and to do what is good towards God, because we don't know enough—John Adams is very good man but he can't teach us any more now, and he don't know enough either—we wish to do what is right, and suppose we get the man we pay great attention and do everything he tell us. Two years since we heard this man coming so we think now he never come." Although the speaker was not named, it was quite likely that it was Robert Young, a very sincere young man, a son of Edward Young and Nancy. When Raine told them that he would do his best for them on his return to England, Young replied, "Oh you good Captain! we like you to not forget us, we never forget you."

Other snippets of their conversation include such gems as, "I drink with you, if you please—I not like any more, my belly full—I so very sorry Captain Raine you go away soon—if my mother not let me go I cry very much. If we pray God always hear us—it is time to say now." The last remark was used to indicate that it was time for prayers.

When shown a mirror, one of the Quintals called it a "pride glass". In regards to money, their reply was, "Money no use to us, if you give me money, I throw it in the sea."

Regarding the island itself, Ramsay recorded, as did Carteret before him, "The Island in the distance seems a high rock out of the water but as you approach it you observe the ridges and valleys in it." On the island, he reported:

We observed clay and clay slate but it seems to consist chiefly of trap. The valleys contain a very rich soil and little cultivation is required. They have cocoanuts, plantains, bread fruit and yams in abundance, tobacco but do not cultivate, also pumpkins, calabashes, and a species of mulberry, the bark from which the women make their clothes, also the oil nut, the kernel of which they use for candles stuck on a wooden skewer.

As for the "grog" which Raine and Ramsay tried when they first came ashore, he goes on to say, "They have another tree with the root of which the sugar cane they make their rum, a strong fiery spirit and of which they drink freely, scarcely diluted, but they say they don't make any, except when a ship comes." In this regard it may be remembered that very few ships had called at Pitcairn, and most certainly the spirits could not be prepared in a matter of hours—from the first sighting of the ship to the landing of some of the crew.

There are a great many other trees which have no edible fruit but are used for carpenters work etc. We left them the seeds of the peach and apricot, walnut, almond, wheat, maize, grape, onions, potatoes—we also gave them several kinds of carpenters tools, books of all descriptions, wearing apparel, plates, knives, combs. The ram which was left them unfortunately died but we supplied one in its place, also left them a goose and gander as likewise firearms and ammunition.

The *Surry* sailed from Pitcairn on 12th April 1821, with the three rescued men from the *Essex* still on board. On arrival back in Sydney on 1st June, it was found that a cargo of wheat had already been brought from Van Diemen's Land, and the *Surry's* supply was sold at a loss.

Of the three men from Elizabeth Island, one made his way to London, and the other two back to the United States.

The whale-ship *Russell* from New Bedford arrived at Pitcairn on 9th March 1822. According to Captain Arthur's log of that date, he went ashore "accompanied by Captain Arcy, in his boat". There appears to be no record of the name of the vessel under the command of Captain Arcy, but it was probably another whaler.

The fame of Pitcairn Island was spreading throughout the world by this time, and the impression gained by the outsiders caused Captain Arthur to have the following notice put up in his ship before they arrived at the island:

It is the impression of the Russell's owners, that the most part of the company were from respectable families, and it is desirable that their conduct towards the islanders should verify the opinion. As the island has been hitherto but little frequented, they will be less susceptible of fraud than a little more general intercourse with the world would justify. It is desired that every officer and man will abstain from all licentiousness in word and deed, and will treat them kindly, courteously, and with the strictest good faith. As profane swearing has become an un-fashionable thing even on board a man-of-war, it is quite time that it was laid aside by whalemen, particularly at this time. As these islanders have been taught to adore their Maker, and are not accustomed to hear His name blasphemed, they were shocked with horror, when they heard some of the crew of an American ship swear, and said it was against the laws of God, their country, and their conscience.

The whale-boat left by Captain King needed repairing, and Captain Arthur had the work carried out on the deck of the *Russell* the day after he arrived.

When the canoe was brought out, Captain Arthur and Captain Arcy each took five of the islanders ashore—under the direction of the islanders, of course.

The day before, a Friday, the islanders at first refused to eat before leaving the ship until they were assured by Arthur that it would do them no harm.

With the help of Robert Young, Captain Arthur climbed to The Edge where he was "met by the venerable Governor, John Adams". After a "most artless yet dignified" welcome by Adams and most of the women and children, the visitors were invited to the village.

"Soon after our arrival a dinner was served up, consisting of two roast pigs, fowls, yams, and plantains; but as they declined partaking with us, on account of its being their feast [fast] day, we concluded to wait till near sunset, at which time they would be at liberty to join us. . . ."

Beds were set up in the house for Arthur, Arcy, and Adams, and after retiring the three men chatted until midnight.

During the next three days, the *Russell* remained off Pitcairn Island, the crew going on shore in relays.

On Monday Captain Arthur went ashore once again to bid farewell to his new friends—"a more affectionate leave than I ever did anywhere except my home". John Adams, Dolly Young, and Mary Christian accompanied Arthur back on board, shortly before noon.

"We gave them a part of bolt of light duck, one axe, two hatchets, four boat-knives, a bag of bread, a few bottles of wine, a roll of old canvass, a little grindstone, and a watch."

Arthur recorded that John Adams and six Tahitian women were the only survivors left from the *Bounty* on the island, and that 49 children had been born, of whom two were dead, making a total of 54 persons on the island. Actually 50 children had been born, and of these four had died.

By this time Thursday October Christian and his wife, Susannah, had three sons and three daughters. Thursday's brother Charles, who was married to Sully, had three sons and four daughters.

Edward Quintal, now married to Dinah Adams, had one son and a daughter. Edward's half-brother, Arthur, was married to Catherine McCoy, and they had four children, two sons and two daughters.

Daniel McCoy and Sarah Quintal had four sons, and John Mills's only surviving child, Elizabeth, was the widow of Matthew Quintal II. She had two sons. George Young and Hannah Adams at this stage were the parents of a baby son.

John Adams was by this time firmly established with Mary (or Teio), who had become blind. Adams was very tender in his care for his wife. Their only unmarried son was George.

Mills's widow, Prudence, had her daughter, Rachel Adams, and Isabella, Fletcher Christian's widow, was the mother of Mary Christian and Edward and Dolly Young—all unmarried. Nancy still had her two sons and a daughter fathered by Edward Young of the *Bounty*. Mareva, the only other surviving Tahitian, and the widow of Minarii, had no children of her own.

Captain Arthur wrote, "There are about eleven active men, who are ready and willing at all times to assist a ship's crew in, or anything else the island affords."

That afternoon the *Russell* sailed from Pitcairn, arriving back in her home port of New Bedford seven months later. Captain Arcy, however, indicated that he intended remaining another couple of days to finish watering.

That same year, 1822, another girl was born, this time the first daughter for Daniel McCoy and his wife, Sarah. Elizabeth Mills married William Young, but unfortunately their first son died within nine months of his birth. The only other birth recorded for 1823 was Simon, a second son for George and Hannah Young.

It was to be about twenty-one months before another vessel was recorded as visiting Pitcairn, again a whaling vessel, this time the *Cyrus* from London, under the command of Captain John Hall.

John Adams realized that he would need help on the island, because he himself was not able to teach the increasing number of children. His requests, and those of the islanders, for a pastor to come among them had not been met, and he asked Captain Hall if he could be of assistance to the island people.

On being approached, one of the crew members volunteered to go ashore and remain to give the islanders both scholastic and religious training. The entry in the Pitcairn Island Register reads as follows:

Dec. 10. Arrived ship Cyrus of London John Hall master
John Buffett and John Evans came on shore to reside,
the former as school-master.

CHAPTER IX

JOHN BUFFETT CAME ON SHORE

THUS the world at large came to know of Pitcairn Island and its inhabitants. The act of mutiny that led to the island's settlement shrank into the past of older generations, and a world once horrified and fascinated by the celebrated mutiny was more interested in the mutineers' descendants.

Without exception, every visitor to the island whose recorded observations have been preserved remarked on the innocence and morality of the islanders.

It is one of the great curiosities of history—irony apart—that an act of lawlessness and the years of violence, drunkenness, and bloodshed, as the principal actors played out the drama of Pitcairn's early days, begot a community of genuine innocence. Notwithstanding similar instances in history, it is doubtful that there has ever been such a *volte-face*.

Dishonesty was unknown on the island. Sexual morality was in keeping with the spirit of the people who coveted neither their neighbour's goods nor their wives; and who, without any enforced puritanism, regarded dancing as mildly sinful unless there was a suitable festive occasion to permit it. And even then, though rhythmically based on the amoral Tahitian dances, their dancing was restrained.

Being without coin, or even the idea of money, the Pitcairners operated a barter system of exchange when not conducting themselves as a single family. In fact, on the latter basis they enjoyed a sort of perfect communism or idyllic utopianism: goods were shared, labour and tools shared, and the resulting personal indebtedness between families was incurred and acquitted in perfect amity.

Adams officiated at weekly Sunday church services which the whole island attended, and, conducting an occasional school for children and adults alike, played the role of pastor, teacher, spiritual director, and personal counsellor. Moreover, his devotion to his wife, Teio, and his family set an example for the rest of his "flock". (If Quintal and McCoy and the others could have seen him—qualified in every respect as a venerable patriarch!)

Small wonder that the younger islanders knew him generally as "our father".

Unversed in the sharp-wittedness and allied "sophistications" of civilization, the Pitcairn Islanders presented to the world and to God a face of Eden-like innocence. They seemed as incapable of guile or wickedness as an infant child. That the ways of both European and Polynesian civilization were unknown to them only underlined their unique position: a new people evolving their ideas and experiences and multiplying in a reasonably bountiful and extremely pleasant environment almost completely isolated from any organized culture.

This is not to suggest circumstance as the reason for their "purity" of mind and intent. Adams, reformed and penitentionally inspired with religion, launched his naive flock on the path of virtue; but they could just as easily have been set on a different course. Yet such is the malleability of human nature and the inconsistencies of the laws of heredity, that the first generation of mutineers' descendants, and subsequent generations, were models of piety and charity living in their own roughly made promised land.

It was into this idyllic setting that the first non-*Bounty*, non-Polynesian settler on Pitcairn came—John Buffett.

John Buffett was born in Bristol on 16th July 1797, and at an early age became apprenticed to a cabinet-maker. The life did not suit young Buffett, and he left his apprenticeship and joined the Royal Navy, serving aboard H.M.S. *Penelope*.

Had he known what lay in store for him at sea, the youthful cabinet-maker might not have changed vocations.

The *Penelope* set sail for Quebec, and on 30th April 1815, in the Gulf of St Lawrence, the ship was wrecked. Of the crew of 120, 42 lost their lives. Buffett was among those saved when a Canadian fishing boat went to their rescue on the snowbound shores of the Gulf. The survivors eventually made their way to the seaboard town of Gaspe, where two transport ships were at anchor. Buffett joined one, H.M.S. *Leander*, and was taken back to Portsmouth.

Undeterred by his initial experience, Buffett continued to follow the sea as a calling and a few years later was serving under Captain McNevin on the brig *Weasel*.

On a voyage from Jamaica to St John, New Brunswick, the *Weasel* had been at sea in bad weather for sixty-two days with the crew on short rations, when the ship ran into a snow-storm rounding Cape Cod. One man had been on watch alone for several hours, and while he went below to get his relief the ship was wrecked on Scituate Beach, south of Boston.

Again, Buffett survived, and went back to sea once more. In 1821 he sailed from London as the mate of an American vessel bound for Canton and Manila. In Manila Bay the ship lost her mizzen mast and fore-topmast in a storm. The ship was sold and Buffett transferred to a ship bound for Chile, the *Lady Blackwood*.

Three weeks out of Manila, the *Lady Blackwood* ran into a typhoon. They went on to one of the islands of the Moluccas for temporary repairs, and then back to Manila Bay where the ship was refitted at Ternate. Leaving the Philippines, she sailed for Oahu, in the Sandwich Islands, and then on to California where Buffett left the ship.

In Buffett's own words:

I remained on shore some months and then joined the whaleship Cyrus of London, John Hall, Master. Having procured 1700 barrels of sperm oil, we touched at Oahu, which we left in October 1823 bound to London. In our passage we touched at Pitcairn's Island for refreshments. The inhabitants being in want of some person to teach them to read, and write, the Captain asked me if I should like to remain there. I told him I should, and was discharged and went on shore.

About 11 a.m. they all assembled at the house of Daniel McCoy, where Adams always resided when a ship visited Pitcairn. There they all stood and sang the 95th Psalm. Buffett said that they chanted, rather than sang, the psalm to a tune Adams had taught them.

Before *Cyrus* sailed, its crew joined the islanders at Edward Young's house, where some of the crew entertained the Pitcairners with their dancing. Adams, "a man about 5 feet 6 inches high, stout made and very corpulent", joined in the fun after taking off his shirt and trousers. European-style clothing was only important when a vessel called at the island, and Adams was not loath to rid himself of them.

Like all the island's visitors, the crew of the *Cyrus* were delighted at their reception and enchanted—so far as sailors can be, at the way of life on the island. When it came time to sail, one other of the ship's company, John Evans, decided to jump ship and stay. Evans hid in a tree until the *Cyrus* had sailed and he was able to come out and join his friend, Buffett.

Pitcairn had gained its second outsider, and Evans was made welcome.

The two men quickly settled down into their new life. Buffett began teaching the island children to read and write, as well as giving them religious instruction. Adams had been teaching them the Old Testament, whereas Buffett taught from the New, and the two had a minor disagreement, but Adams was always willing to listen to Buffett.

The day of his arrival on the island was a Wednesday, and Buffett found the day was still kept in fasting, but, since Captain Arthur's visit, not as strictly as before. Buffett pointed out to Adams that two fast days a week were not good for the health of the inhabitants, and the Wednesday was soon dropped for good.

Nine weeks after his arrival John Buffett married Dolly Young, a daughter of Edward Young of the *Bounty*. Adams approved of the wedding and performed the ceremony himself from the Book of Common Prayer.

John Evans wanted to marry Adams's daughter Rachel, but the old man disapproved of the marriage, on the grounds that Evans, then a little more than nineteen years of age, was several years younger than his prospective bride. But Rachel pleaded successfully with her father to allow the marriage, and at last, on 26th November 1824, the two were wed.

Early in 1825 (3rd January) the first new blood was introduced to Pitcairn with the birth of Buffett's son Thomas.

Buffett by this time was giving religious instruction to the adults as well as children on Wednesdays, while John Adams still conducted the Sunday services. Gradually, however, Adams also relinquished this job to Buffett.

The year following the arrival of John Buffett and John Evans, three ships visited the island: the *Oeno*, George Worth, from Nantucket; the *Maryland*, Captain Obed Folger; and the *Waverly*, from Hawaii, under Captain W. Dana.

In 1825 there were four ships, three of them whalers and the fourth, a warship, H.M.S. *Blossom*, which arrived off Pitcairn on 5th December. Several of the islanders, including John Adams, rowed out to the ship, while it was still approaching an anchorage.

It was the first time Adams had been on a naval vessel since his arrival at Pitcairn. While his eight companions went exploring the ship Adams and Captain Beechey spent the time in going over the events leading up to the mutiny on the *Bounty*. For the first time, Adams admitted his own participation in the mutiny. He was, by this time, quite

John Adams's house

The reason in my opinion that made the majority of the crew yield so easily to the persuasions of Christian was, that the Captain stinted them in their allowance, and that during the greater part of the time the Ship was lying at Otaheite no Ships Provisions of any kind was served out, and the Men were obliged to their own resources, to get a meal, except that when Hogs were received on board. After the Meat was cut from the bones, they were served out to the Crew. If a man was detected in bringing a Yam or any thing else in the Ship so as to for his own use it was taken from him, and he was punished. —

The original quarrel between Captn. Bligh, and Christian occurred at the Cape of Good Hope, and which was kept up until the mutiny occurred in a greater or less degree Captn B, it is said was continually having obliged Mr C. in some manner making him feel the obligation he was under to him, all these aggrevations combined was the occasion of the behaviour of Mr Christian. —

Mr C. was universally esteemed & beloved by the Officers and Ships Company, for his very kind and conciliatory behaviour. —

John Adams.

John Adams's signed statement, given to Captain Beechey

sure that the British Admiralty had no intention of taking action against him.

A statement was taken down and was signed by Adams. The document is now in the Mitchell Library in Sydney and is rather a strange piece of work. In parts Adams refers to himself in the third person, and in other parts in the first.

The Pitcairn Islanders were as curious about everything on the ship as natives would have been.

Having no latches to their doors, they were ignorant of the manner of opening ours and we were consequently attacked on all sides with "Please may I sit down or get up or go out of the cabin or please to open or shut the door." . . . They soon learned the Christian name of every officer on the ship and they were always used in conversation instead of surnames, and whenever similarity to their own occurred they attached themselves to that person as a matter of course.

Several hours after the Pitcairners had been welcomed aboard, the *Blossom* was close enough for a landing to be made.

We followed the guides past a rugged point surmounted by tall spiral rocks known to the islanders as St. Paul's Rocks into a spacious iron bound bay where the Bounty found anchorage. In this bay which is bounded by lofty cliffs almost inaccessible, it was proposed to land. Thickly branched evergreens skirt the base of these hills and in summer afford welcome retreat from the rays of the almost vertical sun. In the distance are seen several high pointed rocks which the pious islanders have named after the most zealous of the Apostles and outside of them is a square basaltic islet.

Because of the sunken rocks near the coast, the visitors were taken ashore by the Pitcairners in the island boat, two at a time. The sight of the boat returning brought great relief on the island, for Buffett had told them the approaching ship was a man-o'-war, and the islanders, especially the women, had become alarmed for Adams's safety.

However, when they saw the boat putting in towards the shore, they set off to meet the visitors. One of Adams's daughters, Hannah Young, raced ahead of the rest and, hurrying up, kissed her father "with a demonstration of the warmest affection". The others soon arrived and made the visitors most welcome.

Captain Beechey recorded that the women wore the Tahitian tapa cloth, made into a petticoat and mantle. The latter they wore loosely slung over the shoulders, reaching to the ankles.

G

Because of the manual work done by the women on the island, they were all quite muscular, "but their features and manners were perfectly feminine, their complexion, though fairer than that of the men was a dark gypsy hue". Their hair was long and wavy, as described by Dr David Ramsay, but Beechey mentioned they wore a chaplet of red or white blossoms to keep it in place.

Beechey was on a survey voyage for the Admiralty determining the correct position of various islands in the Pacific, including Pitcairn. As it was getting late, he told the islanders he would like to get to the village before dark to set up his instruments for making observations the next day. All the equipment was immediately shared among those present for the trip across the island to the so-called village.

The first authentic description of the Pitcairners' homes comes from Beechey. The "village" consisted of five houses, built upon a cleared piece of ground sloping to the sea, and commanding a distant view of the horizon through a break in an extensive wood of palms. Beechey said the cottages were built "more substantially than neatly".

Farther up the hill were three or four more cottages, one of which belonged to Adams, who wished at this time of his life to have some peace and quiet. To the east were four other cottages belonging to the Youngs and Quintals. Each cottage had a smaller building attached to it in which the women made the tapa cloth from the bark of trees.

The women took it in turns to carry out cooking duties for the day. Like their clothes, the cooking was in the Tahitian style.

An oven is made in the ground sufficiently large to contain a good size pig and is lined throughout with stones nearly equal in size which have been previously made as hot as possible. These are covered with some broad leaves, generally of the ti plant, and on them is placed the meat. If it be a pig, its inside is lined with the heated stones as well as the oven. Such vegetables as are to be cooked are then placed around the animal. The whole is carefully covered with leaves of the tree and buried beneath a heap of earth, straw or rushes and boughs, which by little use becomes matted into one mass. In about an hour and a quarter the animal was sufficiently cooked and is certainly more thoroughly done than it would be by fire.

After the tent had been erected for Beechey's instruments, the visitors from the *Blossom* ate at the home of one of the Christians. Grace was said, then, at the words, "Turn to", they fell to eating. None of the locally made spirits was served, and Beechey said that only water was served, "with the exception of some wine we had brought with us".

Light was supplied by candles made from doodoe nuts (*Aleurites triloba*) stuck on palm leaves, but they gave out considerable heat and crackling, and were most unpleasant to anyone sitting close by.

The Tahitian custom of distinction between the sexes was kept up on Pitcairn, and because there were not enough seats to accommodate all the visitors as well as the islanders, the women were obliged to wait until the men finished their meal, before they themselves could dine. This, however, did not seem to worry the women. The explanation of the men was that as man was made first he should on all occasions be served first.

When those of the ship's company that had gone ashore had retired to bed they heard the whole family chant a hymn in the middle of the room. Early in the morning they were awakened by the sound of another hymn being sung, but went back to sleep while the islanders busied themselves with their daily chores.

In the house, the top part was used for sleeping. There were also several beds on the lower floor, though no partitions divided the sleeping quarters from the living. A ladder led to the upper part of the house through a trapdoor.

There were no windows, as such, on the houses, but sections of the wall could be removed, and were during the hot weather.

Not far from the village was the now famous Pitcairn banyan-tree, then measured by Beechey as being two hundred paces in circumference. Beneath some palm-trees not far from the village were the graves of the few islanders who had died, and also apparently of the mutineers who had died during the massacre.

During his stay Captain Beechey was taken over most of the island, travelling over the narrow and precipitous paths which led down into the valleys and up to the ridge overlooking the village. He was taken to see the cave where it was said Fletcher Christian had planned to hide if ever a vessel had called.

At Beechey's request the islanders agreed to give an exhibition of their dancing. This consisted of basically Tahitian movements, but done in a much more decorous manner, consisting of little more than the islanders snapping their fingers and gliding past each other. Music was supplied by a gourd, a kettle from the *Bounty*, and a piece of "musical wood". Arthur Quintal, who led the musicians, held the piece of wood between his toes and struck it with two sticks. Dolly Buffett accompanied him with the gourd, from which she produced a tattoo by beating it rapidly with the palms of her hands. The exhibition, although apparently enjoyed by the participants, did not last long as they considered it "too great a levity".

The following day Beechey found some stone axes which had apparently belonged to the inhabitants of the island before the arrival of the *Bounty*. These were at the bottom of "the Rope", a cliff so called because a rope was needed to get to the bottom of it. Beechey was also shown primitive characters crudely drawn on a rock at the bottom of the Rope. These he copied.

As the weather was not promising, Beechey left the observatory in charge of one of his men and went back on board, accompanied by John Adams. The wind came up and for several days there was no communication with the shore.

Again the islanders held some apprehension for the safety of their patriarch, and each day they would climb to a high point of the island to watch out for the ship.

On board, however, Adams was enjoying his stay. He joined in the various activities aboard, including the dances and songs of the fo'c'sle.

Once the weather moderated, on 16th December, Adams was once more put ashore. Before leaving, Adams asked Beechey if he would perform the marriage ceremony for his old blind wife and himself. This Captain Beechey agreed to do, and on the following day John Adams and Teio were legally married. It was duly entered in the register of "Births, Deaths, Marriages and Remarkable Family Events".

The island was increasing rapidly in population, and at the time of the *Blossom's* visit there were 36 men and 30 women living there. Of these, only six remained of the original 28 arrivals from the *Bounty*, and the rest, other than John Buffett and John Evans, had been born on Pitcairn.

Because of the increasing population Adams asked Beechey to request the British Government to make some provision for the migration of the inhabitants of Pitcairn to some other place where they would be assured of a surer future, as they considered that all the land that could be cultivated was already under cultivation.

To this, Beechey readily agreed, and on his return to England he passed Adams's request on to the Admiralty and the Colonial Office. Both agreed that they would help the Pitcairners to any place they might choose.

When the *Blossom* was ready to leave, after staying longer than any ship had hitherto remained at Pitcairn, George Adams requested permission to sail on the ship. However, his mother sought such assurances of his safe return that Beechey was forced to refuse him passage.

From his writings and observations, Beechey emerges as a sensible, engaging man who warmed to the islanders and took a deep interest in their problems. A youthful romance lay behind George Adams's desire to leave the island. He had fallen in love with Polly Young, but because Polly had said she would never marry him she now felt that she could not break her word. Beechey did his best to convince the two youngsters that such a promise need not be binding, and suggested that they forget their earlier quarrels and marry. But it was more than a year before Polly eventually relented, and the two were married on 1st April 1827.

The year following the departure of the *Blossom* saw three more ships visiting lonely Pitcairn.

On one of these, the *Lovely Ann*, a brig from London under the command of Phillip Blythe, the second islander to leave Pitcairn sailed away. This was Jane Quintal, who upon being severely punished by her brother Edward for some moral lapse, persuaded Blythe to take her to the island of Rurutu. There she married the local chief and raised a large family.

Earlier in the same year, 1826, Fletcher Christian's second son, Charles, was widowed. Sully of the *Bounty* had died. She was about thirty-seven when she died, leaving Charles with four sons and four daughters, the oldest being about fifteen and the youngest, Isaac, being just over a year old—the age Sully herself had been when taken ashore in a bucket from *Bounty*.

So the days passed, chronicled in Buffett's register—somebody married; somebody died; someone was born. Everyone attended church on Sundays. The children went to school daily. On Wednesdays they and the adults received religious instruction from Buffett.

Otherwise they tilled their land or tended their vegetables. Sometimes the men went fishing. The women still went collecting birds' eggs. Sometimes, on someone's birthday, there was dancing; and life on the island generally was conducted in gentle good-humour and charity, with truth and godliness the touchstones upon which the Pitcairn Islanders built a community of unity, amity, and good order. They might have had need of a teacher and a minister as they had when they sought Buffett's services; they had no need of a policeman.

During 1827 another three vessels are recorded calling at Pitcairn: the *President* from Nantucket, Captain Winslow, called on 2nd February;

the *Connecticut* from Norwich, Captain Chester, a fortnight later; and towards the end of the year, on 10th December, the *Discoverer* from Valparaiso, under Captain Lindsay.

John Buffett was still teaching the children to read and write, and was also conducting most of the religious services on the island.

Buffett's wife already had two sons, Thomas and John, when on 27th May 1828 she gave birth to their third son, David. However, the same year, on 1st October, Buffett made the following entry in the register: "Mary B. Christian born", to acknowledge another of his offspring. Her mother was one of Buffett's pupils, Mary Christian, aged seventeen, the daughter of Thursday October.

In spite of this adventure out of wedlock, Buffett was allowed to continue teaching the children, and held considerable sway over the islanders.

A few weeks after Mary Christian was born a small vessel was seen approaching the island—a much smaller vessel than any that had previously called there.

CHAPTER X

GEORGE HUNN NOBBS

THE Pitcairn Island Register contains the following entry made by John Buffett and dated 5th November 1828: "George Nobbs came on shore to reside."

This entry was probably not made for some months after the event. It does not record that on his arrival Nobbs was accompanied by a big bearded American named Noah Bunker.

Nobbs's background is the stuff of which legends are made and romantic novels written.

George Hunn Nobbs was born in Ireland in 1799, by his own account the son of Francis Rawdon-Hastings and Jemima Ffrench. At an early age he moved to Wingate in Durham County, England, where for a number of years he was brought up by a family called Nobbs, and from them he took his name.

Nobbs joined the Royal Navy "by being placed on the books of H.M.S. *Roebuck*" at the end of 1811. In 1813 he was serving aboard H.M.S. *Indefatigable*, "a naval storeship", under Captain Bowles. It was aboard this vessel that Nobbs arrived in Sydney early in 1815, taking out to New South Wales 198 convicts.

On his return to England, Nobbs left the Navy and remained ashore until joining a vessel of eighteen guns which left England early in 1816 to aid the "patriots" of South America in their fight against the Spanish. The role of nineteenth-century soldier of fortune suited him.

For sixteen months the vessel cruised as a privateer along the South American coast, sinking several Spanish ships and capturing others.

Nobbs was in charge of a prize ship when it was retaken by the Spanish Royalists. He was taken to Callao and forced to work on the fortifications of the port. As time went by supervision of the prisoners became lax, and by bribing an American captain in the port Nobbs was able to escape from Callao and eventually to rejoin his ship about a hundred miles up the coast.

The privateers carried the war across the Pacific to the Philippines. Cruising off Manila, Nobbs's ship joined in what was in effect a remarkable feat of piracy—the cutting out from its escorts of a rich Spanish merchant ship from Cadiz, *La Minerva*. The success of this venture netted Nobbs two thousand dollars as his share of the prize, enabling him to pay off some of the debts he had incurred in South America.

In November 1819 he became prize master on a ship of forty guns sailing under the colours of Buenos Aires.

An able master, and a ruthless antagonist, Nobbs captured several more prizes before deserting with his pockets well lined and making his way to the port of Guayaquil. There he boarded an English packet which landed him at Talcahuano in April 1820.

At midnight on 7th May 1820 the port was attacked and captured by a leader of the Spanish Royalists, Benavides, and his Indian troops. Benavides had turned traitor to the "patriotic" cause after being taken fighting for the rebels, and became one of the most feared of the royalist fighters. He put the Chilean garrison to the sword and took many of the inhabitants, including Nobbs, prisoner.

Next day rebel troops from Concepcion stormed the port, put Benavides to flight, and freed the prisoners.

George Nobbs then joined the Chilean Navy under Lord Cochrane, the British Admiral leading the rebel navy.

Late in 1821 he was ordered up the Azapa River to recover British and American property taken by Benavides. The launch had gone only sixteen miles upstream when it was ambushed by a party of cavalry from the banks of the river. Of the 64 aboard, 48 were killed or wounded. The dead and badly wounded were thrown into the river, and the rest were stripped, dressed in rags, and sentenced to be shot.

Each morning, three or four at a time were selected at random, taken behind the prison, and shot. When only four, including George Nobbs, were left, Benavides agreed to exchange them for four of his officers— one was his brother-in-law—captured by the rebels.

After his release, Nobbs went to Valparaiso, paid off from the Chilean Navy, and returned to England. Not long afterwards his mother died, and he returned to the sea.

For the next six years Nobbs sailed on various merchant ships, but ill-fortune seemed to dog his path. In October 1822 a Neapolitan vessel on which he was sailing between Naples and Messina foundered. A year later, as Chief Officer on the ship *Gambia*, Nobbs went to Sierra Leone.

Of the nineteen aboard, only four lived to return. The next year, apparently as master of the same ship, Nobbs once again went to Sierra Leone, and there he spent six weeks suffering with fever.

On his return to England, Nobbs resigned his command and began the most important voyage of his life—back to South America. According to Nobbs's later version, he met in South America a semi-invalid, Noah Bunker, who was prepared to sail with Nobbs to Pitcairn Island on condition that he, Nobbs, refitted the small boat of twenty tons that Bunker was supposed to own. Nobbs asserted that he spent £150 on the refitting, but in later years he made no mention of any other crew, or of sealing equipment aboard the vessel when they arrived at Pitcairn.

George Nobbs said that it took Bunker and himself six weeks to reach the island from Peru.

The best account of their arrival has been given by a Belgian, Jules-Antoine Moerenhout, in his *Voyage aux Iles du Grand Ocean*. Moerenhout arrived at Pitcairn Island on 20th January 1829, and for the next few years was to prove a friend and protector of the Pitcairn Islanders. He had sailed from Valparaiso early in December 1828, on a small schooner bound for the eastern Tuamotu Islands. He describes this as a "schooner of 180 tons, measuring 86 feet long by 26 wide, a true walnut-shell, the body of which, hardly out of the water, was shallow enough to cause fear, whilst its mast seemed to want to touch the clouds; a fine set of sails, always as much under the waves as over and well worth of its name *Volador* (flying fish)".

The master decided to call at Pitcairn to recruit pearl-divers.

Shortly after the schooner's arrival, Moerenhout was told there were two strangers on the island, and that one of them was very ill. The man who was ill had asked to see someone from the ship and Moerenhout went to him immediately.

He was met by George Nobbs, "well clad and well mannered", who thanked him for his kindness in coming, and took him to see his friend.

I saw a man lying on a mattress which partly covered the floor. Near him was a woman who was waving small branches to chase away the flies. At my approach, the sick man signalled me with his left hand for me to sit down. His appearance contained something sinister. He was a man about thirty five years old; with black beard and hair, a thin and very pale face, a covered forehead; very large eyes and thick eyebrows; and upon his features, extraordinary in their entirety, could be read at the same time suffering and an unusual exaltation of spirit, which, while despairing of life, knew how to struggle against sorrow.

Noah Bunker, for this was the sick man, asked Moerenhout to get him some medical supplies from the schooner, particularly laudanum. He said he had been ill when he arrived on the island, and that eight days before, he had fallen 150 feet over a cliff, and had broken his right leg, and also his arm in several places.

To Moerenhout, the two men unfolded a strange story. They had, they said, arrived at Pitcairn Island three months before in a decked vessel of about twenty tons. They told the people of Pitcairn that they had left Peru six weeks before with the express intention of settling on Pitcairn.

The islanders appear to have been somewhat uneasy at this, but, because Bunker was ill, they gave provisional approval for the two to land.

Edward and Dinah Quintal took Noah Bunker in, and the women of their household cared for him as best they knew how. When asked who owned the vessel on which they had arrived, Bunker replied that it was his. However, the same question put to Nobbs elicited the reply that it belonged to both of them.

When doubts as to either of them actually owning the vessel were expressed by the islanders, both because of the different answers to their question and the presence on board of gear for catching harbour seals, the sick man told them that he had in fact promised Nobbs a half-share of his boat if the latter would accompany him to Pitcairn. As for the sealing gear, he admitted that eight men had set out to catch seals so that the two would have enough money for clothes and other goods when they left eventually for Pitcairn. At Pisco, about 130 miles south of Callao in Peru, he claimed that six of the crew had deserted, and the pair had decided to make straight for the island.

Bunker appeared to get worse each day and so was allowed to remain for the time being. Nobbs begged to be allowed to stay as he could no longer stand the vices and irreligion of civilization. Finally the islanders agreed that both could stay.

The small vessel was beached and Nobbs slipped easily into the island community. Soon he was teaching the young boys and girls of the island, taking over to some extent the duties of John Buffett, and something of the latter's standing, for to the islanders Nobbs presented an image of unparalleled devotion and piety.

Bunker's illness became worse, and when several times he threatened to kill himself, much greater care was taken of him. Anything which he might use to commit suicide was removed from his reach. But Bunker's "death-wish" was strong. About a week before the arrival of Moerenhout, he had his bed moved to a place near the window. At night he complained about the position of the candles, until they were moved to the other end of the room, leaving him in semi-darkness.

The girl looking after him left him alone for a few minutes, and when the others returned from reading the Bible by candlelight at the far end of the room, they found Bunker had disappeared. A search party was organized immediately.

The search during the night proved fruitless, but in the morning two men, with the help of a dog, sighted the missing man groaning on a rock nearly two hundred feet down a cliff. With great difficulty, Bunker was taken to the top of the cliff and back to Edward Quintal's house on a makeshift stretcher. Many bones had been broken, but he was still alive.

Thus Moerenhout found the injured man—an uninvited guest, taxing the islanders' hospitality to the limit of care and patience and still determined to commit suicide, for not long before he had asked a child playing near by to get him a knife.

When Moerenhout went back on board the schooner he found John Adams aboard. With his permission, Moerenhout sketched the old mutineer.

The next morning Moerenhout was returning ashore when Edward Young swam out through the surf to guide the schooner's boat to the Landing Place.

Of all Fletcher Christian's conditions for an island home, the one Pitcairn most fulfilled was that of inaccessibility. The Landing Place was barely approachable.

A narrow gap between rocks grants access, but at all times the sea creates a surging, eddying surf that not only threatens to capsize any boat seeking to enter, but if entry is gained angrily pursues the ingoing boat so that it will be dashed against the rocky shore unless the helmsman can master the drive and ebb of the waves. And only the Pitcairners were expert at this.

A good example of the help Moerenhout received on his second trip ashore is recorded in his journal:

It was midday when I climbed down into the canoe with one of the deck officers, four sailors, two natives, and an Englishman who had been living on Pitcairn for five years. We put away from very near the NNW coast. There was that day a strong swell from the north, which made us feel almost in the water; also the sea, rolling in long waves, was breaking with such a crash on the rocks, with which the island is surrounded on all sides, that the latter appeared to us inaccessible, even for the lightest landing parties. At last we reached the landing place but without being able to make out the little bay, because of the violence of the seas. Then one of the natives, a young man of about twenty-five years, six feet tall, and strong as Hercules, demanded the rudder, looked at the sea and held us for a few minutes, during which several great waves came, each in its turn, lifting our landing party to their top, as if to smash it with them on the nearby rocks. After having thus let pass three or four, our young pilot, who had not stopped looking around, suddenly called "Now, now, pull away, pull!" and, in next to no time, we found ourselves safe and sound in the little bay.

When Moerenhout returned ashore he called to see Noah Bunker again, to find out if he had received his medicine and also if there was anything else he wanted.

Bunker seems to have been in a rather talkative mood for once, and spoke about Valparaiso and several people there whom they both knew personally. He told Moerenhout he had once commanded a Chilean ship.

When asked the reason for undertaking the voyage from Peru to Pitcairn in such a small boat, the patient answered, "As you may imagine, the reasons were very powerful ones, but I cannot tell you what they were."

As to whether he wanted anything done in Valparaiso, Bunker, referring to a mutual acquaintance, replied, "Tell him that you have seen Bunker, the condition he is in, and that he is dead; for long before you return to Chile I shall be dead."

"What, don't you want to get better?"

"I have neither the wish nor the will to do so," Bunker replied. "I do not regret life, and death is nothing. . . . Here or elsewhere, now or later on, it is all the same. Everything would be well if one could die when one wants to and without suffering before doing so, as I am suffering."

After taking his farewell of John Adams, and meeting his old blind wife, Moerenhout left the island, taking with him several of the young men for his pearling expedition. In return, to help the islanders, he had left ashore his carpenter.

On their return, Moerenhout found that death and disease had visited the island. The carpenter from the *Volador* had died, and so, too, had Noah Bunker.

Bunker had taken an overdose of laudanum given him by the captain of a visiting American whaler, and, after sleeping for more than twenty-eight hours, had regained consciousness for five minutes, and then died without a word.

The whaler, *Independence*, had called at Pitcairn a month before, on 26th January, shortly after Moerenhout's departure, and had sent four men, ill with fever, ashore for a few hours. Every member of the crew of the *Independence* had had the fever, and some had died. The islanders gave the four men every care during their short stay ashore, and consequently the fever had spread throughout the island.

Fever had killed the carpenter from Moerenhout's schooner, and many of the islanders were ill, catching the fever as they tended the sick and thus spreading it still more. John Adams had come down with it and was very ill.

Moerenhout went to see him, but, except for a short spell, he found the old man delirious, speaking at random about England, the *Bounty*, and Tahiti.

But more than illness had struck the island.

The following day, being Sunday, all the islanders dressed in their best clothes, most of them having European clothing, which had been sent to them from time to time.

Moerenhout recorded:

I also learned that George Nobbs, the survivor of the two strangers who had come in the little vessel from Peru, and of whom I have already spoken, was to preach and say prayers in one of the houses; while Buffett, the Englishman who had been here for five years . . . was to do the same in another house.

I was very surprised to see that now they were going to hold services in two different places; and it was not long before I gathered that George Nobbs had already succeeded in making a split among these people who, before his arrival, had lived together in harmony.

After a few minutes, Nobbs began the service by reading several passages from the Bible; then some hymns were sung. After these he gave a long sermon, which sent Mr. Brock to sleep, although the sermon was fairly good and well delivered. The service ended with a special prayer, the principal fault of which was that it included too many things; but when he was praying for old Adams, there were tears in every eye.

The next day, when Moerenhout arrived at the village, he was given the Spanish papers left by Noah Bunker. These were the ship's licence, the bill of health, and the list of the crew of the vessel. George Nobbs had taken the rest of the papers when Bunker died, and had burned them, so he asserted, at the request of the dead man.

The crew list showed Bunker as captain and Nobbs as chief officer, but the name of the owner on both the ship's licence and the bill of health was not that of either man.

Nobbs arrived a moment later. I took him on one side and told him frankly what I thought. I told him, quite clearly, that it was ridiculous and absurd for him to act as pastor to people who were kind and simple enough to receive him without knowing him—and that after the life he had led in Peru, where one of our officers had known him, and had ended up by offering him a passage to Tahiti. He hesitated for a moment; and then said that having come here with the express intention of living among these people, he would not leave unless compelled by force to do so. It is to be hoped that this man, who does not lack ability, and who also appeared to have a very mild character, may, at least, be sincere. But in view of the seeds of discord he has already sown among the Pitcairn Islanders, to what dangers will they not be exposed when they lose the old man who has guided them up to the present time?

Moerenhout took stock of the island resources and maintained that some at least of the islanders would have to migrate when they became more numerous. At the time of his visit, the population numbered seventy-eight. He could see that a shortage of water was a distinct possibility.

But Moerenhout considered that the most serious danger to the island was that when Adams died they could come under the rule of some stranger without morals and principles. He expressed surprise that the London Missionary Society had not sent out a pastor to care for the inhabitants, especially since he considered that they would make ideal missionaries for the Pacific area as they spoke both English and Tahitian.

Unconcerned with such a possibility, the islanders learnt—apparently from Nobbs, for there was no sign of any will—that Bunker had bequeathed half his property to the community in general. Edward Quintal was to receive half the vessel in which the adventurers had arrived. "The other half was claimed by Nobbs, the survivor of the two. The gift was all the more valuable as all the houses on the island were built of wood, and planks were very scarce, for they could only be obtained by hard work."

Some of the islanders claimed that Buffett, and not Nobbs, should have a share of the vessel. Edward Quintal supported the claim of George Nobbs. Nobbs took matters into his own hands, and had a house built from the planks of the small vessel. With Quintal and some of his relations supporting Nobbs, and others supporting Buffett, there was soon a division on the island. Two church services were conducted each Sunday—one by Buffett and one by Nobbs.

John Adams was still very ill, most of the time in a coma. During his short spells of consciousness he expressed the wish that the inhabitants of Pitcairn should elect one of their number to take over control of the island when he himself should die.

Then, on 5th March 1829, surrounded by members of his family, John Adams, ex-mutineer and patriarch of Pitcairn Island, died.

His wife, blind and bedridden for many years, sorely missed the loving care and affection of her husband, and on 14th March Teio, or, as she was generally known, Mary, died also.

In the early days of the settlement she had acted as midwife to the little community, and was highly regarded by the whole population. When she died three of her four children were living. Her first child, Sully, had died three years before in 1826, leaving seven children still living. Her son Daniel McCoy had eight children; her daughter Catherine McCoy, who had married Arthur Quintal, had seven; and her last son, George Adams, had two—a total of twenty-four grandchildren.

Adams himself had four children, including George, living when he died, and ten grandchildren. Between them John Adams and Teio left six children and thirty-two grandchildren living on the island when they died. Including Buffett, Evans, and Nobbs, the population of Pitcairn at this stage was seventy-six, therefore half the inhabitants were descended from either Adams or his wife. One child had been born between the death of Adams and his wife.

Edward Young, a son of the original Edward Young of the *Bounty*, took over the leadership of the island, but only in an unofficial capacity. Under his firm guidance, the differences that had arisen over the disposition of Noah Bunker's goods were settled. He also managed to bring about a reconciliation between John Buffett and George Hunn Nobbs.

On 18th October, little more than seven months after the death of Adams, George Hunn Nobbs married Sarah Christian, a daughter of Charles Christian and Sully. Nobbs was then about thirty, and Sarah was aged nineteen. (Her birth, according to Captain King, occurred about 1810.)

Chapter XI

MIGRATION TO TAHITI

AFTER his talks with John Adams about the uncertainty of Pitcairn Island's being able to support its growing population, Captain Beechey had written to the Second Secretary to the Admiralty, Sir John Barrow, about the problem.

In the letter, dated 21st December 1825, Beechey reported Adams's request that the British Government arrange for a vessel to take the islanders to New South Wales or Van Diemen's Land. Although Adams had convinced him of the necessity for migration, the captain said, he would have preferred the Pitcairn people to remain on their island, but if they should leave they should be kept together, for "it would be a pity to separate their little colony, as they are all so much attached to each other and their manners are different from and superior to the People whom they would have to mix with".

When Sir John Barrow received the letter from Captain Beechey he immediately sent a letter to R. W. Hay of the Colonial Office in which he suggested that he would be happy if "They could all of them be transported to some Settlement on the eastern coast of New South Wales; the higher up the better on account of the warmth of the climate—Or, on Bathurst's Island opposite to our Establishment on Melville Island."

It happened at this period that the Reverend Henry Nott was in England on leave, after spending many years as a missionary at Tahiti. Nott had brought with him a letter from the young king of Tahiti, Pomare III, asking for protection for his domain, and for permission to fly the British flag.

The Colonial Office discussed the problem of Pitcairn with Nott, who suggested that Tahiti would be an ideal home for the descendants of the *Bounty* mutineers. Not only could they speak, or at least understand, the Tahitian language, but they were also partly Tahitian themselves. As it was widely known that the Pitcairn Islanders were deeply religious, Mr

John Adams's house

George and Hannah Young, with their daughter Dinah

Nott undoubtedly felt that they would facilitate the work of the missionaries in converting the Tahitians to Christianity.

Accordingly, a letter from the Secretary of State, Earl Canning, written a few months before his death, was given to Henry Nott to take back with him on his return to Tahiti.

F.O. London, March 3ᵈ 1827

Mr Secretary Canning
  to
Pomare, Chief of the Island of Taheite
Sir,

I take advantage of the opportunity which is afforded to me by the return of Mʳ Nott to Taheite, to address you upon a subject which has lately come under the consideration of this Govᵗ:—

It has, from various circumstances, become desirable, that certain Individuals, (the descendants of an English Subject) who have been living for many years past on Pitcairn's Island, should be removed from thence to some other Settlement in the Pacifick.—His Majesty has therefore given Orders that a Ship shall be employed for the purpose of conveying them and their Families to Taheite, provided you may be willing to receive them into your Dominions.

The British Govᵗ persuades Itself that you will not refuse your consent to this arrangement, as the modest and amiable manners of these people, and their moral and religious sentiments, are such as to have excited a strong feeling in their behalf, in the minds of H.M.'s Officers who have visited Pitcairn's Island, as well as on the part of the British Nation at large.

I have therefore to request that you will grant them a favourable reception, and will be pleased to extend your Protection to them, and permit them to fix their Residence in such quarter of the Islands under your Govᵗ as they may see fit to select, or may be chosen for their residence by their Friends & Connections in the Island of Taheite. His Majesty trusts that their peaceable and industrious conduct will be found to justify the hospitality & kindness which you may be pleased to shew to them.

Mʳ Nott, who is the Bearer of this Letter, will explain to you more fully the particulars connected with the intended removal of these individuals.

By the time Nott arrived back in Tahiti King Pomare had died and had been succeeded by his half-sister, Aimata, known as Queen Pomare. However, Canning's letter was read to the chiefs of Tahiti, and they agreed that the people of Pitcairn could find domicile among their people.

Paofai, the Secretary of the Tahitian Government, wrote to the Foreign Office on 2nd March 1829 that the "persons now residing on Pitcairn's

H

Island . . . shall be kindly received, and well treated whenever they shall arrive on these islands".[4]

Commander Laws of H.M.S. *Satellite* wrote to John Croker, the Secretary to the Admiralty, in a letter from Tahiti dated 11th March 1829, that he had attended a second meeting of all the principal people of Tahiti. Among other things, the request of Canning was further discussed, and permission was given for the migration to take place.

The result of this meeting, as translated by one of the missionaries, reads as follows:

We have agreed to the wish of the British Government, in receiving the Pitcairn's people, and in giving them land. We wish to live in peace, and behave well to the British flag, which we consider our real friend. We want an officer, a consul, at Tahiti, as representative of the King of Great Britain, that he may assist us: it is of no use depending on the consul at the Sandwich Islands [Charlton]; we have long known that we can obtain no advantage from him. We wish much that a British ship of war would come frequently to Tahiti, to take away to their own land, those bad foreigners who trouble us. We wish to do our duty towards the Britons.

You are powerful and rich, but we are weak children—On behalf of Pomare the Queen,

> APAAPA, *Secretary of State.*
> TEPAU, *Judge.*
> ARUPAEO, *Governor, and a Judge.*
> TEPOEA, *One of the Seven Supreme Judges.*
> MARE, *a District Judge.*

On 3rd May 1829, on his return to Port Jackson, Commander Laws wrote to Rear-Admiral Sir E. W. C. R. Owen, Commander-in-Chief in India: "The project of removing the people from Pitcairn's Island to Otaheite, referred to in my Letter to J. W. Croker, Esque., of the 11th March, 1829, may be easily effected by a Ship of War on the New South Wales Station with the assistance of one of the Colonial Vessels; the distance being only 600 Miles, one trip will convey the whole as the number does not exceed one hundred persons."

The following year, while these discussions were still going on, H.M.S. *Seringapatam,* under Captain the Honourable William Waldegrave, called at Pitcairn on 15th March. As usual, the visitors were most favourably impressed by the hospitality they received from the islanders and by their piousness.

Waldegrave wrote: "I had the gratification to hear William Quintal

say part of the catechism, and answer several questions as to his knowledge of the redemption in Christ." He also remarked that he "heard two
little girls repeat part of a hymn, which showed to me how well they
had been instructed", and that he had "attended at their evening prayers".

In his private journal, Waldegrave wrote: "In the evening we walked
to see Christian's and Adams' graves. They are at some distance from
each other,—the grave of the former near the spot where he fell, murdered, about one third from the summit of the island; the latter is buried
by the side of his Otaheitan wife, at the end of his cottage-garden."

In fact, the whereabouts of Christian's grave is unknown. In verse
later, George Hunn Nobbs pointed this out:

> *Where are they now! The infatuated band,*
> *Whose outraged feelings urged them on to crime,*
> *Proscrib'd, they wandered on from land to land*
> *To Pitcairn's came and perish'd in their prime.*
>
> *What need I tell their hapless leader's fate;*
> *(Slain by the hand of one he deem'd his slave)*
> *Save to the rash I would this fact relate,*
> *Nor e'en a hillock marks his dubious grave.*

Captain Waldegrave stated that the islanders appeared quite happy and
that there was no complaint or fear of famine.

The *Ganges*, which called at Pitcairn at the same period as the first
visit of Moerenhout, arrived in Tahiti in February. The Reverend Mr
Nott wrote to the Directors of the London Missionary Society on 25th
April 1829:

Several vessels which have lately been at Pitcairn's Island and have touched
here, have informed me, that the people expressed no wish to remove
from that Island. The ship Ganges, Captain Coffin, an American was here
two months ago, and had her cabbin full of fine yams, and had many
more below, which she obtained at Pitcairn's Island. I enquired of the
Captain if the people expressed any wish to leave the island, he said no,
not at all, he did not hear any complaints.

In his letter, Nott also suggested that he was now against any ship's
being sent to Pitcairn to remove the inhabitants, and that in all
probability dry seasons may have caused the fear of a future shortage of
food which Adams expressed to Captain Beechey.

However, on 15th December 1830 one of the missionaries from Tahiti,

Mr Crook, arrived in Sydney. He met the Governor of New South Wales, Major-General (later Sir) Ralph Darling and discussed with him the suitability of Tahiti as a new home for the Pitcairn Island people.

Communications had been back and forth by this time from Britain and from Sir Edward Owen on this subject.

Darling informed Captain Alexander Sandilands of H.M.S. *Comet* on 24th December that "I no longer see any objection to your proceeding direct to Pitcairn's Island, as coupling the information which I have received from Mr Crook with that contained in the Report of Captain Laws of His Majesty's Sloop Satellite, there can be no doubt that the people, whom it is proposed to remove from Pitcairn's Island, will be received without hesitation at Otaheite".

At this point, the whole affair—perhaps speaking volumes for the concern of His Majesty's Government for even its most distant subjects and attesting to the virtuous intentions on their behalf engendered by the Pitcairners' unique and pious position—provides a striking illustration of benevolent bureaucracy knowing no bounds.

The only people who had not been consulted about the proposed move were the Pitcairners!

Yet from John Adams's chance request—and he an old mutineer at that—the whole machinery of the Admiralty, the Foreign Office, and the Colonial Office, distant governors and consuls, had been put zealously to work to improve the lot of the happy, soon to be hapless, Pitcairners.

Captain Sandilands was ordered to proceed direct to Pitcairn in the *Comet* with the Government Barque *Lucy Ann*. Those of the islanders who wished to go to Tahiti were to be conveyed on this vessel of 208 tons, one of the four vessels owned by the New South Wales administration. Samuel, the eldest son of the missionary, William Henry, was to accompany the expedition as he was well acquainted with the Tahitian people, and should prove "useful" in the movement of the Pitcairn Islanders to their new home.

Darling also wrote: "I have further given directions that some articles as Presents for the Chiefs and Natives be provided and placed at your disposal. They will I have no doubt be a means of facilitating the object of the Service on which you are employed, and of strengthening that good disposition which the Natives have always evinced for the English."

These "Articles", valued at £228 16s., included tools, cloth, food, beads, and "2 Umbrellas" at eight shillings each. Mr Henry was to receive fifty pounds for his services.

Captain Sandilands sailed from Port Jackson on 28th December. His report, dated 26th May 1831, at Port Jackson, gives an account of the migration.

Both ships . . . arrived off Pitcairn's Island on the 28th of February; and being guided on shore by the natives, who came off in their canoes, I landed the same day, and made known to the inhabitants the subject of the expedition. On the second day, I assembled all the heads of the families, and having most fully explained to them that they were perfectly at liberty, either to remove to Otahite or remain where they were, I directed Mr Henry, who was employed by the Colonial Government of the colony to accompany the expedition, to give them every information in his power—which, from his being thoroughly acquainted with the manners and laws of Otahite, as well as being present at the meeting held by the late King [*sic*] Pomare and the chiefs, when the promise of land, protection, and assistance was made to Captain Laws, of H.M.S. Satellite, as set forth in his letter to the Secretary of the Admiralty,— he was well calculated to afford. One half of the inhabitants gave me in their names, having resolved to remove to Otahite; and on the following day, the remainder came to the same resolution. The whole immediately commenced making preparations for embarking, by carrying down to the landing-place yams, potatoes, and household goods, which were continued to be embarked on board the ships until the 7th of March, on the morning of which day all the inhabitants were embarked on board the Lucy Ann, being eighty-seven in number. I have very great satisfaction in reporting to your Excellency that this service was executed in the short space of four days, the merit of which is entirely due to Lieut. H. F. Peake, of this ship, whose zeal and judgment in directing the embarkation, under the great natural difficulties he had to contend with in the face of a most perilous surf, entitle this officer most fully to this public expression of my acknowledgements. I arrived at Otahite, and anchored in Papiete Harbour on the 23rd of March; and found the island, under the government of Queen Pomare, daughter [*sic*] of the late King Pomare, I regret to say, upon the very eve of a civil war; but which, I have great pleasure in making known to your Excellency, terminated by the opposing parties coming to actual hostilities; and that previous to my leaving Otahite, the governors of provinces, and the chiefs opposed to the Queen and her party, having amicably arranged their difficulties, had returned from Papiete to their own provinces, with their numerous armed followers. Although the island was in the most disturbed state on my arrival, I was greatly relieved from the anxiety for the situation in which I was placed with the inhabitants of Pitcairn's Island, by receiving from the Queen and her chiefs on the one side, and the hostile party on the other, assurance that the promises made by her father the King Pomare and them would be most strictly executed. I therefore, at the request of the Queen, landed the people of Pitcairn at the residence of the Queen, about three miles from the anchor-

age, where houses were provided for them, and at which place they remained until the contending parties returned to their homes; when the
Queen gave up for their use a large dwelling, belonging to herself, in the
town of Papiete. Previous to their removing to this place, a beautiful tract
of very rich land, and belonging to the Government of this island, was well
examined by the Missionaries, myself, Captain Welpole, and Lieut. Peake,
and determined to be a very eligible territory for their future residence.

Having made known to the Queen this determination, the Queen
assembled the chiefs of the district in my presence, and formally communicated to them that she had assigned this land to the inhabitants of
Pitcairn—giving orders at the same time, that her people should immediately commence the construction of houses, when they had made an election of a site suited to their wishes; and the materials for erecting those
houses were in considerable forwardness previous to my departure. It will
be gratifying for your Excellency to know, that a feeling of great regard
was universally manifested to this people by the Otahitians, who endeavoured with great diligence to find out those who were their relatives, in
which they were often successful; and in one instance, a woman came a
considerable distance and discovered in one of the four remaining Otahitian women a sister. I have been this particular in these points, in order
to show upon what ground I conclude there is every reason to hope the
change from Pitcairn's Island to Otahite will be attended with advantage
to them. On my arrival at Pitcairn's Island, I found them exceeding distressed for water, and what they had was procured with difficulty; and
although the fertility of this island has reared a comparatively numerous
population, yet this very circumstance, from their increasing numbers,
renders the necessity for emigration the more obvious. The gentlemen
composing the Christian Mission at Otahite afforded me every service in
their power. My thanks are due to Capt. Walpole, of H.M. 39th Regiment, who accompanied me, in the interest he took in the transactions of
this voyage, was well as to my officers and crew.

Hoping that your Excellency will approve of my proceeding,

I have the honour to be, &c., &c.,

(Signed)   ALEXANDER SANDILANDS,
Commander.

To His Excellency, Rear Admiral Sir E. W. C. R. Owen, K.C.B.,
Commander in Chief.

This report no doubt was quite pleasing and satisfying to His Excellency, but unfortunately it does not give the true picture of the migration
to Tahiti. Nor does a similar report from Captain Sandilands to Governor
Darling, dated 19th April 1831.

Before leaving Pitcairn for Tahiti, many of the islanders had asked
that they should be brought home if their new land was not what they

had been led to believe. Before the *Comet* and the *Lucy Ann* arrived, some of them had even written to the British Government asking to be allowed to remain on Pitcairn, but there is no record of the letter's having arrived. Once the two government vessels called at the island, they decided to at least try out the migration. Although Captain Sandilands did not promise to return them to their old home if the new one was unsatisfactory, the people were counting on the possibility of such a return.

The two ships entered Papeete Bay about noon on 23rd March—the Pitcairn Island Register records the date as 21st March, and Moerenhout as 31st March—to find, as Sandilands recorded, a civil war about to break out.

Moerenhout happened to be there when they arrived, and he soon hastened on board the *Lucy Ann* to renew his acquaintance with his old friends. The islanders related to him the events that had occurred since his departure two years before.

The Belgian was not at all happy about such people being brought to live among the amoral inhabitants of Tahiti. He refrained, however, from voicing his disapproval, so that they might have the chance of deciding for themselves if their new home was suitable or not.

They had not long to wait. That very night they were to witness scenes which, to their minds, were horrifying. About fifty Tahitian women came aboard the *Lucy Ann* and their actions with the men on board, both on deck and below, were enough to decide their future there and then. Next morning they approached Captain Sandilands demanding to be taken home to Pitcairn, as they had no wish to remain among such people as the Tahitians.

Queen Pomare herself was as amoral as her subjects, and was a devotee of the part-Christian, part-heathen sect of Momaia, then sweeping the island. She did, however, try to help the new-comers. She allotted them land at Outuaiai, about three miles from Papeete, and the rest of the Tahitians treated them with every courtesy. But the island system of morality was something the Pitcairn people could not tolerate. Their lustful mutineer forebears might never have existed.

Arrangements were made with a Mr J. G. Bicknell to feed them for six months, Captain Sandilands taking it upon himself to authorize the payment on behalf of the Government.

Each man was to receive 3 lb. of meat a week, with half that amount for each woman and child. The men were also to be given 1½ lb. of vegetables a day, with the women and children each receiving 1 lb. The fresh meat was to be supplied at 3d. a lb., and the vegetables at 5s. a hundredweight.

With the threat of civil war settled between the Queen and her subjects, land at Papaoa, to the north of the island, was set aside for use by the Pitcairn Islanders.

Until houses of their own were built, the migrants were forced to share the homes of the Tahitians in the area, and so they were forced to witness Tahitian morals at first hand.

Within a short space of time they all returned to Papeete, where they moved into a large house owned by Queen Pomare, and there kept as much to themselves as possible.

Except for the three Englishmen, all the migrants from Pitcairn Island had some Tahitian ancestry, and seventy-six of them were at least Tahitian in blood.* This fact, combined with the desire to please the British Government, no doubt made them most acceptable migrants to the ruling class of Tahiti.

The Queen even went so far as to formally adopt Reuben Elias, the six-months-old son of George and Sarah Nobbs. The child, however, remained with his parents.

The new migrants were very young, the average age of those born on Pitcairn being only 14½ years. Even including Nobbs, Buffett, and Evans, and the four original Tahitian women, their average age was still only lifted to about 17. Forty-nine of them, or more than 56 per cent, were under the age of 15. It was a tender age to be exposed to moral danger, but the more immediate danger to the once-sheltered Pitcairners was physical.

The following entry in the Pitcairn Island Register gives an indication of what was about to happen: "Soon after the arrival of the people at Tahiti they were attacked with fever."

Thursday October, the first son of Fletcher Christian, was the first to succumb, and on 21st April he died.

Three days later, John and Dolly Buffett with their four sons, together with Robert Young, Charles Christian III (Little Charlie), Matthew Quintal, and Frederick Young, sailed in a small schooner of thirty tons to return to Pitcairn. Adverse winds caused the vessel to land them at "Lord Hoods Island", now called Marutea, before it returned to Tahiti.

The day after the ten islanders sailed, the infant daughter of Arthur

* A list of the 48 males and 39 females from Pitcairn is given at Appendix II, the age, family group, and percentage of Tahitian blood being given for each individual.

and Catherine Quintal, Lucy Ann, who had been born on the voyage from Pitcairn, also died.

Then followed Prudence (Vahineatua), the widow of mutineer John Mills, who died on 29th April; George Young on 4th May; Kitty Quintal, aged 12, on 15th May; Polly, the 17-year-old wife of Edward Young, the following day; and Jane McCoy on 4th June at the age of 9. Then, on 6th June, Dinah Quintal gave birth to a daughter whom she named Nancy.

Kitty Quintal's mother, Catherine, died on 8th June. And the next day, Nancy (Toofaiti) also died. She was the Tahitian who had come to Pitcairn on the *Bounty* with the Raiatean, Tararo, and had later gone to live with Jack Williams—the original cause of trouble on the island.

The disease that had struck the Pitcairn Islanders continued to take its toll, and on 25th June Thursday October's son Charles died; two days later 17-year-old Daniel McCoy died, and the very next day his brother Hugh, aged 15.

Their old friend, Moerenhout, was distressed to see the Pitcairners' unhappy state. He arranged with Captain Mauruc of the French brig *Courier de Bordeaux*, to pick up the people stranded on "Lord Hoods Island" and take them on to Pitcairn. On arrival they found that on 3rd June Edward Christian had also died of the disease.

The *Courier de Bordeaux* arrived at Pitcairn on 27th June. There the islanders found that during their absence the hogs had gone wild and destroyed their crops, and that their cottages had been broken down by natives from Bora Bora, who had been on board the *Courier de Bordeaux* when she visited Pitcairn when it was deserted. Buffett and the others immediately set to work repairing the damage.

Moerenhout was now determined to help the rest of the Pitcairn people to return home. He offered to buy a schooner belonging to the missionaries if the Pitcairners would help him recoup some of the expense by diving for pearlshell in islands about one hundred miles from Pitcairn. This they readily agreed to do.

The missionaries refused to sell their schooner, *The Messenger of Peace*, however; so when Captain Driver arrived on the American whaler *Charles Doggett*, he was asked to take the rest of the Pitcairn Islanders home.

Payment was made with copper and other goods left by Captain Sandilands, and by contributions from Pritchard, Simpson, Wilson, and Nott, missionaries of the London Mission Society stationed at Tahiti. These men had been a great comfort to the Pitcairn people during their stay at Tahiti, especially George Pritchard, who was later to become British consul. Other white residents, including Moerenhout himself, made up the difference.

At last, on 14th August, after spending more than twenty weeks at Tahiti, the remaining Pitcairners sailed for home. They arrived on 2nd September.

They found that Robert Young, who had been engaged to Mary Christian, had died on 18th August.

The effects of the disease continued, and on 6th November Edward Young died, and on the twenty-fourth of the same month Joseph Christian was the next victim.

In the short period of thirty-one weeks from April to November 1831, sixteen deaths had occurred—thirteen of them in less than ten weeks.

The cost of the migration to Tahiti was defrayed from the Military Chest, "the resources of the Empire being more properly chargeable with services of this nature". Excluding the overall cost of wages for the crew of the *Lucy Ann* and the members of the 39th Regiment which accompanied them, the main charges were made up of £50 as remuneration to Mr Henry for accompanying the Expedition, £228 16s. for the purchase of articles for the use of the people of Pitcairn and presents for the natives of Tahiti, and £125 for the supply of meat and vegetables by Mr Bicknell while the Pitcairn Islanders were living at Tahiti.

At Port Jackson on 7th July 1832, G. H. Macmurdo, Acting Commander of His Majesty's Sloop *Zebra*, wrote to the Governor of New South Wales, Richard Bourke:

As no direct Communication can have reached your Excellency respecting the Pitcairns People, I beg to inform you that, although every possible attention and kindness was shewn them by the Queen, the Chiefs and the Tahitians in general, and although every want was amply provided by the Agent appointed to supply them, they became so wretched and melancholy, and pined so much after their Native Island, that, after five Months' residence here during which period twelve of their Number died, the Missionaries, with that Christian feeling which marks their Character, raised a subscription of six hundred and fifty Spanish Dollars, and Chartered a Vessel which took them to Pitcairn's Island in September last.

Little good, if any, resulted from the venture to Tahiti. The only event of worth on Tahiti was the birth of Charles Driver Christian, the son of Maria Christian, born in August. He was named Charles after his father and Driver after Captain Driver of the *Charles Doggett*. In later life Driver Christian, as he was to be known, was to play an important role in the religious life of the descendants of the *Bounty* mutineers. Together with George Hunn Nobbs, he was responsible for some of the beautiful hymns, including the famous "Ship of Fame", which are still sung today on both Pitcairn and Norfolk Islands.

In the meantime, with the death of Edward Young, the islanders lost their nominal leader. On their immediate return they practised their religion with their usual fervour, but soon some of them began to drink much more than usual, and visiting whalers reported that although the inhabitants of the island were as friendly and hospitable as ever, their character in general was not as high as before their ill-fated migration.

CHAPTER XII

CAPTAIN JOSHUA HILL

ON 28TH OCTOBER 1832 the barque *Maria,* under Captain Thomas Ebriel, arrived off Pitcairn Island on a pearling expedition from Tahiti.

On board was a passenger from Papeete, Joshua Hill—a most extraordinary person.

Hill had left England for South America in June 1830. He had eventually arrived at New Bedford, and then sailed on a whaler to Paita in Peru. From there he sailed to the Sandwich Islands where he remained until he was refused a grant of land by the Governor of Maui. He then set off for Tahiti, where he arrived in October 1831, a few weeks after the *Charles Doggett* had sailed for Pitcairn.

On his arrival, he had the best houses pointed out to him. The best one, he decided, belonged to the missionary, George Pritchard. Although the owner of the house was absent at the time, Hill selected a room for his own use and informed Pritchard on his return that he had given him preference over the others.

Hill let it be known that he had been sent by the British Government to take the Pitcairn Islanders to some other place, and that he had a "secret mission" in regard to all the islands in the area. When introduced to Queen Pomare, Hill remained sitting during the interview, even though the missionary acting as interpreter stood the whole time as an act of courtesy.

Moerenhout claimed that Hill "exhibited a puerile vanity: a bombastic pride: a dangerous fanaticism: and an implacable hatred of anyone who dared to oppose his plans in any way whatever". Baldly, he was a confidence trickster, who had not even the virtue of being a merry rogue, for he had the humourlessness of the paranoic. But Pritchard at first accepted him on face value and gave him free board—and paid for his laundry.

It is not out of character that Hill later had nothing good to say about Pritchard, whereas he set high store on himself.

Referring to the Pitcairn Islanders in a letter to Viscount Goderich dated 20th November 1831, Hill wrote: "I have brought out with me from England certain things for them, such as Bibles, elementary School Books, &c. But hereafter possibly they may stand in need of some trifling necessaries, as common Duck for Frocks and Trowsers, &c., with strong threads, needles, Fish-hooks and Soap."

He also said, "It seems that they are pretty well supplied with the most essential articles for the present except common soap, which they have no means of obtaining, and are, it is also said, becoming rather negligent as to their ablutions."

Hill must have long had it in mind to practise his "grandeur" on the Pitcairners, for at various times since 1828 he had correspondence with various government officials in England about the islanders, offering his services when they were to be shipped to Tahiti. This offer had been refused.

Now he had come direct to the Pitcairners.

He was taken ashore in one of the canoes that came out through the surf to greet the barque on its arrival. John Buffett, who had been waiting near the Landing Place watching the islanders return from the ship, came forward and invited the visitor to supper.

Buffett found the new-comer to be very tall and aged about fifty-nine —he was actually born on 15th April 1773. He had rather a stern demeanour, as is shown in the pencil drawing of him done in 1837. His manner was that of a man who was accustomed, and expected, to be obeyed.

Hill introduced himself to Buffett as Captain Joshua Hill, saying that he had been sent out by the British Government to "adjust the internal affairs of the island"—a complete untruth. This should not take long, said Hill, as H.M.S. *Dublin* would shortly arrive from Valparaiso expressly for the purpose of conveying him to the Marquesas Islands in a diplomatic capacity.

After supper, Buffett took his guest to the schoolhouse to meet George Nobbs, who immediately on hearing of his mission gave him a room for his use while he was on the island. The families of Pitcairn all agreed to supply Hill with his meals each day in turn.

Almost eight weeks later Hill was to claim that on the day of his arrival, a Sunday, Nobbs was in such a state of drunkenness that he was incapable of performing his duties as acting pastor, and that he himself had conducted the evening service.

At first all the inhabitants, including the Englishmen, took Joshua Hill at face value, just as the missionaries had on Tahiti. Later John Buffett was to claim that he doubted Hill's integrity from the beginning, as the Naval List showed Lord James Townshend to be the commander of the warship *Dublin*, and not Lord George Townshend, with whom Hill claimed to be "intimately acquainted". Nevertheless, Buffett did some carpentry for the new-comer, and was promised "something good" would be done for him in return.

Within three weeks of his arrival Hill was visiting the various families on the island, proclaiming to the women that he would soon become a little king among them.

He attempted to induce Evans's wife, Rachel, to leave her husband to look after him, and told her that he would take her under his protection and supply her with everything she wanted. "I will cause the first captain of a man-of-war who arrives to remove these lousy foreigners from the island," promised the island's newest arrival.

Very upset, Rachel told her husband what had been said, and from then on enmity existed between Joshua Hill and John Evans and his family.

The next to clash with the "little king" was John Buffett. Again it was through the wife. In her turn, Dolly Buffett brought Hill his meal, to be greeted not with gratitude, but with the accusation: "I know your husband does not like to feed me." Dolly replied that whatever belonged to her also belonged to her husband. Hill, however, persisted in his assertion that Buffett was against him.

On being informed of this, Buffett, deciding to take Hill at his word, told his wife to have nothing further to do with Hill. Having alienated Buffett and Evans, the arrogant new-comer now turned his attention to the third "foreigner", George Hunn Nobbs.

Early in December Hill informed Nobbs that he must change his method of teaching and follow that laid down by himself. Dumbfounded, Nobbs refused and was summarily dismissed from his post as teacher. Hill then took the extraordinary step of expelling Nobbs from his own house, and took it over for his own use.

In a way, it is probably remarkable that some earlier visitor than Hill did not take advantage of the Pitcairners' gentleness of nature and lack of suspicion. Their kindly temperament and hospitality made them easy marks for the first one that came along with that intention. And their devoutness and naivety led them into accepting Hill's word as law for no other reason than that "people don't tell lies", and therefore the backing of the British Government must lie behind Hill as he claimed.

There was, however, some uneasiness.

It found a climax in Hill's treatment of Nobbs, which incidentally suggests from the compliance of the victim that life with the Pitcairners had made a changed man of the once fire-eating soldier of fortune and privateer commander.

At all events, eight of the men, including Edward Quintal, signed the following statement, dated December 1832:

We, the undersigned, heads of families at Pitcairn's Island, do hereby certify that Mr George H. Nobbs has conducted himself to our satisfaction ever since he has been on this island; also we have no fault to find with his manner of keeping school for the space of four years; and the reason why Mr Nobbs is dismissed from teaching and school-keeping is in consequence of a disagreement between Mr Nobbs and Mr Joshua Hill, who has lately come to reside on this island amongst us.

How Hill dealt with this "boldness" is not recorded. Disdainfully, no doubt; but his next step was to prevail on the inhabitants of Pitcairn to form a temperance society. In this he was successful and the stills on the island were destroyed, though in some cases reluctantly. Hill had tried to induce the missionaries of Tahiti to form such a society, but had met with considerable opposition from the missionaries themselves.

The islanders were at this stage convinced that Hill had only to send word to the Commander of the South American Station at Valparaiso and a force would be sent to Pitcairn to punish any who dared to oppose his will.

On the other hand, they were informed that anything they required on the island could be sent from London or New South Wales on a request from Hill, and that all previous gifts from the British Government had been sent through his influence.

So it was that through a combination of fear of antagonizing the British Government, and hopes of gain, the Pitcairners came more and more under Hill's influence.

George Adams now became Hill's confidant.

He agreed to inform "the little king" of any happenings on the island and its general mood, provided the source of information was not revealed. However, very shortly the two broke up and became the most bitter enemies.

On 10th January 1833 H.M.S. *Challenger*, under the command of Captain Charles Fremantle, arrived off Pitcairn Island.

In his report to the Secretary of the Admiralty, George Elliott, dated 30th May 1833, Fremantle wrote:

I found on the island a Mr Joshua Hill, a gentleman nearly seventy years of age, who appears to have come from England expressly to establish himself amongst these people as a kind of pastor or monitor. He had not been on the island more than two or three months, and was officiating as schoolmaster, and had quite succeeded in supplanting the Englishman who had acted previously in that situation. He informed me on his arrival, he had found the island in the greatest state of irregularity. He landed on a Sunday, when he found Nobbs, who acted as their pastor, intoxicated, and in such a state from the effects of drunkenness, as to be incapable of performing his duties; and he had taken them upon himself, wishing to render as much service as possible to the islanders. It appeared to me so extraordinary a circumstance—a gentleman of Mr Hill's age and apparent respectability, coming from England—that I at first thought he must be some adventurer, more likely to do harm than good, in the cause he had undertaken; but from the papers he showed me, he having been in communication with my Lords Commissioners of the Admiralty, the Colonial Office, Captain Barclay, and many respectable gentlemen, offering his services, in the first instance, to remove the people from the island when it was first proposed, I was induced to think he must be interested in them; and as he had succeeded in restoring them to some kind of order; by putting a stop to the intemperance which existed, as he had broken up their stills, and had formed them into a Temperance Society, I gave him all the assistance in my power to support him in his situation; the other Englishman having clearly proved by his conduct, that he was unfit for it.

Captain Fremantle also stated that on his arrival he found that the islanders were not improved by their visit to Tahiti and that on their return they had indulged in intemperance by distilling a spirit from the ti root. He trusted that "they may continue to live in that state of innocence and contentment they did previous to their departure for Tahiti; which, it is to be hoped, they may, if they do not return to the use of that spirit they have so well learned the art of distilling, and which was brought about by the Englishmen, a specimen of which I obtained. It was not unlike whisky, and very good."

As for the "art of distilling" being brought about by the Englishmen, the islanders were already making "grog" from ti roots and sugar-cane at the time of Captain King's visit aboard the *Elizabeth* in 1819—four years

John Adams shortly before his death, by Moerenhout

Queen Pomare

before the arrival of Buffett and Evans, and nine years before Nobbs and Bunker.

The population at this period was seventy-nine. Fremantle stated that he had no hesitation in saying that they had lost much of their simplicity of character, but that they were "still a well-disposed, well-behaved, kind, hospitable people". They were well dressed and had the appearance of Englishmen.

The *Challenger* remained off the island for two days, and "having given all the assistance and advice in my power on the island, and arranged their little disputes to the best of my abilities, I left this little colony".

Before leaving Pitcairn, Captain Fremantle wrote to Joshua Hill that he would pass on Hill's views with respect to sending to the island a clergyman to look after the spiritual needs of the inhabitants.

It appears obvious that Fremantle, after his first few doubts as to the integrity of Hill, was quite impressed by him. When Nobbs did not deny that he had "partaken of the spirits distilled by the natives", Captain Fremantle confirmed Hill in the position of schoolmaster.

When asked what he intended doing, George Nobbs replied that it was his wish to leave the island. Fremantle agreed that "under existing circumstances" it was the best thing he could do, but that he was not compelled to leave.

After the departure of H.M.S. *Challenger*, Hill continued to increase his power over the islanders. His right-hand man was now Edward Quintal.

A form of government was set up with Edward Quintal, Arthur Quintal senior, and William Young as elders. Later John Quintal also became an elder. Hill himself was appointed president, and three of the islanders were set up as councillors or sub-elders. Three of the Quintals, Arthur junior, William, and Matthew, were given the title of cadets.

Six weeks after the departure of the *Challenger*, on 22nd February 1832, another ship of war called at the island. This time it was a Russian warship, the *Amerika*, which was circumnavigating the world. The vessel, of 655 tons, was under the command of Captain-Lieutenant Vassily Stepanovich Khromchenko of the Imperial Russian Navy. The *Amerika*, with a complement of 60 men, stopped only briefly at Pitcairn on her way from San Francisco to Rio de Janeiro.

The next ship to visit Pitcairn was an American whaler, the *Ballance*,

I

from Rhode Island. On her were some books sent as presents for the islanders by their old friend, Captain Doggett.

Joshua Hill received word that one of the books was written by Thomas Paine. A book by the author of *The Rights of Man* and *The Age of Reason* was not likely to meet with the approval of such a man as Hill. He immediately inquired as to its whereabouts, and, hearing that Jack Evans had it, he had him questioned. Evans denied ever hearing of the book, upon which Hill gave him the nickname of the "Big fool with the woollen cap".

The little dictator of Pitcairn, for such had Hill become, now introduced censorship on the island. He told the people that "all books coming on shore must undergo my inspection and such as I condemn must be burned by the common hangman".

The day after the arrival of the *Ballance*, Hill wrote to the British Consul-General for Chile at Valparaiso, John White, that, since the *Challenger* had sailed, "I have experienced considerable trouble by the presence of two or three foreigners . . . residing on the island; and till they are compelled to leave it, there will no peace be upon Pitcairn's".

He requested that Lord Townshend, the British Commander-in-Chief, be asked to "give the necessary directions for the removal of these foreigners (Englishmen) from this in other respects happy little island".

White sent the letter to Townshend on the assumption that the Commander-in-Chief would have power to exercise his authority in this case. Townshend passed on the complaint of "a Mr. Joshua Hill, who it appears is a resident on Pitcairn's Island" to Rear-Admiral Seymour. If only the Pitcairners could have seen a reference to "a Mr. Joshua Hill", as appearing to be resident of their island.

However, Townshend in his turn sent the letter from Rio de Janeiro on 3rd September 1833 to Captain Elliott of the Admiralty with the request that the Admiralty "acquaint him how far the act of removing the individuals of whom Hill complained would be justifiable, provided the majority of the inhabitants should express their wishes to that effect, and the captain of the ship visiting the island would consider such a measure benefitial to the harmony and prosperity of the community in general".

Meanwhile, back on Pitcairn, Edward Quintal was continuing as Hill's right-hand man. On 6th April he wrote—or his son William wrote on his behalf—to George Pritchard: "Our good friend, Captain Hill, has been, and is doing all in his power for our general welfare; and I am sure that his plans are well calculated to insure both our present and future happiness."

However, the following month Hill added to the "present and future happiness" of Pitcairn by having a prison built on the island!

When Moerenhout heard of this he wrote: "A prison at Pitcairn—My pen drops from my hand at the mere thought of it, poor unfortunate people: endowed with so many virtues: goodness: and a quite angelic gentleness, is this what they are leading you to?"

In the same month, Hill's little government passed an act depriving all the children of the Englishmen of their lands, and forbidding any of the islanders to marry them. Their land was to be confiscated and disposed of as Hill saw fit. The confidence trickster was now a paranoic dictator.

After conducting the evening religious service on Sundays he would deliver a lecture to the islanders on astronomy or any other subject he saw fit to deliver himself for the benefit of his bemused subjects. The congregation would then leave and the government, or court, established by Hill would sit in secret to enact laws or decide on punishments.

After one service Hill announced that the next day all the men would be employed cutting timber for one of the elders, Edward Quintal. Charles Christian senior remarked to Matthew Quintal that they might as well get their axes, for there was not much difference between talking about cutting timber on Sundays and doing it. When these words reached Hill he summoned his court.

Hill and two of the elders were for flogging Christian, but the others refused to sanction such a punishment. After much discussion it was resolved that Christian be sentenced to work on the public road.

One must give Hill grudging credit for improvements made to the road and the Landing Place at Bounty Bay. They were carried out under his direction and were long overdue.

In July Hill's progression to total power brought an act passed in regard to "high treason"!

Jack Evans claimed later that on his requesting a copy of the law for his guidance, Hill flew into a rage, and shortly afterwards Evans was taken to the church where he was tried for contempt. No witnesses were allowed. On being found guilty he received one dozen lashes with a cat-o'-nine-tails, "each tail being the size of a man's little finger".

Shortly afterwards, Hill learnt that John Buffett was the father of Mary Christian's two children, a son having been born on 30th May 1832.

Even though these births had occurred before he arrived on Pitcairn, Hill regarded the matter as one for his court. John Buffett was brought into the church and put on trial for his opposition to Hill as well as for his previous conduct.

Buffett was sentenced to "three dozen lashes with a cat, upon the bare back and breach, together with a fine of three barrels of yams or potatoes, to be paid within one month, or in default thereof, an extra barrel will be required for this re-iterated contempt of court".

The same day Buffett was ordered to leave the island, with or without his family, by the first available ship, otherwise he would be imprisoned.

When the sentence was passed Buffett was tied up in the church and given about two dozen of the lashes by Edward Quintal. It was also ordered that should Buffett not show proper respect to the "public functionaries" he would be given the rest of the lashes due to him.

The next two weeks were spent by John Buffett in bed recovering from the effects of his punishment. Even though his wife was ill and had four young boys to care for, the family were allowed no visitors, not even Dolly Buffett's half-sister, the elder Mary Christian.

Charles Christian, who was now the oldest man born on Pitcairn, protested against the flogging of Buffett and the treatment of the family. Several of the women also complained about these actions.

Hill, now calling himself the President of the Commonwealth, wasted no time in dealing with any murmurings.

The next Sunday the inhabitants were warned that visits would be declared "illegal meetings" and anyone causing any disturbance could be shot by the authorities. While the congregation was in church the firearms of all who could be considered as enemies or potential enemies of Hill were confiscated.

From that time forth, the "President of the Commonwealth" attended church services with a loaded musket.

Most of the islanders now felt not so much respect for Hill as fear of him and those around him. His word was law. Families were divided and a feeling of uncertainty was apparent everywhere.

Yet on 3rd October 1833, almost a year after the arrival of this man, a letter was signed by the "public authorities" and some of the other islanders expressing their sincere gratitude for all that Hill had done for them. In the letter they requested Hill to remain with them a while as "so long as one of these profligate foreigners is among us on Pitcairn's, we never shall be able to go on aright, or resist their corrupting or destructive practices".

This letter was apparently handed to Hill after the evening service, and the following day he replied, "I would say that, notwithstanding the importance of time, I shall not, with the blessed Lord's will, think of leaving you until hearing from home, i.e. from the British Government, nor until my presence becomes no longer necessary in furtherance of the established welfare of your commonwealth and beloved little island."

Hill next imposed his own will on Nobbs again. For when Nobbs within the next few weeks became very ill he was refused visitors and was not allowed to use the medicine chest of which he was part owner. Nobbs at this period was confined to bed for about three months.

It seems strange that in the atmosphere created by the mad Joshua Hill—for mad he must have been—the Pitcairners were still able to pursue their usual activities as the seasons came and went. They did so, but there was little that Hill did not pry into or interfere with, still less escaped his notice, and all needed to wonder who would be next to cross him, or how some chance remark or action might incur his wrath.

Early in January the following year birds known to the islanders as "men of war hawk" appeared again at Pitcairn on their annual migration. They were regarded as a table delicacy, and were often shot. (Incidentally, this was no longer possible, now that Hill had confiscated all weapons.)

On one occasion when the birds were quite prevalent, John Buffett was working in the field with Edward Quintal. He mentioned to Quintal that if Mr Hill would let him have his gun he might shoot some of the birds. He also suggested that Edward Quintal was only being polite and working in with Hill for his own ends.

The next day, 11th January 1834, Buffett received a communication from Hill castigating him for his words to one of the "magistracy of the commonwealth".

Still later on the same day, Buffett received a note from the elders and Joshua Hill saying: "You are hereby strictly and positively forbidden to hold any intercourse or keep any communication whatever with George Nobbs whilst thus upon the Island."

Apart from the absurdity of sending pompous notes around the island, which may not have occurred to the Pitcairners, some of the islanders considered that this act was not quite fair, as Nobbs was still ill. Arthur Quintal, one of the elders, told Hill that he knew it was not proper to act in such a manner, and that actions of this kind could not be loving your neighbour as commanded by the Bible. Upon being asked who was his neighbour, Quintal replied that everyone was. As usual when his authority or wisdom was brought into question, Hill became angry and told Arthur Quintal, "No, I am your neighbour, your teacher. He [Nobbs] is not your neighbour!" This extraordinary outburst was typical of Hill.

Moerenhout blamed the religious societies of England for the advent of Hill. He maintained that they should have looked after the interests of the islanders much better than they had, and as they had been requested to do on several occasions.

While Hill was still on Pitcairn, Moerenhout wrote, "Even now Joshua Hill, whether hypocrite or sincere, but certainly a fanatic, has made a serious attempt to substitute an intolerant, rigid, and cruel religion for the simple, kindly one that Adams taught his pupils."

It is worth recalling again his remarks on Hill during the latter's stay in Tahiti, a man who "exhibited a puerile vanity: a bombastic pride: a dangerous fanaticism: and an implacable hatred of any one who dared to oppose his plans in any way whatever".

Chapter XIII

THE EXILES

THE whaling ship *Tuscan*, under Captain Stavars, arrived at Pitcairn Island from London on 8th March 1834. On board were some missionaries of the London Missionary Society bound for Tahiti.

Captain Stavars, the surgeon, Mr Bennett, and two of the missionaries went ashore. On being informed of the dissension ashore, the captain offered to take the Englishmen and their families off the island to Tahiti.

George Nobbs, John Buffett, and Jack Evans accepted the offer for themselves, but decided to leave behind their wives and children for the time being.

Dr Bennett lent a sympathetic ear to the story told by the three unhappy exiles, and helped them make copies of several documents relating to their lives on Pitcairn.

Nobbs wrote a petition to Commodore Mason, the Officer Commanding the South American Station, in which he gave details of his arrival at Pitcairn and his undertaking of duties as teacher and acting pastor. He did not, however, make any reference to the early dissension caused by his arrival—though it could hardly be compared to that caused by Hill—or to the death of Noah Bunker.

Nobbs enclosed with the petition the "certificate of office" signed by the islanders in December 1832, and another signed by the missionaries at Tahiti, Pritchard, Nott, and Wilson which declared: "The whole of the people belonging to Pitcairn's Island having mutually agreed to receive Mr Nobbs as their sole teacher and minister, we, whose names are undersigned, do hereby testify our approval of this arrangement, and do most sincerely hope that he may prove a great and extensive blessing to the whole of the inhabitants." This was signed at Tahiti on 13th August 1831, while most of the Pitcairn Islanders were still in residence at Papeete.

Nobbs also informed Mason that Hill had claimed that he, Mason, had served under Hill on one of the East India Company ships of which he had been in command. He asked that he should be allowed to return to his family on the island, but with no official position, being content to simply employ himself in agricultural pursuits for the support of his family.

John Buffett wrote a similar petition dealing mainly with his own case. In this he claimed that his flogging was the result of his making known that Hill intended to have him and his family sent off the island. He also enclosed a copy of his sentence.

The third petition, in a similar vein, was written by Jack Evans.

Commodore Mason received these letters late in 1834. He replied to the three men, and wrote to George Pritchard that it was his firm conviction that Hill had no right to assume any authority on the island, much less inflict corporal punishment, or to send any of the inhabitants from Pitcairn.

Edward Quintal took the opportunity of the departure of the *Tuscan*, with the three exiles aboard, to write once more to George Pritchard in praise of Joshua Hill and in condemnation of the "foreigners". "Captain Hill has all along acted like a father to us all," he wrote, "and we really owe him more than we shall ever be able to discharge." We shall see later that Hill himself was probably the author of this and other similar panegyrics, including the earlier plea to him never to leave the island.

About three months after the exiles arrived in Tahiti, Captain Ebriel, who had carried Hill to Pitcairn, offered to transport their families to Lord Hood's Island.

On 12th June 1834 the *Pomare* left Pitcairn, having carried the exiles briefly back to Pitcairn to pick up their families: Sarah Nobbs and three children, Dolly Buffett and her four sons, Rachel Evans and her two sons, and also George Adams, Hill's first confidant, who had decided to join the exiles on Lord Hood's Island.

Finding it proved unsuitable as a home, Ebriel carried them on to the Gambier Islands, three hundred miles from Pitcairn. But the Buffetts and George Adams returned to Tahiti on the *Pomare*. Nobbs decided to stay on to do missionary work. Strangely enough, Jack Evans elected to remain with Nobbs rather than return with his friend Buffett, on whose account he had jumped ship more than ten years before.

Nobbs was really more a teacher than a missionary, but he had been promised a retainer by the missionaries at Tahiti if he would instruct the inhabitants of Gambier in the Christian religion.

Three Jesuit missionaries—Caret, Laval, and Columban—who arrived at Gambier from Valparaiso on 7th August 1834, saw him there. The priests were the vanguard of attempts to establish the Roman Catholic religion in this area of the Pacific.

Monsieur Caret wrote on 8th August: "Yesterday, we anchored at the Gambier islands. We met there an Englishman, who has been some weeks resident, with another of his countrymen, and a Kanac." The two Englishmen were, of course, the recently exiled George Hunn Nobbs and Jack Evans.

Caret continued: "Without being exactly a missionary, he is here to instruct the people. The Protestant missionaries at Otaiti have promised him a salary, and this may induce him to remain. I do not think the man will hurt us; he has even offered us the use of his hut till we can construct one."

Back on Pitcairn Island, Hill's egotism was revealed to the full. He penned what was perhaps the most astounding document ever to come from that little island.

In a "memorandum" to Lord James Townshend, Joshua Hill claimed to have visited the four corners of the globe, to have dined with, visited, or been visited by, a collection of the most notable people of the day.

Among other things, he wrote that he had

... given the arm to Lady Hamilton. ... I have entertained Governors, Generals, Captains (R.N.) on board my ship. ... I have visited the Falls of Niagara and Montmorency, the natural bridge in Virginia, the great Reciprocating Fountain in East Tennessee, the great Temple of Elephanta at Bombay. ... I have visited and conversed with 'Red Jacket' the great Indian warrior. ... I have dined with a principal Hong merchant at Canton. ... I was at Napoleon's coronation. ... I have had a beautiful Egyptian Lady write to me. ...

He also said that he was "decidedly against the use of ardent spirit ... tobacco, &c. ..."

The memorandum, however, begins, "I am aware that pedantry and egotism become no one, and myself perhaps less than any. (Pro. xxvii, 2.) But for certain reasons, the following credentials, as a memorandum, I hope will be pardoned on the present occasion—they are truths."

Although he was against "ardent spirit", wine was a different matter, provided of course that it was the "very best". "I have had a fine band of music on board my ship, and my four kinds of wine on my table."

In a covering letter, Hill told Townshend of his voyage to Pitcairn, and of the help he had been to the missionaries at both the Sandwich Islands and at Tahiti. He blasted the missionaries of Tahiti for not forming a temperance society at his suggestion. He also stated that there had been relief in the recent removal of Buffett, Evans, and Nobbs, and their families.

With Hill's letters were sent "the Humble Petition of the Principal Native Inhabitants of Pitcairn's Island":

We, the undersigned public functionaries of Pitcairn's Island, humbly beg leave to address your Lordship, and thus implore, that your Lordship will be pleased to have pity on us, and take cognizance of our truly unfortunate case. Your Lordship will, in the first place, be pleased to understand, that ever since the death of old Mr John Adams (i.e. Alexander Smith, of H.B.M.S. Bounty), now about five years, we have been divided in party spirit, through the presence alone of three worthless fellows (runaway English sailors, whom, alas! we allowed to stop on the island), by the names of John Buffett, George Nobbs, and John Evans. At times we have had two schools and two churches, whilst at other times we have had neither the one nor the other, and at best very deficient, as may naturally be supposed; until the month of October, 1832, when Mr Joshua Hill, an English gentleman (our actual teacher and pastor), providently, as we conceive, arrived here in the barque Pomare from Tahiti, where, it would seem, he had been doing them all the good in his power, as it seems he had previously done at the Sandwich Islands. . . .

This letter was later published in Honolulu and was widely believed. It accounts for the disrepute in which Nobbs was for quite some time to be held. It was revealed later that "so far from expressing the sentiments of the community, not more than three persons were acquainted with its contents. The rest of us were ignorant of its existence till we saw it published. . . ."

The islanders also stated that the part referring to Nobbs had been publicly retracted, and an apology was sent to the same newspaper.

The truth, of course, lies in between. Nobbs was not, in the early days, the popular figure on the island that later writers would have us believe. That he did later become popular and was highly esteemed by the Pitcairn Islanders is also true.

As for the "Humble Petition" itself, the style is so obviously that of Joshua Hill that it is probable that he himself was, in fact, largely, if not wholly responsible for its composition.

Not long after these letters were written, there occurred an incident in which Hill was to deprive himself, in the long run, of much of his power.

Arthur Quintal's daughter, Charlotte, was found guilty of stealing some yams. Hill declared that the offender ought to be executed!

Charlotte Quintal was then twelve years old. Understandably her father, who was one of Hill's original elders, strongly objected and still opposed Hill's "second offer" that she should at least be made to suffer severely. Quintal declared that she should not be subjected "to the will of the merciless man".

Joshua Hill is reported as then having threatened Quintal with a sword, declaring at the same time, "Confess your sins, or you are a dead man." Quintal, who was dressed in only a pair of "trowsers", said later that his blood ran cold at the feel of the sword against his neck. But he grasped the blade of the sword with his bare hands and forced Hill to his knees. On being allowed up to discuss the matter "in a Christian manner", Hill immediately made a grab for his sword again.

Several young men of the island had been attracted to the school-house by the uproar. They entered before Hill had done any more harm than inflict a few slight cuts to Quintal's neck. The sword was taken from Hill and not returned until he was leaving the island.

The issue of Charlotte Quintal and the yams was dropped.

On 16th September 1834 George Adams and the Buffett family returned to Pitcairn Island, where, despite the protests of Hill, they were allowed to land. John Buffett himself was employed as mate on the ship that brought them, the American brig *Olivia*.

The islanders wrote a petition to Nobbs pleading for his return and offering to pay any expenses incurred. Captain Kendal of the *Olivia* delivered the petition to Nobbs at Gambier, as well as the letter from Commodore Mason referred to previously.

Nobbs and Evans returned to Pitcairn with their families on the *Olivia*, arriving on 13th October. Hill claimed that the letters from Mason to the three Englishmen were forgeries, but the islanders, for the most part, were now determined to defy the old man and allow the families once more to settle among them.

The long tyranny of Hill was drawing to a close.

Commodore Mason wrote from Callao to George Elliott, Secretary of the Admiralty, in a letter dated 2nd January 1836.

I had the honour to receive, on the 28th ult., your letter of the 3rd October, 1835, enclosing copies of letters from the Secretary of the Admiralty and Mr Hay, with other documents relative to the Pitcairn Islanders, and desiring me to go or send a vessel there, to investigate the conduct of Mr

Hill, and to undeceive the people as to his authority. In reply, I beg to inform you, that I have always felt a very strong interest for that most exemplary and Christian Society, and that nothing but the revolutionary state of Peru, since February last, and a foreign war since June, which has put the persons and property of His Majesty's subjects, in common with other foreign merchants, to great hazard, together with the loss of the Challenger, has prevented my going or sending; but in consequence of various letters which I received, as far back as December 1834, I wrote at various times to the victims of Mr Hill's tyranny and oppression, and to Mr Pritchard at Tahiti, informing them of my firm conviction that he had no right to assume any authority on the island, much less to use corporal punishment, or to send any of the inhabitants away. I will however, take the earliest opportunity of going, or sending a vessel, there, and hope to hear that the letters I wrote produced the effect I wished, of releasing the inhabitants from Mr Hill's tyranny and oppression, and of restoring to the island those whome he had driven away.

During a storm on 10th January 1837 the British warship *Actaeon* arrived off Pitcairn Island from Tahiti.

This, and the following day, were so squally, and the sea ran so very high, that we were nearly bearing up for Valparaiso, as we could not work to windward; but fortunately on the 12th, the wind moderated, and our captain landed.

Three canoes came off to the ship, through a heavy surf. In these were Edward, John, Matthew, and Arthur Quintal, George Adams, and Charles Christian. Edward Quintal brought a note from a Mr Hill, and he delivered in due form.

In the *Nautical Magazine* for 1838 (pp. 514-22), referring to Joshua Hill, one of the crew wrote that

We had heard of this man at Valparaiso, and consequently were very much prejudiced against him.

Mr Buffett was a passenger with us from Valparaiso. . . . He was flogged by Edward Quintal, (Mr Hill's right hand man).

We were heartily welcomed by all the island, to whom Mr Hill, or, as we jocosely called him, Lord Hill, from his supposed importance, was very unpopular.

When the captain, Lord Edward Russell,* landed, he was met by the inhabitants who were most eager for him to settle their disputes.

* The story that Hill was known as "Lord" Hill because he had claimed to be related to the Duke of Bedford, and had been exposed by the son of the Duke, who happened to be Lord Edward Russell, does not seem to be borne out by contemporary reports.

Lord Russell called a meeting of all the islanders. It appears that the proceedings of the meeting provoked much laughter. The spell of Joshua Hill was broken and, with the exception of Edward Quintal and his family, the islanders turned on him. Quintal was the only one to support Hill to the end, and the year before had even called his son Henry Joshua in honour of his benefactor.

Hill was ordered to leave the island at the first opportunity. Lord Russell declared, however, that he personally did not consider that he had sufficient authority to carry out the deportation.

George Nobbs, "another Englishman, was elected schoolmaster, by the general voice, and, although not so good a man as could be wished, still will be of much service to them".

Even though Nobbs was once again the teacher, and he himself had been exposed as an impostor, Joshua Hill continued to try to exert his sway over the inhabitants. A proof of his persuasive powers is the fact that some of them once again, to some extent, came under his influence for a while.

At the end of the year, on 6th December, H.M.S. *Imogene*, under Captain Bruce, arrived at Pitcairn Island. Later belief was that the ship had come specifically to remove Hill, but in fact Captain Bruce did not even know of the controversy. However, the state of dissension among the islanders is revealed by Bruce's report to the Admiralty. It is a fascinating and detailed account of the island and its inhabitants. In the comments on Buffett, Nobbs, and Evans the depths of the dissension and the side animosities that must have been aroused are revealed. There is no other way of accounting for Captain Bruce's impressions.

At 2.30 P.M. of December 7th we made Pitcairn's Island, bearing E. by S. ½s. 8 leagues, and carrying on thro' the night, passed to the Eastward of the Island and hove to in "Bounty Bay" at 7 A.M. the 8th, its appearance exactly corresponds with the sketch of "Captain Beechey" on the Small Chart; The water in the Bay and off it, is beautifully clear, and a sandy and rocky bottom visible at 20 fathoms depth.—Most of the native men immediately came on board in their canoes though blowing fresh with, a tumbling swell, being rejoiced at the sight of an English Ship of War "from home", as they term England. They are a [*sic*] very kindly hospitable, and strikingly virtuous and correct, though among the natives it is to be regretted that two cases of deviation from the course of strict morality, have, not long since, occurred; and I am sorry to find that among the three English settlers, there have been cases perpetrated of deep, base, and disgraceful profligacy; the names of these men are

"George Nobbs," John Buffett, and "John Evans" all of whom the people are desirous should be removed from the Island—"Nobbs" is the Teacher and Tailor, "Buffett" a joiner; "Evans" who seems to have preserved his integrity as far as I can learn, to be without reproach, is a sailor by profession, and with respect to the community, a mere vegetating animal. "Mr Hill" a fourth Englishman, who had established his residence here, I brought away at his own request; he had made himself very obnoxious to the natives, having assumed a power and control over them,—which he had neither authority to do, nor ability to execute effectually, and some being led away to side with him, the seeds of dissension among the people were thus sown—it is probable however, that he produced more good than evil amongst them, as with the exception of some arbitrary proceedings, his conduct was marked by the strictest moral integrity; his removal being accomplished, I think harmony will be restored in the community of the Islanders; who nevertheless are most desirous to be relieved of the presence of the three above-mentioned persons, instead of whom they would gladly receive a competent Religious Instructor; and it would be a great boon to this most amiable and deserving people, were our Government to send them a duly authorized person of character, intelligence, and ability to preside over them and their interests; their own Youthful community could now furnish a person competent to instruct the children, under the direction of a clergyman, in the usual branches of general knowledge, reading, writing, arithmetic, geography and history, and without these aids I should much fear that the approaches of depravity and wickedness will scarcely be effectively repelled from the state of society which affords so many temptations. The houses of these islanders are much superior to those of the Sandwich or Society Groups, both in building, accommodation, appearance, and cleanly comfort; the food of the people is simple; principally sweet-potatoes, yams, plantains, and bananas, either baked or made into cakes, and sometimes either pig, or goat, both of which abound, with fowls, as well as fish and vegetables; the island also yields bread-fruit, and sugar cane, and wild tobacco in great profusion; there are two cows and a bull the increase of which the people do not seem to desire to any great degree, as they have no fences sufficient to keep them out of their yams, and potatoe patches; there are also two donkeys for burthen; the soil of Pitcairn's is a rich mould; the land of the whole island would maintain about 300 people. Water is now in abundance, as they have two large reservoirs, but they depend greatly upon the rain to fill them; There is a great deal of wood, in clearing which for cultivation, human skeletons have been dug up always having a pearl shell under the head:—a shell foreign to Pitcairn's; a proof, with others, of the Islands having been inhabited and deserted before the arrival of our countrymen there. It is all strikingly beautiful and picturesque, both on shore, and from the sea; And is very healthy, the only diseases known being asthma, dysentry, and rheumatism. All the articles of food, both animal and vegetable, are very superior in quality.—Two females of the original settlers yet Survive, and are Strong and health-looking; they are "Isabella" or /Mainmast/ Christian's wife, and "Susan" Wife of Young:—both Tahetian Women, who accompanied the Mutineers on their first Settling at Pitcairn's.—The landing at "Bounty Bay" has not improved since Beechey's Visit, and the islanders congratulate themselves on the Security afforded them by it; they however pilot the Boats in Successfully through the Surf, watching the Smooth always, and are most active and expert assistants. To get off Stock, a large Boat should be Anchored outside the Surf, and every thing brought to her in the Canoes; a white flag will be hoisted at the Village on the approach of an English ship, when landing is practicable in Bounty Bay, and the Ship can heave to close inside Adam's Rock.—We had So Strong a Westerly Current during the two days we remained as with Easterly Winds, to find a diffi-culty in Keeping our place. The other landing place as indicated on Beechey's Admiralty Chart, on the West-end, is a Very good one with East, S.E. or N.E., but the Walk over the Hill is a Stiff one. The only Vessels that have touched here Since H.M. Ship "Actaeon," were the "Colocolo," a "Chilian," and the "Hobomok," an American whaler. These primitive people do not now like thoughts of leaving their island, unless to see England, /home as they call it/ which all of them would like to do; Yet in time some of them will find it necessary to Emigrate, when perhaps the Younger families will go. The island of "Toubouai" would be an Advantageous place for the whole Pitcairn's Population to be removed to, it has good landing and a harbour for Small Vessels;—Wood and Water in Abundance, a fertile Soil; with only 74 inhabitants 2/3 of whom are Males; and, I was informed by Mr Consul Charlton, it might be purchased for £100—

Having done all that was in my power for the Advantage of these primitive and Amiable, and most interesting islanders, and having wit-nessed undoubted proofs of their great attachment to the Countrymen and land of their Fathers, the whole Scope of my instructions was fulfilled, with the exception of returning to "Valparaiso"; for which end at 7. P.M. on Saturday December 9th. we Stood away to the Southward.

Included with this report was a chart showing the number of people on the island, divided roughly into adults and children of each family. The population on 10th December 1837 is given as 95.

As this account shows, Joshua Hill managed to convince Captain Bruce that he was leaving Pitcairn at his own wish, and he obtained a statement to this effect from the captain.

With the departure of H.M.S. *Imogene*, the saga of Joshua Hill comes to an end. In spite of the dissension he caused, he had at least stopped excessive drinking on the island and had caused some improvement to be made to the roadway and to the Landing Place—a small tally for five years' sojourn.

On the other hand, he had divided the people, much more than had the rift between John Buffett and George Nobbs. Above all, he had destroyed their innocence, after abusing it by seizing power without warrant or justice.

Hill was put ashore at Valparaiso and eventually made his way back to England.

In 1841 Captain Hill wrote another "Memorandum", this time to the British Government, claiming payment for the time he had spent attending to the needs of the Pitcairn Islanders. In this document he included a vitriolic attack on George Hunn Nobbs and John Buffett, accusing them of the most outrageous deeds since they had arrived on the island.

The last public record of Joshua Hill appears to be in 1844, when at the age of seventy-one he wrote to the Government a bitter condemnation of the morals of the missionaries who had been at Tahiti during his visit there twelve years before.

George Pritchard, British Consul on Tahiti

passing the previous part of his life in affluence and comfort,) to throw himself upon the bounty of his gracious Sovereign for the means of closing his days in tranquillity and respect as a faithful christian teacher.

And your Memorialist, &c.

(Signed) *Joshua Hill*

London, *1841,*

27ᵗʰ May.

Signature of Joshua Hill

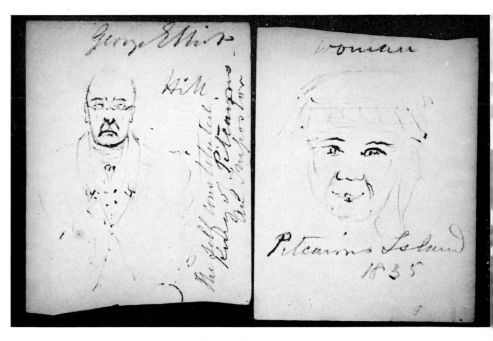

Sketch of Joshua Hill

CHAPTER XIV

THE PITCAIRN ISLAND RECORDER

Well now I am resolved to keep a journal
Not in a Magazine or Album stile
Nor by the month or week,—but hodiernal
A faithful Chronicle of Pitcairn Isle.—
Whatever haps to come within my knowledge
Relating to our City or our College

I write because sojourners bid me do so
They say 'twill interest the folks at home
I write because reports a little so so
By Malice propagated, current roam.
Respecting what is past I would stand neuter
But shall with scandal grapple for the future.

GHN

ON New Year's Day of 1838 George Hunn Nobbs began keeping a journal which he called "The Pitcairn Island Recorder".

It is an invaluable record of life on Pitcairn, and, in passing, it reveals something further of Nobbs himself.

On the first day of the journal, Nobbs recorded that since the departure of the *Imogene* (meaning, of course, Joshua Hill), all the inhabitants were united, "with the exception of one family" who "keep aloof from the rest, neither do their children attend the public school".

The family, of course, was that of Edward Quintal, Hill's former right-hand man. Old enmities died hard, but the island code of morality shines through Nobbs's entry for 17th February.

After the school was dismissed Hannah Young sent to say she wished to speak to me. On going to her house, she said the reason for sending for me was to enquire whether I had any objection to make against her sending Louisa Quintall (daughter of Edwd Quintall) to school—this child

K

being Hannah's god-daughter. I told her I certainly had none; but sincerely wished Edward Quintall would send all his children to the public school—Hannah remarked that she had promised in the sight of God to procure instruction for this child; and that I had done the same therefore we ought not permit her to remain in ignorance if we could help it—I replied that I could not charge myself with any fault on that head; for it was well known that as soon as Hill left the island I went to Edwd Quintall and requested him to send his children to me for instruction but he declined doing so; therefore no blame can attach itself to me. However, said I, if you can obtain permission for the child to attend school send her, by all means, and I will do my duty by her, let her father's conduct towards me be what it may.

At this period Edward Quintal had three children of school age—Edward, aged 13½, Abraham, 11, and Louisa, 9.

Then, on 5th March, Nobbs sent oranges he had collected to each of the families on the island for their children. Edward Quintal refused the gift.

About forty pupils attended the school, which began each morning, Monday to Saturday, at 7.30 a.m. and continued until noon. Sometimes there was a second session in the afternoon, but Nobbs often had reasons for cancelling the second one.

On New Year's Day the school was dismissed early in the morning because the rest of the day was to be spent helping divide some grounds belonging to Sarah, the widow of Daniel McCoy. On 3rd January there was no afternoon class, the time being used in the construction of the first public toilet on the island. And on the fifth, instead of keeping school, Nobbs recorded that he was busy digging ground and planting potatoes.

Of the children attending school at the beginning of the year, 22 were learning to write and 13 to do arithmetic. In general, Nobbs reported, the children learnt readily enough, but on such matters as money and time they were liable to make ludicrous mistakes, there being neither money nor timepieces upon the island.

The entry for 8th January reports that because of incessant rain from the night before until 2 p.m. there was no school that day.

Being much troubled with rheumatism, and having no coat or jacket fit to keep out the rain.—(the distance from my house to the school being considerable) I was afraid to venture out. Obtained some duck cloth from Mr Adams and Mrs Christian 2nd and set about making a coat which when finished I intend to cover with paint which of course will render it water proof, and then I hope the wet weather will be no obstruction to the school.

Nobbs complained bitterly on 12th March at being asked to help with the cleaning of the water reservoir after he had cancelled the afternoon class.

These reservoirs are not cleaned out more than once in two years and it is not six hours work yet the man who is engaged all the week teaching their children cannot be excused from taking part in this scavenger like employment; Oh! the [un]enviable situation of a teacher on Pitcairn Island, God grant I may be relieved from this thankless office before many months hence:

The Recorder gives an interesting account of the manner in which the Pitcairners went fishing. The entry for Saturday, 6th January, reads:

Some few of the inhabitants gone on the rocks in quest of fish, others hunting goats, in order to provide meat for the sabbath: while those who can afford it have made up their minds to kill a pig or some fowls.—I presume this mode of conduct will require some explanation which it is my design to give as clearly as I can. First, it must be borne in mind that animal food is by no means plentiful on Pitcairn's;—Fish has ever been their main stay but that too is becoming scarce. No family on the island can afford to eat land meat more than two days in the week, upon an average, the whole year round. Fish may, or may not, be obtained three days more so that at least two days in the week; yams or potatoes mashed up in a villanous compound of cocoa nuts and common water, and which in smell is but one remove from Russian train oil, forms the general fare: But let the food be what it may, the remainder of the week; every effort is used to procure meat for saturday evening and sunday.—If the weather is favourable six or eight canoes put to sea about eight o'clock on saturday morning and remain fishing the greater part of the day; if successful they procure a sufficiency for their own families and are enabled to impart a little to others.—generally speaking they take enough fish to last till the following monday. Sometimes, though, they are not so fortunate and after being exposed to a scorching sun all day; and perhaps losing a hundred fathoms of line, five or six pounds of lead and a lot of hooks into the bargain they return in the evening half famished and but two or three small fish to repay their toil. Another method of procuring fish is upon the crags of the level of the sea, where the surf breaks with appalling violence. This mode of fishing is not confined to the day only, but is also practised frequently at night, of night fishing I shall speak hereafter, Those who have made up their minds to go upon the rocks, start early in the morning, the parties generally consist of one or two men and several women or girls. the men are armed with slender poles each from

ten to twelve feet long. a blunt knife and a basket. Having descended to
the rocks, which are from two to three hundred feet below the common
level of the island, the men with practised eye watches the influence of
the surf. As soon as the foam occasioned by the dash of the last billow is
a little cleared away they run out to the extremity of the crags, which
frequently terminate very abruptly, and search around for a blue fish
which generally keeps near the shore and is considered by inhabitants
who eat it raw a very great dainty. Should one of these fish be within
reach of their weapon they make a sharp thrust at it; not permitting the
staff to go out of their hands;—if their intention is accomplished they
retreat as fast as possible from the returning surf with the fish still
struggling on the barbs. Sometimes, if the fish is not sufficiently near to
justify the attempt they watch its motions till the surf, which returns
at short intervals, is approaching with fearful rapidity; they then start
inland and generally eludes its violence. There is a great deal of daring
and danger in the amusement, as they frequently term it: for the recur-
rence of the surf is so frequent that if they did remain on the crags till
the very last moment their chance of securing a fish would be small.
Again to stop too long, independent of the danger attending it would
mar their sport; for should any part of their body get wetted by the salt
water the fish, whose taste or smell is very acute, disappears instantly
If the fish proves shy as is sometimes the case they chew a piece of raw
crab and spit it into the water which generally succeeds in bringing it
within reach. One singular method they have, which notwithstanding the
incessant swell, and the numberless rugged proturberances under the
water, they frequently practised with success—But this is Saturday afternoon and as there are no boats out fishing, the weather being too rugged,
I must fish in the hog sty for meat for supper to night and for tomorrow
consequently, being prest for time I must defer the remainder of my
description to another opportunity.

Line-fishing, the Pitcairners would sometimes be troubled by sharks,
which would eat the fish caught before they could be brought in.

The usual day on the island was spent by the women "busy Cooking,
Nursing, Washing, or making Hats", and by the men "either pulling
down or building up; or per adventure sharpening their tools preparatory
to doing so".

On 9th January it was decided after consultation among the men to
build a house for Arthur Quintal senior, the one intended for Thursday
October Christian being deferred. Quintal was determined to begin rebuilding his immediately, and as several of the islanders had been helped
by him in building their own houses, "those who are indebted to him are
fearful if they go on with Christian's house they will not have an opportunity to discharge the obligation they are under to Arthur Quintall".

However, after preparing nails, cutting timber, and collecting leaves of the pandanus-tree to thatch the house, the building was commenced. In little over three weeks the rebuilding was finished, and as usual when a community effort was involved, Quintal killed a pig so the workers could celebrate with him.

When John Buffett built three tables for George Adams, John Quintal senior, and George Nobbs, they celebrated the occasion with a pig killed by Adams for the four of them.

A week after Arthur Quintal's house was finished, the tools were once again prepared for building, this time for Thursday October Christian's house.

One of Nobbs's complaints was that presents were given to the islanders by the crews of various ships calling at Pitcairn, but that he and his family usually missed out. "The sailors on board a ship think it would be insulting me (A teacher and of course in their idea a great man) to offer me any trifle they may have to spare. And the Captains think it is more charity to give it to the natives."

Poor Nobbs!

On 30th January we find the account given by George Nobbs of the manner in which the Pitcairners made oil:

Last evening after dark several of the natives came to assist me in the preparatory process of making oil from the cocoa nut This is technically called Scraping the dry nut which is effected by means of a slender iron bar about three feet long pointed at one end, and flattened and brought to an edge at the other; the pointed end is stuck into the ground in a slanting direction, and the inside of the cocoa nut (after being broke exactly in the middle) is brought into contact with the flatted edge, which in a short time, owing to the skillfulness of the operator, reduces the meat of the nut into thin flakes resembling snow. After a sufficient number of cocoa nut have undergone this operation the meat is closely pressed into a large wooden trough and covered with leaves where it remains six or seven days and acquires great heat, which causes a considerable quantity of the oil to separate from the grosser substance. The oil thus obtained is always the best, being the clearest and sweetest. During the heating process a considerable quantity of a particular leaf is cut up fine and mixed with the cocoa nut mass which in great measure prevents the offensive smell which the rotting cocoa nut would acquire, it serves also to give it a consistency when put into the press. In about a week the oil is fit for pressing; the hotter the day the greater is the quantity of oil obtained;—it is first spread in the sun for three or four hours and then put into small canvas bags and press'd by a simple lever about eight or nine feet long with four or five men and boys seated on the end farthest from the fulcrum. This is the whole process of making oil on Pitcairn Island. It takes about fifteen nuts on an average to make a quart of oil. Some of the women have resumed their laborious but necessary employment of beating tappa. The process will be described at length at some future time.

Unfortunately, the Recorder ends in May without the descriptions which Nobbs postponed to a future time.

When the surgeon aboard H.M.S. *Curacao*, Dr William Gunn, gave a great deal of assistance to the islanders during an epidemic in August 1841, Nobbs presented him with the Recorder. It is now in the Mitchell Library in Sydney.

CHAPTER XV

A BRITISH CROWN COLONY

ALTHOUGH they were not in actual fact British subjects, the people of Pitcairn had more or less regarded themselves as being under the patronage of the British Government.

In his report to Rear-Admiral C. B. H. Ross, the Commander of H.M.S. *Fly*, Russell Elliott, wrote from Callao on 25th January 1839, that he had arrived at Pitcairn Island on 29th November the previous year.

He reported that there were then ninety-nine inhabitants on the island, and that they were most anxious to have someone in charge of the island for their internal regulation and government:

. . . but more especially to meet the difficulties and dangers which they had already experienced, and were again threatened with, by lawless strangers in whale ships; there having been cases of recent occurrence, where half the ruffian crew of a whale ship were on shore for a fortnight, during which time, they offered every insult to the inhabitants, and threatened to violate any woman whose protectors they could overcome by force, occasioning the necessary concentration of the men's strength for the personal protection of the females, and thereby great damage to their crops, which demanded their constant attention; taunting them that they had no laws, no country, no authority that they were to respect— American vessels denying that they were under the protection of Great Britain, as they had neither colours nor written authority.

Elliott did find, nevertheless, that the Pitcairn Islanders were flying a merchant Union Jack given them by an English vessel.

Because he did not know the British Government's intentions in relation to Pitcairn, Elliott decided to confer "the stamp of authority on their election of a magistrate or elder, to be periodically chosen from among themselves, and answering for his proceedings to Her Majesty's Government".

Russell Elliott drew up a few "hasty regulations" and an election was held. The unanimous choice of the Pitcairn Islanders was "a most able and superior senior of their number", Edward Quintal.

The date, 29th November 1838, is now regarded as being the time from which Pitcairn Island became a British Crown Colony, though it was not formerly annexed by Elliott.

The regulations set down that an elder or magistrate was to be elected by the free votes of all the inhabitants born on the island—male and female—who had reached the age of eighteen. Anyone living on the island for five years also became eligible to vote, but not to stand for office.

The franchise being given to its women in 1838, Pitcairn can perhaps make another historic claim apart from its *Bounty* fame.

The Chief Magistrate was to hold the main authority on the island and settle all differences that might arise. Any problems he was unable to iron out were to be decided by the captain of the next man-of-war visiting the island.

Two councillors were also to help the Magistrate, one to be nominated by the Magistrate and the other to be elected at the same time as the Magistrate.

The original ten regulations reflected the special requirements of the island, and were later expanded and amended. They are unique in the laws of the world.

No. 1—Laws and Regulations of Pitcairn's Island

The Magistrate is to convene the public on occasions of complaints being made to him; and, on hearing both sides of the question, commit it to a jury.

He is to see all fines levied, and all public works executed; and every one must treat him with respect.

He is not to assume any power or authority on his own responsibility, or without the consent of the majority of the people.

A public journal shall be kept by the Magistrate, and shall from time to time be read; so that no one shall plead ignorance of the law for any crime he may commit. The journal shall be submitted to the inspection of those captains of British men-of-war, which occasionally touch at the island.

No. 2—Laws for Dogs

If any one's dog is found chasing a goat, the owner of that dog shall pay a fine of one dollar and a half; one dollar to the owner of the goat or goats, and the other half to the informer.

If any dog kills or otherwise injures a goat, the owner of the dog so offending must pay the damages; but should suspicion rest on no particular dog, the owners of dogs generally must pay the damage. The foregoing law is of no effect when the goat or goats are upon cultivated ground.

Persons who have fowls or hogs in the bush may take dogs to hunt them, but should the dogs commit damage during the hunt, the person taking the dogs to hunt must pay the damage.

No. 3—Law for Cats

If any person under the age of ten years shall kill a cat, he or she shall receive corporal punishment. If any one, between the ages of ten and fifteen, kill a cat, he or she shall pay a fine of twenty-five dollars; half the fine to be given to the informer, the other half to the public. All masters of families convicted of killing a cat shall be fined fifty dollars; half of the fine to be given to the informer, the other half to the public.

N.B. Every person, from the age of fifteen and upwards, shall pay a fine similar to masters of families.

No. 4—Laws for Hogs

If a pig does any damage, the person who sustains the damage may take the pig so trespassing, no matter whether he sees the pig committing damage, or another person see the pig committing damage. If any person or persons, see a pig, or pigs, committing damage, and neglect to inform the person sustaining the damage, the person guilty of such neglect must pay the damage.

No. 5—Law Regarding the School

There must be a school kept, to which all parents shall be obliged to send their children, who must previously be able to repeat the alphabet, and be of the age of from six to sixteen.

Mr. Nobbs shall be placed at the head of the School, assisted by such persons as shall be named by the Chief Magistrate.

The school hours shall be from seven o'clock in the morning until noon, on all days except Saturdays and Sundays, casulties and sickness excepted.

One shilling, or an equivalent as marked below, shall be paid for each child per month, by the parents, whether the child attend School or not.

In case Mr. Nobbs does not attend, the Assistant appointed by the Chief Magistrate shall receive the salary in proportion to the time Mr Nobbs is away.

Equivalent for money:*		s	d
One Barrel of Yams	valued at	8	0
One Barrel of Sweet Potatoes	„ „	8	0
One Barrel of Irish Potatoes	„ „	12	0
Three good Bunches of Plantains	„ „	4	0
One Day's Labour	„ „	2	0

* The value of yams and potatoes has also been recorded as two dollars, the plantains as one dollar, and the day's labour at half a dollar.

The Chief Magistrate is to see the labour is well performed; and goods which may be given for money, shall be delivered, either at the market-place, or at the house of Mr. Nobbs, as he may direct.

No. 6—Miscellaneous

If any person wants to cultivate any lands, he is to give notice of it to the public; and any person wanting any wood is to go on the aforesaid land and get it. If any person cuts more wood than is sufficient to build his house, the wood that remains after his house is finished is to be given to the next person who may want it to build a house. This extends only to the mero and borou timber.

Any person who may want any trees to break off the wind from his plantations or houses, is to make it known; and no one is allowed to cut them down, even if they be upon his own land.

At any meeting which may take place, there shall be no bringing up things that are past to criminate others, with a view to prevent justice with the case before the magistrate. Any one doing so shall be punished by such a fine as a jury may think proper to award.

The Magistrate is to appoint churchwardens, four in number, beginning on the first of every month.

Any person detected in shooting, or in any way killing white birds (unless it be for the sick) shall, for each bird that is killed, pay a dollar.

No. 7—Laws for Wood

If any person goes to cut logs, to enclose a piece of ground, or any other purpose, he is not to cut any fit for building a dwelling-house. The Magistrate is to appoint four men to inspect the logs after they are brought home; and should any be found serviceable for building dwelling-houses, they are to be taken from him and given to the next person who builds a house.

The third year from the time a person commences cutting wood he is to pick a share of thatch for covering dwelling-houses.

If the wood is left longer than the time specified, it is to be taken from him and given to the next person who builds a house.

Any person cutting logs, must not cut green ones until no more dry ones can be found. Any person without a pig-sty and wanting one, is allowed to cut green logs to make it with, if dry logs are not to be found.

No person is allowed to cut down any trees for logs on which there are young ones growing, which may become serviceable for building in future.

Any person having a large enclosure round his pig-sty, cutting down any tree on which there is any good logs, is not allowed to take the logs, but he is to leave it for the benefit of those who have no enclosure. He is also bound to inform those who have no enclosure where the logs are to be found; but if they do not cut them at the end of two weeks, any one may be allowed to cut them, and keep them for such service as they please. No one may cut green logs to repair his large enclosure, save what he may find on trees which have been cut and left above two weeks.

No. 8—Laws respecting Landmarks

On the first day of January, after the Magistrate is elected, he shall assemble all those who should be deemed necessary; and with them he is to visit all landmarks that are upon the island, and replaces those that are lost. Should anything occur to prevent its accomplishment in the time specified (the 1st of January), the Magistrate is bound to see it done the first opportunity.

No. 9—Laws for Trading with Ships

No person or persons shall be allowed to get spirits of any sort from any vessel, or sell it to strangers or any person upon the island. Any one found guilty of so doing shall be punished by fine, or such other punishment as a jury shall determine on. No intoxicating liquor whatever shall be allowed to be taken on shore, unless it be for medical purposes. Any person found guilty of transgressing this law, shall be severely punished by a jury.

No females are allowed to go on board of a foreign vessel, of any size or description, without the permission of the Magistrate; and in case the Magistrate does not go on board himself, he is to appoint four men to look after the females.

No. 10—Law for the Public Anvil &c.

Any person taking the public anvil and public sledge-hammer from the blacksmith's shop is to take it back after he has done with it; and in case the anvil and sledge-hammer should get lost by his neglecting to take it back, he is to get another anvil and sledge-hammer, and pay a fine of four shillings.

Such were the original laws of the new British Crown Colony of Pitcairn's Island.

Edward Quintal was re-elected Chief Magistrate on 2nd January 1839. Fletcher Christian II was elected as one of the councillors and Edward Quintal chose his son William as the other councillor.

A whaling vessel called the *Cyrus* called at the island on 19th July that year, thirty months out from New Bedford. The captain allowed the carpenter to remain ashore for a couple of weeks. He was very popular with the islanders, and became especially friendly with George Adams.

Upon leaving the island, he was presented by his new friend, George Adams, with the original Bible taken ashore from the *Bounty*.

The Bible eventually found its way into the hands of the Historical Society of Connecticut. A headmaster on Pitcairn Island, Mr A. W.

Moverley, wrote to the Society requesting that the Bible be returned to the people of the island. To this the Historical Society agreed, and in 1937 the Bible was handed over to the British Ambassador at Washington to arrange for its return to Pitcairn. It is now the most prized possession of the religious people of Pitcairn Island.

When Pitcairn Island issued its first postage stamps the twopenny one carried as its centre piece the *Bounty* Bible.

Captain Elliott had proposed that a British ship-of-war should visit the colony at least each twelve months. H.M.S. *Sparrowhawk*, under the command of Captain H. Shepherd, arrived at Pitcairn Island on 9th November 1839.

George Nobbs, who had taken over the task of keeping the Pitcairn Island Register from John Buffett in July that year, recorded that when the captain and several of the officers landed at 11 a.m. they brought with them General Ramon Freire of Chile. When Nobbs was a mercenary under Lord Cochrane he had met Freire, who was then a colonel. Friere had become the Chilean dictator, but, defeated in 1839, had fled the country, his life spared by his opponents. For Nobbs, while Freire's visit lasted, the long hand of his past revived old memories and old wounds.

At the time of the *Sparrowhawk's* visit, Lieutenant James Lowry recorded that the population was then 51 males and 51 females, and that "Some of the girls and young women were very pretty, and would be considered beauties in Old England, and all were good-looking".

Of Fletcher Christian's only daughter, Mary Ann, he wrote: "There has been only one old maid on the island, and she is now nearly fifty, and is as cross and crabbed as any old maid need be; she rails against the early marriages most heartily."

The last five marriages before the arrival of the *Sparrowhawk* show that the Pitcairners of the second generation were indeed marrying young. On 30th October 1836 there had been two marriages. Charles Christian III, aged 18, married Charlotte Quintal, aged 14, and Matthew McCoy, aged 17, married Margaret Christian, also aged 14.

In 1837 Arthur Quintal II, at the age of 21, married his fifteen-year-old cousin, Martha Quintal, on 22nd October. And on 5th November John Quintal, at 17, married Dinah Young eleven days before her thirteenth birthday. Dinah was still attending school when the warship called at Pitcairn, though by then she had a son, John Quintal III, who was born on 23rd December 1838.

There were no marriages in 1838, and the only marriage in 1839 was on 24th March, between Thursday October Christian II, aged 19, and Mary (Polly) Young, who was then only 14.

The average age of the first generation at marriage was 22 for the males and 21 for the females. However, up to this period, the average age of marriage partners of the second generation was 18 for the males and only 14 for the females.

The community was divided into thirteen family groups at the end of 1839.

After Captain Shepherd had decided several cases submitted to him for decision by the Chief Magistrate, Edward Quintal, the *Sparrowhawk* sailed for Tahiti on 12th November.

Lowry also recorded that "Some years ago, they managed to distil a spirit which made them all drunk; when, after a short time, they felt it hurt the constitution, they made a law that no more should be made, since which time drunkenness has not been known on the island."

Left to themselves, the Pitcairners had no need of Joshua Hill's autocratically imposed temperance society to safeguard themselves.

As for thoughts of once again migrating to some other place, Lowry said that they would not be anxious to leave their home again, and that "they themselves seem quite aware that they are far better off and happier than the generality of mankind".

CHAPTER XVI

ROCK OF THE WEST

GROWN comfortable with respectability and serene with the leisureliness of life on the island, the Pitcairners came to call their island home the "Rock of the West". For so it still seemed—like a great rock jutting out of the sea; but the apt description also fitted the sense of security and solidity the Pitcairners drew from their home soil, set as it was in isolated loneliness in the vast Pacific.

The tightly knit little community was a happy one. As a romantic corner of the British Empire, once a year it received an official visit from a British man-o'-war; while other ships that called—and every year the number of such visitors increased—brought supplies of stock, seed, books, Bibles, and medicines. In return, the islanders' hospitality was such that Pitcairn was famous amongst the world's mariners, and the Pitcairners were renowned for their kindness, honesty, and sincerity.

Witness the farewell to the ship *Pandora* that called in 1848, the sentiments of the islanders being recorded in the island Register by George Hunn Nobbs: "that the good ship Pandora and all her gallant crew may escape the perils of the deep, and before many months have elapsed show her number some early morning at Spithead is the wish of their friends residing on the 'Rock of the West' ".

Nobbs had taken over the task of keeping the island's Register in the middle of 1839.

At the year's end, he issued a simple statistical report on the island's progress:

Number of births this year, eight, Marriages, one Deaths, three. Thirteen ships have touched here this year: a greater number than ever arrived before in the same space of time. Fifty two scholars attended public school, Number of inhabitants 106, 53 of each sex.

In January the following year, the annual elections for Chief Magistrate and councillors over, Nobbs formed the island's first Sunday-school, which he himself undertook to teach. He was now Sunday-school teacher, unofficial minister, recorder, and doctor.

His status was disputed by very few, but especially by Hill's old ally, Edward Quintal. However, it seems that Quintal, an honest but severe and straight-laced man, was hostile anyway to the three strangers on the island—Nobbs, Buffett, and Evans. The last-named had grown increasingly quiet with the passing of the years, and Buffett was in every respect but the accident of his birth an islander. He sometimes used to stand in for Nobbs when the latter was ill. And running right through the Register is a record of Nobbs being ill—as he was for several days in the middle of April 1840, at the time of one of the violent storms which still frequently strike the island.

On the evening between the eighteenth and the nineteenth of April experienced a heavy gale of wind from the W.N.W. which did considerable damage to the Bread Fruit, plantains; orange trees &c: some large pieces of the Banian-tree* were broke off; and considerable fears were entertained by some of the inhabitants for the safety of their houses. But through the mercy of Him who "rideth on the storm" no accident occurred. At day light the gale broke. Mem. The wind blew with greater violence than at any other time these twelve years past. In consequence of the ill health of the teacher no school have been kept for some time past.—Mr. Buffett officiating on the Sabbath.

On 2nd May Edward Quintal and John Evans came to blows. The cause of the dispute is not recorded. The fact that Evans received "several bruises" is, however, and the fight probably stemmed from the animosity Quintal held for Evans. The fracas quite astonished the other Pitcairners, who were now little used to violence or bloodshed.

The extent of quarrels amongst the Pitcairners was usually confined to what they termed "arguments of the tongue". The London Missionary Society was astounded that Nobbs should record what seemed a trifling affair, but it probably served Nobbs to underline the bad feeling between Quintal and the Englishmen. It also underlines, by inference, the general peaceableness of the islanders.

The London Missionary Society took considerable interest in the little community, yet for some reason never sent a fully ordained minister to Pitcairn, despite repeated requests from the islanders sent through numerous captains of ships that had called at Pitcairn. In addition, Moerenhout

* It is under this banyan-tree, the famous banyan-tree of Pitcairn Island, that John Adams lies buried.

had pointed out, and evangelical-minded churchmen and friends in England agreed, that the Pitcairners, being not only deeply religious but part-Polynesian, would have made ideal missionaries for the Pacific islands.

In November of the same year that Quintal and Evans fought, 1840, the missionary packet *Camden* arrived off the island bearing the Society's Reverend Mr Heath and presents from the Governor of New South Wales, Sir George Gipps, and from the Bishop of London.

Mr Heath was fêted as an honoured guest, and the *Camden* was made even more welcome than other ships.

Pitcairn Island thrived on visitors. A glimpse of distant sail meant new friends, and another tantalizing glimpse of the great world not only beyond their shores, but almost beyond their ken. Yet the visits were not without troubles.

As regularly as ships called, the sheltered islanders fell victims to fevers. Each year from 1841 to 1847, fever or influenza took a steady toll. In 1845, after half the population had suffered fever, Nobbs wrote in the Register:

I will now say a few words respecting the salubrity of the island; it is generally supposed to be a healthy spot; indeed appearances seem to justify such a conclusion: but the reverse is found by experience, to be the fact. Asthmas, Rheumatism, Consumption, Scrofula and last but not least Influenza under various modifications is prevalent. Five times within the last four years have the fever been rife among us, and though it has not been so severe latterly as it was on its first appearance this I think may be accounted for by the teacher becoming more acquainted with the nature of the disease (thanks to Dr Gunn) and also with the appropriate remedies,—when the influenza first appeared among us it did not spread so rapidly as it has done at its subsequent reappearance, but the cough was more violent then, than it has been since. This I attribute to the teacher's not having giving them emetics as soon as the disease attacked them; since then he has invariably given them vomits on the first appearance of the disease; which seems to prevent any considerable degree of cough But there is one particular in which the recent fever differs from the previous ones, viz in the total absence of a cold fit at the very commencement. I have seen some of the patients when first attacked tremble as violently, and apparently from the same causes, as ever I saw a anyone [*sic*] under the influence of ague. Now, in this last sickness it was not thus; only one person complained of cold and he was but slightly affected. —the first person attacked was a man of full habit of body, plethoric and subject to fits, he had attended Divine service in the morning, it being the Sabbath, after evening service I found him under the influence of a raging fever; his eyes seemed ready to start from their sockets and the heat of his skin caused a disagreeable sensation to those who touched him;—he complained of violent pains in his head, back and thighs and said he felt as if "live things were creeping between his flesh and skin." Fearing it might bring on one of the fits to which he was subject the teacher bled him, and gave him a suporif which had a good effect; the next day a dose of calomel and jalap was administered, and two days after that he was well; though very weak.

I do not think the fever was infectious; and though in the space of six days not less than sixty out of one hundred and twenty two were attacked yet I attribute it solely to the peculiar state of the atmosphere; whenever we have been visited by this epidemick the circumstances, as respects the weather have been invariably the same. A long drought succeeded by two or three weeks of wet; and the wind settling into the north west; in fact a north west wind is always the precussor of rheumatism, catarrh, and slight febrile affection. Bleeding is not to be recommended; vomits are the sovereign remedy for certainly no community of persons secrete greater quantities of bile than the inhabitants of this island.

At the beginning of the epidemic in 1841, the man-o'-war *Curacao*, under Captain Jenkin Jones, happened to arrive from Callao. The ship's surgeon, Dr William Gunn, stayed on shore for three days treating the stricken people, and Nobbs, after receiving instruction from Dr Gunn on the continued treatment of his patients, presented the good doctor with his "Pitcairn Island Recorder".

One of the worst stricken was the island's first Chief Magistrate, the stiff-necked Edward Quintal; and despite patient nursing by his former antagonist, Nobbs, Quintal died on 8th September. As he was one of the most important of the first generation of native-born Pitcairners, Quintal's death could be regarded as the end of an epoch on the island.

His opposition to the English "foreigners" on the island, which had included forbidding his children to attend Nobbs's school, had been tempered by one of fate's ironies. When Chief Magistrate, he had been responsible for seeing that all children on the island attended the public school. For his term of office, the cantankerous but high-minded Quintal saw to it that his children attended.

Eleven days after his death, another figure notable in the island's history followed him to the grave. This was Mauatua (or Maimiti), Fletcher Christian's widow. The famous Tahitian, whom Christian called Isabella, claimed until her death that Captain Cook's first arrival at Tahiti was "perfectly remembered by her". Her age was unknown, but she must have been more than eighty when she died.

Mauatua's death left only one of the original *Bounty* people on the island—Teraura, or Susannah, the widow of both Midshipman Edward Young and of Fletcher Christian's eldest son, Thursday October. She survived until 15th July 1850, when she died, aged about seventy-five.

Susannah was amongst those of the islanders—and most of them were present—on a day early in 1845, when the young men of the island, carrying ropes, slipped beneath the waters of Bounty Bay on a historic salvage mission—to bring up the guns of H.M.S. *Bounty.*

With the sea-wind idling in the bay, and the surge and fall of the water at a propitious ebb, the descendants of the men who had tended and manned the cannon watched and waited for the first trace of the ship to reappear.

The able-bodied men stood to the hauling ropes once the swimmers had fastened them to the sunken *Bounty's* guns. (Did they take the rope a turn round the tree against which *Bounty's* hawser had fretted and rubbed in the days when the mutineers were first ashore?)

The slack taken up on the rope, the guns resisted. Then, abruptly the first jerked free, and the islanders could feel the heavy weight dragging clear of the sunken hulk. Gradually, foot by foot, the guns came to the surface.

For fifty five years they had been deposited at the bottom of the sea on a bed of coral guiltless of blood,—(during the time so many thousands of mankind in Europe became "Food for cannon") but on saturday last one of these guns resumed its original vocation; at least the innoxious portion of it, to wit, belching forth fire and smoke, and causing the island to reverberate with its bellowing: the other gun is condemned to silence having been spiked by someone of the Bounty's crew.

So Nobbs recorded. Coral-encrusted, hoary with seaweed, the guns had to be cleaned down; but Nobbs, the one-time master-gunner and soldier of fortune, says no more of the islanders' sentiments or the state of the cannons.

Life continued on the island, placidly and harmoniously, with little of moment to mark the passage of time. Life was uneventful, almost humdrum, until the second week of April 1845. Then, on 16th April, Nobbs made the following lengthy entry in his Register:

For several days past the weather have been cloudy with occasional showers; winds very variable. Yesterday the wind blew from the S.S.E. and it began to rain in good earnest; as the day declined the wind increased; at sunset it blew a gale. All hands busily employed securing the roofs of the houses and making all snug before dark.—a dirty night was anticipated and our fears were more than realized; at 10 o'clock the wind shifted four or five points to the westward and the sheet lightning began to break the monotony of the lurid atmosphere: By midnight a perfect typhoon raged above and around us; the whole concave of the heavens was in a continued blaze and the roar of the thunder, though not so very loud (with the exception of one burst) was incessant.—From the position of the wind, which veered and hauled four or five points, the houses were a good deal sheltered from its violence or they would, most assuredly have been prostrated; therefore the most of us, though we passed a sleepless night, were in mercy permitted to remain quiet in our houses.—Very frequently through the night loud crashes were heard, which we supposed were the trees in the higher parts of the island yielding to the fury of the storm;—the noise did proceed from the falling, and smashing of trees, but from a cause, of which we were, at that time happily ignorant.

At daylight a man, much alarmed, came to my house saying "a part of the island had given way and was going into the sea;"—From the door of my house I obtained an imperfect view of the spot from which a portion of the earth had been detached and felt certain it was an avalanche occasioned by the wind acting upon the trees, and the torrents of rain which fell detaching the earth from the parts above it. So great was the consternation and amazement of many of the natives that although they had seen the spot from which the earth had slidden almost every day of their lives, yet they could not so far collect their ideas as to remember the original appearance of the place, whose property it had been;* nor the locality of the parts near it;—As to the cause of the disruption various opinions prevailed some said it was occasioned by a water-spout, others that a thunderbolt had fallen there and a third party were anxiously enquiring if it were not probable the sea had perforated a hole from the under side of the island and so washed it away.—That they had considerable occasion for alarm cannot be disputed, and what may easily be referred to natural causes (and those not very recondite either) would to persons so inexperienced as our community, appear mysterious and awful. I will endeavour, in a few words, to describe what presented itself to our view at daylight. On going out of doors we saw that a considerable portion of the earth had been detached from the side of the [word omitted] but to what extent we could not then ascertain;—the place in question was situated at the head of a ravine which debouched into the sea; the rain mixing with the falling earth (which was of clayey nature) brought it to the consistency of thick mud but sufficiently liquified to glide very slowly down the inclined plane of the valley;—nothing with which it came in contact could resist its force,—the large trees at the head of the ravine, and immense pieces of rock, were borne slowly but unresistingly along and about three hundred cocoa nut trees were torn up by the roots and swept into the sea.

* The first two weeks of September the year before, had been spent adjusting boundary landmarks and making a survey of the island.

So tenacious was the heterogeneous stream that some of the cocoa nut trees from forty to fifty feet in height, after being displaced from their original situation remained in an upright position some minutes, and when they fell it was many yards from the spot in which they had come to maturity.—A considerable portion of this aquatic lava (for indeed its appearance had a distinct resemblance to the molten streams of an active volcano) had reached the sea before daylight: and when some of our people ventured to the edge of the precipice, they found to their dismay the boat houses, and boats left there, had disappeared. Two families whose houses were adjacent to the ravine removed their household goods, fearing the foundation of their dwellings might become undermined, and whelm them in the ruin;—but in a few hours the stream ceased to flow, and confidence was in a measure restored. We had now time to turn our attention to other parts of the island; at Bounty Bay a great quantity of earth had been washed away, a yam ground containing a thousand yams totally disappeared, several fishing boats destroyed, the Bounty's guns washed to the edge of the surf and large pieces of rock so encumbered the harbour that if a ship should come it is doubtful whether a passage could be found for her boat to pass through. In the interim all the plantain patches are levelled, about four thousand plantation trees are destroyed, one half in full bearing; the other half designed for the year 1846 so that this very valuable article of food we shall be without for a long time to come. The fact is, from this date until August we shall be pinched for food; but "God tempers the wind of the shorn lamb." I humbly trust the late monitions of providence viz Drought sickness and storm which severally have been inflicted upon us this year may be sanctified to us, and be the means of bringing us, one and all, into a closer communion with our God; may we remember the rod and who hath appointed it; may we flee to the cross of Christ for safety and for succour in every time of need; always bearing in mind our heavenly Father doth not willingly afflict the children of men.

But the shorn lambs of Pitcairn, placing their trust in God, prospered and lived through storm and calm, good season and bad.

By the end of 1846 there were 134 people living on Pitcairn, fishing and farming, the young ones among them attending school and Sunday-school, and all at church on the Sabbath. Sickness continued to occur, and ships to visit. The islanders wed, and gave birth, and died. Imperial Britain, no longer affronted by the mutineers, viewed its tiny possession as a most romantic outpost of Empire.

But daily life on the island was not without hazards.

On 20th February 1847 Reuben Nobbs, the eldest son of the teacher, accidentally shot himself through the thigh while out hunting goats. The accident left the young man a cripple. On an island whose terrain made no allowances for the lame, Reuben Nobbs became a supernumerary. So after persevering with his lameness for two years, he left Pitcairn on an American brig sailing for Valparaiso, and there settled, becoming a clerk.

A death by misadventure, in the same year Reuben was shot, was that of William McCoy. A large splinter in McCoy's foot became so infected that, despite the administration of laudanum and meal poultices, he was dead in a fortnight.

Nobbs recorded in the Register: "As a member of the community William McCoy's conduct was ever worthy of imitation. A dutiful son, a loving brother and a firm friend. Being unmarried he left no issue.— His lands he bequeathed to his niece, Jane McCoy, daughter of his brother Matthew McCoy."

Matthew himself had only narrowly escaped death the previous year when his canoe overturned in the surf on the western side of the island. Two friends, however, were near by and went to his rescue when they saw he had been injured by the violence of the wave and a collision with his upturned canoe.

All told, the islanders were fine seamen, as they are to this day. They were familiar with every shore and cove round the narrow coast, and alert to fickle whims of sea and weather. They were more familiar, perhaps, with the island waters than with many parts of the island itself. Its precipitous ridges and cliffs had left a number of areas inaccessible, including the regions of the mysterious markings and hieroglyphics left by some earlier inhabitants. But in 1848 interest was renewed in the inscriptions by the surgeon aboard H.M.S. *Calypso*, Dr Domet.

In spite of being informed of the difficulty of descent down the Rope on the eastern side of Pitcairn, Dr Domet tackled the climb to see them for himself. He managed the climb, and that same afternoon two officers from *Calypso*, Lieutenant McCleod and Midshipman Lock, went down. None of the three could throw any light on the possible origins of the markings, but all returned with their curiosity satisfied and their courage, or agility, proved. The markings are still visible to the intrepid visitor willing to go down to see them. An expedition of anthropologists and students from Otago University set out for the island in February 1964 to try and determine their origin.

The islanders were as ignorant of natural history, outside their own experience, as they were of prehistory. Nobbs's entry in the Register for 7th September 1849 reads:

A large hair seal captured on the West side of the island. Fletcher Christian first discovered it among the rocks, and was much alarmed at the sight of it: he feared to go near it least it should be a ghost (of which he has a great horror) or some other beast of prey; but quickly ascended the hill which overlooks the town and gave the alarm. Some persons went over to his assistance and shot the animal just as it began to make the retreat to the water.

So at last a seal was sighted on Pitcairn, more than forty years after Mayhew Folger had first arrived at the island seeking them.

The year 1849 drew to a close.* It had been, as Nobbs remarked in the Register, an "unprecedented" year in the annals of Pitcairn.

We have been visited by two British ships of War; the Pandora Capt. Wood, and the Daphne Capt Fanshawe. The commanders of these ships and their officers treated the inhabitants with the greatest kindness and were pleased to express their entire approval of all they saw and heard. The Daphne brought us a bull and a cow, and some rabbits, with a variety of other articles from the Rev. Wm. Armstrong, and other friends in Valparaiso;—the cattle and the rabbits produced a great sensation.

Another (to us) wonderful occurrence is the arrival of so many other ships under British colours viz eight from the colonies, (bound for California) and one whale ship from London,—in all nine merchantmen and two ships of War!!!

American ships have dwindled down to seven—six whalers; and one Brig from California,—in her Reuben E. Nobbs embarked for Valparaiso. Number of ships touching at the island this year eighteen.

George Adams saved the life of a female child alongside a British ship in the offing.

The inhabitants, with scarcely an exception have suffered severely from sickness during the months of August, September and October. The school was discontinued, the children were too sick to attend, and the teacher was fully (and thank God efficiently) employed in ministering from house to house. Some of the cases were quite alarming, and the disease (the influenza) in general was more severe and considerably modified from that of former years—violent spasms in the stomach and epigastric regions were frequent in all stages of the complaint.

At the close of the year the community are in the enjoyment of restored health. May the recent affliction so teach us to number our days that we may apply our hearts unto wisdom.

The rescue recorded by Nobbs was made when George Adams jumped fully clothed into the water to save a small girl who had fallen overboard

* Summary of the year 1849: Number of births, 10 (males 3, females 7); marriages, one; deaths, one. Number of inhabitants, 155 (males 76, females 79). Forty-seven children attended the public school.

from a visiting ship bound from Australia to California. The grateful father tried to express his gratitude with a gift of money, but Adams refused. One did not accept money as a reward for such a service on Pitcairn Island.

On 23rd January 1850 the islanders celebrated the sixtieth anniversary of the settlement of Pitcairn—or, more exactly, sixty years since the burning of H.M.S. *Bounty*.

At daylight one of the *Bounty's* guns was fired to awaken the islanders. At ten o'clock divine service was held in the church, followed by a reading of various letters from the British Government and influential friends of Pitcairn.

At midday a volley was fired under the flagstaff. The now famous bell of Pitcairn was rung throughout the afternoon to celebrate the day, and at sunset the *Bounty's* gun once more was fired.

Thus, the first record of an official celebration of their origins. It was probably about this time that George Hunn Nobbs wrote his paean for Pitcairn—"Fenua Maitai". *Fenua maitai* is Tahitian for "the good land".

FENUA MAITAI

O Pitcairn, I love thee, though, lone, 'midst the ocean,
  Thou standest exposed to the tempest and storm
Though thy shore, ever white with the surf's rude commotion,
  Rugged lava and wide yawning chasms deform;
Yet oft, 'mongst those chasms, with joy have I rambled,
  In the "Pools," down "the Rocks," and down "Isaac" have gamboll'd,
Or have join'd my companions, by moonlight assembled,
  To sing forth thy praizes Fenua Maitai!

Though discord and strife mark'd the dawn of existence,
  Nor yet were the days of our children more bright,
And, but for the efforts of female assistance,
  The black man had surely o'erpower'd the white.
But why harrow up recollections of sorrow?
  From the past for the future a lesson we'll take;
And draw a close veil o'er those dread scenes of horror,
  When blood stain'd thy valleys, Fenua Maitai!

To happier moments now memory turning,
    When Youth, Hope, and Love gave to Fancy full scope
I have clim'd the rude cliff at the first break of morning,
    To see the sun rise from "the ridge of the Rope:"
Or down "T'other side," with his last ray ascending,
    Over mountain and valley, in one glory bending,
My rapturous gaze o'er the prospect extending.
    I have fancied thee "Eden," Fenua Maitai!

By torch-light the haunts of the white bird exploring,
    Perch'd high on the "big tree's" aerial bridge,
How quick beat each heart, as the death-wail came soaring,
    From the ghost that still lingers on "Talaloo's ridge!"
Or with arrow and grains, on the calm nights of summer,
    When the "Davy" recedes from the shores of Tahtama,
The tribes of the ocean, allured by the lamma,
    Are the meed of thy children, Fenua Maitai!

"Ship-landing"—"St. Paul's"—"Water-drop"—"Vaibebea's"—
    "Eteaa"—"Arlehow"—"Menalee's-stone"—
"Alah," where the lore of the Indian appears,
    Momento of hordes, long extinct and unknown;
From the heights of "Look-out," where the wild goats are bounding,
To the coralline groves where the "Toaw" is sounding,
    Sweet Rosebud of Ocean, Fenua Maitai!

Our Sires—to their mem'ry this day is devoted;
    Our friends—may they prosper in every land;
Ourselves—may our blessings be gratefully noted,
    Our errors deplored, and Religion expand!
May the flag of old England for ages wave o'er us!
    Be Victoria our Queen! May our Queen be victorious,
And this Rock of the West oft resound with the chorus,
    "Pitarnia hinaaro, Fenua Maitai!"

                                          G. H. N.

CHAPTER XVII

THE REVEREND GEORGE HUNN NOBBS

To THIS good and bountiful land then, the author of "Fenua Maitai" returned on Sunday, 15th May 1853, as a fully ordained minister—the Reverend George Hunn Nobbs—his official status in Holy Orders settling once and for all the controversy that to some extent had always surrounded his position on the island.

Like many prophets unsung in their own land, Nobbs had been lionized abroad. In England he had been fêted wherever he went. Given an audience with Queen Victoria, who was intrigued to meet a man from distant Pitcairn Island, he came away with an autographed photograph of the Royal Family; a memento he bore proudly back to Pitcairn to the wonder of its ingenuous inhabitants.

Between fêting and invitations, Nobbs studied for the ministry. The time normally required for ordination however, had been reduced in Nobbs's case through the influence of Admiral Fairfax Moresby, whose ship, H.M.S. *Portland*, had carried him to England; and through the good offices of the Reverend Mr Murray, an "admirer" of the Pitcairners.

On 30th November 1852 "George Hunn Nobbs, Clerk" was "licensed to perform the Office of Chaplain to the Inhabitants of Pitcairn's Island" by the Lord Bishop of London.

The journey home, again on H.M.S. *Portland* with Admiral Moresby on board, took Nobbs to Valparaiso and a reunion with his crippled son, Reuben Elias. Reuben, ill and homesick, took advantage of the ship's visit to return home with his father. Jane Nobbs, who had accompanied her father abroad, was the first native-born Pitcairner to visit England.

Although the islanders welcomed back their "new" pastor warmly, they were sorry to see Mr Holman leave. Mr Holman, the Chaplain aboard *Portland*, had remained on the island during Nobbs's absence. Both during and after his sojourn on Pitcairn the islanders named three of their infant children in his honour: Rebecca Holman Ascension McCoy, Elizabeth Holman Adams, and William Henry Holman Christian.

Nobbs found little had changed, though one death had occurred: Matthew McCoy had died within a month of being elected Chief Magistrate for the year 1853. Even the circumstances of the visit of H.M.S. *Portland* were to be expected: within days "several of the people were attacked with influenza".

One of the chores Nobbs resumed was that of keeping the island Register. He made the last entry but one on 14th February 1854, referring to an accident to Frederick Young.

Five months later the chronicle, into which so much of the lives and stories of the island had been compressed was closed off in the following manner:

This book has become so dilapidated from getting wet with salt water when taken on board the Virago at the commencement of last year, during my absence, that it is necessary to prepare a new book by copying the contents of this into it and then continue from this date. It is my intention to send this Imperfection; to my well beloved friend the Rev. T. B. Murray, thinking it may serve to amuse him over his after dinner toast and water: though I think either my honoured friend or his sedate and most amiable spouse will find it difficult to translate many of the original autographs in the shipping list; and I think much of my own unrivalled penmanship, will be attended with similar difficulties.
Pitcairns   July 1854

GEORGE H. NOBBS

The original Pitcairn Island Register is now in the hands of the London Missionary Society. The copy, which makes many corrections to the original, is in the Dixson Library in Sydney. With this copy is also the actual ordination certificate of the Reverend George H. Nobbs.

The closing of the Register was somehow symptomatic of the general mood on Pitcairn—the restless, uneasy feeling that life on the island was also drawing to a close.

Nobbs's return came at a time when speculation and anxiety about their future were at a peak amongst the island's people. For nearly a decade it had grown increasingly clear that Pitcairn could not continue to support an expanding population. The unhappy prospect before the Pitcairners—especially unhappy for the older ones, mindful of their brief stay on Tahiti—was migration.

The idea that migration from Pitcairn would one day be necessary had arisen as early as 1844 when, on 7th September, the acting British pro-consul at Honolulu, Crichton Wyllie, wrote an account of the life of the Pitcairn Islanders from information he had received from visitors to the island, including Lieutenant Hunt of H.M.S. *Basilisk*.

After giving the population as 58 males and 61 females, Wyllie concluded by saying, "The island is still capable of supporting that and a greater population, but the time will soon arrive, when they will require more space, and Mr. Hunt thinks that the Bonin islands would be an eligible place to transport them to."

Within four years Nobbs himself had been moved to act on the problem. For in 1848 the permanent British Consul in Honolulu, General William Miller, wrote to the Foreign Secretary in England, Viscount Palmerston, on 8th April:

I have the honour to enclose herewith to Your Lordship, a letter which Mr. Nobbs, Pastor and Schoolmaster on Pitcairn's Island, has addressed to me, describing the embarrassing position in which the interesting and praiseworthy little Community there is placed, and setting forth the necessity that exists of, at all events, some of them seeking another place of abode, in consequence, of the present insufficiency of land fit for cultivation to support their increasing number, which already amounted to 139, of whom 72 were Males, and 67 Females.

In my reply to Mr. Nobbs, of which I also herewith transmit a copy, I have suggested that one or two Families, or about twenty of the Inhabitants of Pitcairn's Islands, avail themselves of the first good opportunity to remove to the Sandwich Islands where, I am of opinion they could be comfortably located as British Subjects. I have offered to contribute, if requisite, two hundred dollars towards defraying the expenses of their passage after their arrival here, and then to have them properly attended to until they get settled, which I trust will meet with Your Lordship's approbation.

Miller had offers from a Dr Wod, who owned Koloa Estate on Kauai, to employ and assist any Pitcairn migrants, and from a Mr Brown, an Englishman, to do likewise. Miller was of the opinion that Mr Brown "being an Englishman and have his wife and family with him, would be, it appears to me, the best person of the two to attend to such Members of that interesting little Community who might make their appearance here".

The Consul-General at this stage did not consider it worth while contacting the Government of the Sandwich Islands about the project. On 7th September 1848 Lord Palmerston wrote to Miller that:

It appears to Her Majesty's Government to be very desirable to provide the means for enabling the surplus Population of Pitcairn's Island to remove to some other Islands in the Pacific where Land can be allotted to them sufficient to maintain them, and where their Industry and good conduct may contribute to the wellbeing of such Islands.

Palmerston authorized the payment of three hundred dollars towards the project. Nothing happened, however, until Miller again wrote to Palmerston, on 21st May 1849:

Mr. Buffett, who came here upwards of two months since to undergo a Surgical operation will avail himself of this opportunity now afforded to him to return Home and explain to his Fellow Inhabitants of Pitcairn's Island the nature of the Locations which a portion of them may count upon at the Sandwich and Society Islands should they remove to either of these Groups.

Miller considered that Kauai offered the most inducement, as near the main port of the island, Hanalei, there "reside two respectable English Families possessing an extensive Estate and a large Coffee Plantation, with much good land uncultivated, whilst at a distance of fourteen miles from the same port another English Family is residing on a fine property of their own".

Again, on 4th June 1849, Miller wrote that "It now remains for the British Inhabitants of Pitcairn's Island to make known to me their further wishes respecting the removal of some of them as contemplated to Huahine or to the Sandwich Islands".

Between times, there were various other pressures on the island's small, industrious community to move.

The Queen of Huahine, one of the Society Group, offered them an extensive tract of land; Juan Fernandez, a Chilean possession, was thought of; and there was even an offer forthcoming from King Kamehameha III to transport the whole of the island's population to his royal estates in Hawaii.

The Society Island offer and King Kamehameha's proposals were ruled out by Miller's insistence that the islanders would have to go as British subjects—a condition unacceptable to the Polynesian good Samaritans. Juan Fernandez, of course, belonged to Chile.

The Pitcairners themselves were doubtful, as Nobbs explained in a letter to Miller on 14th January 1850.

Whether any of my people will avail themselves of the various offers made them, as regards emigrating, I cannot at present say definitely; for although the necessity exists, and its imperative demands cannot be much longer avoided, such is the affection existing between the members of this unique society, that they are intent only upon putting off the "evil day" of separation. Another cause, and that not a slight one is the great and paramount influence the French are exercising in these seas. Now, to persons whose manners, customs, and every idea are intrinsically "English", to be obliged to succumb to the dictates of those against whom an instinctive dislike has been implanted in their breasts, by their ancestors of the Bounty, is more than a trifle. Here they enjoy the favour and protection of the British Government; and though often put to great straits, and the difficulties are daily increasing, yet they will, I presume, remain for some time to come, where they can, amid all their privations, worship God without molestation, and behold, on Sundays and other occasions, the British flag wave over their isolated and rocky abode. They had not, when I wrote to the Consul General some time ago, so serious a consideration as they have since; and when the generous offer made them by your honourable uncle and other gentlemen in Oahu, and, through your kind solicitude, by the chiefs of the Society Islands, came to their knowledge, and they began to inquire which among them would avail themselves of the very favourable and disinterested invitations, their hearts failed them; they could not brook the idea of separation, and settled down to their accustomed avocations, until the suggestions of their necessities should become more peremptory.

It is interesting to see Nobbs, not then ordained and still resented by some of the islanders, refer to "my people".

At the same time, John Buffett also wrote to Miller in support of Nobbs: "I wrote to your honour by H.M.S. Daphne; since that time there has been no alteration in the views of the inhabitants. The fact is, they will not emigrate till obliged to by sheer necessity."

However, Buffett pointed out that he did not think it would be long before the "sheer necessity" would force the migration. He gave the population as 155 and said that "About ten couple are now marriageable, and the increase will be rapid".

He finished his letter to General Miller by asking for "a fig-tree and a rose-tree".

In March 1852 Miller again wrote to Palmerston that the removal of the Pitcairn Islanders to an appropriate island would "extensively augment the number of Moral and Loyal British Subjects on the South Sea Islands, an object so desirable especially looking to the future".

However, on 30th March 1853 the Consul-General wrote to Addington that the Pitcairn Islanders did not want at that time to change their domicile.

Some Landed Proprietors at the Sandwich Islands are becoming desirous to offer Homesteads to any of the Families who would like to come here; but it would be, I think a pity for them to live under any other than the British Flag; indeed such is their enthusiastic Love and Veneration for the Queen that I do not believe they would, under any circumstances, consent to change their colours.

And despite the offer of land and care in Hawaii, and financial assistance from the British Government towards the cost of their removal, the Pitcairn Islanders refused all inducements to leave their home.

CHAPTER XVIII

NORFOLK ISLAND

ON THE other side of the Pacific, five thousand miles distant from Pitcairn, lay Norfolk Island. If Pitcairn was unique and renowned throughout the world for its hospitality and the gentle lives of its inhabitants, Norfolk was equally famous as a place of suffering.

Discovered by Captain Cook in 1774, and settled by Lieutenant King (later Governor of New South Wales) within a month of the arrival of the First Fleet at Sydney Cove, as a food source for the new colony, Norfolk Island became the final place to which convicts transported to Botany Bay could still be sent: an island of no escape, except in death, and of no hope, except for death.

Almost as precipitous as Pitcairn, the island was as barren of landing places along its steep coastline, and its lovely pine-clad hills had about them a darkness, a quality of brooding sorrow that seemed to rise from the suffering of men for whom the final horror was no longer the gibbet, but a degradation and inhumanity almost unimaginable.

And when, in the increasing enlightenment of the mid-nineteenth century, transportation and the convict system came gradually to be abolished in Australia, one of the last bastions of the system to fall was Norfolk Island. When it did, it was suggested that Norfolk would be a suitable home for the Pitcairners.

The first suggestion appears in a book by Walter Brodie, *Pitcairn Island and the Islanders in 1850*, published in London in 1851. "Should the Home Authorities," wrote Brodie, "finally decide upon abandoning Norfolk Island as a penal settlement, which report says there is a chance of then a more beautiful or suitable location could scarcely be found."

Norfolk Island was suitable not only because of its size and fertility, but, being uninhabited once the convicts had departed, it would enable a move *en masse* and would not involve the dispersal or assimilation of another community. A further advantage was the presence on the island of substantial buildings—barracks, administration blocks, cottages, stores, kilns, salt houses and mills—erected by the suffering convicts. In addition, considerable areas of land were already under cultivation, there was some stock, and the fishing in the surrounding waters was excellent. Climatically, Norfolk and Pitcairn were alike, and geographically there was sufficient similarity of appearance between the two to lessen the nostalgia of the Pitcairners and hasten their period of "settling in".

To all concerned, it seemed a good idea. The islanders appear to have been told of the possibility of Norfolk as an alternative home during or shortly after the visit of Admiral Moresby, Commander-in-Chief of the Pacific Naval Station, in August 1852—the voyage in which he took George Hunn Nobbs to England for ordination.

A year later the Pitcairners were resigned to leaving the island. Their final choice—conveyed to the British Government through the British Consul in the Society Islands, Mr B. T. Nicholas—lay between Norfolk Island or Sunday Island in the Kermadec Group.

When Nobbs returned the weight of opinion had swung in favour of Norfolk Island. Accordingly, a letter was written to Admiral Moresby on 18th May 1853, requesting the transfer to Norfolk Island. In a practical way, few would be sorry to leave, for the Pitcairners, Nobbs found on his return, were suffering grievously. Famine and disease were rife. For weeks, the islanders had been living only on pumpkins, berries, coconuts and beans. "In one week there were not more than ten persons capable of attending to their own wants—it was for some weeks actual starvation."

Brodie's book containing the suggestion of Norfolk Island as a possible home, meanwhile, had stimulated considerable interest in England in the islanders' future, and ultimately funds were established in the mother country to assist the Pitcairners. Brodie used his book as a means of establishing a fund for the provision of medicines and other necessities. The movement gained impetus when Nobbs arrived in England in 1852 and lectured extensively. A committee was formed and raised nearly one thousand pounds.

Finally the project received official recognition by the British Government when it was suggested to the Secretary of State for the Colonies, Sir John Pakington, that Norfolk Island should be reserved for the Pitcairn Islanders. Sir John then requested a report on the island from the Lieutenant-Governor of Van Diemen's Land, Sir William Denison.*

* Although Sydney and Brisbane were the Australian settlements closest to the island, it came under the control of the Lieutenant-Governor of Van Diemen's Land.

Bounty Bay and Village of Pitcairn

George Hunn Nobbs

Denison's reply was enthusiastic. The British Government gave its approval to the transfer. The decision was forwarded to the islanders by the British Consul in the Society Islands on 5th July 1854, "in accordance with your wishes".

It only remained then to confirm the decision with the Pitcairners and verify their choice. Accordingly, the Admiralty instructed Captain Fremantle of H.M.S. *Juno* to go to Pitcairn and find out the wishes of the inhabitants regarding migration to Norfolk Island.

After leaving Sydney on 6th August 1855, Fremantle arrived at Pitcairn Island on 17th August. The entire population assembled in the schoolhouse to hear Fremantle explain the reason for his visit. George Nobbs followed Fremantle and read out a description of Norfolk Island prepared by Sir William Denison.

Although rumours of the British Government's decision had already reached the island, the Pitcairners asked for a day or two to discuss so vital a question.

The following evening, at a meeting of the community, most of the Pitcairn people decided to accept the offer of Norfolk Island. Those who spoke on the proposal did so very briefly—in many cases those in favour confined their answer to a single word, "Go."

However, some of the older inhabitants, remembering the abortive migration to Tahiti twenty-four years earlier, were doubtful. George Adams and thirty-three others decided not to accept the offer. But the decision had been taken by the majority: "Go." John Adams II wrote out the decision, which was then signed by Frederick Young and George Nobbs.

At ten o'clock on the morning of 21st April 1856 a sail was reported coming in from the southern end of Pitcairn Island. By 4 p.m. the vessel rounded St Paul's Rocks and a pennant was seen flying on board. "As soon as she hove to, a canoe went on board (both of our whaleboats having been knocked to pieces during the stay of the Dido) and we were anxiously waiting for the preconcerted signal if indeed it should prove to be *the* Ship, as was generally conjectured."

When no signal came quickly from the islanders who had boarded the strange vessel, doubts were expressed as to its being *the* ship. Finally one of the men appeared on the ship's taffrail and waved his cap seaward, signifying that this indeed was the ship for which they had been waiting.

M

Now there was a great revulsion of feeling many who had been impatient for the means of removal began to feel their attachment for their native place stronger than they imagined, & I believe there was scarcely one among us who would not have consented to put off the long desired day a little longer.

The *Morayshire*, a vessel of 830 tons, had come to take them to their new home, and all those

. . . who were disposed to accept of Her Majesty's most gracious offer of Norfolk Island, & all that appertains thereto, for the sole use of themselves & their families, were to embark forthwith time being allowed to embark such articles of property as we were disposed to take with us. Such an unqualified offer of so beautiful a spot, is easier to imagine than to realize, but it is a bone fide reality to us and yet there is more than one family among us who demure [*sic*] at going.

The next day the *Morayshire* worked up to Bounty Bay and with difficulty, because of the lee current and the wind being off-shore, she came to her anchorage.

So, too, the islanders might have remembered, did the *Bounty* a little more than sixty-six years earlier.

The air was oppressive with memory. The soil, their soil, was redolent of days past and time remembered. The scuffling dust would blow along deserted tracks, crops would go to seed, and seed to jungle. Vines would cloak the farming lands, and empty houses watch, silent sentinels. Living voices would indeed be heard no more in the land; Fletcher Christian's ghost would be free to go where it might on the island, and Mat Quintal's and Bill McCoy's and Neddy Young's, and all the others, with perhaps old John Adams's voice to preach to them all.

Grass would grow across their bones, with the *Bounty's* bones still below in the bay, fetched to and fro by the tides.

And who would not remember that day Nobbs and Bunker arrived, or, with wry grins, "Lord" Joshua Hill's stately stepping-ashore, or perhaps the night of the big storm when the banyan-tree was struck, and the landslide that so terrified them?

But it was not these so much as the wrench of small things, the countless minutiae that they would leave behind. As any family uncovers aching years of memories when it "moves house", so the whole island discovered afresh all the days, all the years that had gone by since the turbulent mutineers and their women had come ashore.

The last complete census before their departure, taken by William Quintal on 19th September 1855, showed a total of 187 living on Pitcairn —92 males and 95 females. The population was divided into 23 family groups, the largest single family being that of George Hunn Nobbs. The most common name was Quintal, which group numbered 47. There were 45 inhabitants with the name of Christian, 22 were called Young, 18 Buffett, 17 Adams, 16 McCoy, 13 Nobbs, and 9 Evans.

At last all had decided to leave. The thirty-three who had rejected the offer at the time of Captain Fremantle's visit had, in the time of waiting for the ship to take them away, changed their minds, except for George Adams, and he, too, was now persuaded to go with the rest.

Adams's concern was for his family, one of whom—his grandchild, Phoebe Cleaveline—was seriously ill. Until the baby improved, neither George Adams nor the baby's parents, Jonathan and Phoebe Adams, had been prepared to sail, "the idea of burying the child at sea was one of his principal reasons for not coming".

But it was a time of doubt, anxiety, and heart-searching for the whole island. All had their problems, but also their hopes. It was not a time of good weather, either, and the days were depressing with rain squalls and rough grey seas. The move, in fact, could not get under way for several days, but as the weather abated the loading began.

Everything was brought off as safely as possible, and without the slightlest risk to man or boat. We brought away everything belonging to them except the bare houses, with the old tables and stools in them, and four canoes. On the Monday following, the day we arrived, Jonathan's child rallied a good deal; and so old George and all his family decided upon coming. By the Tuesday night we had everying off except the people themselves; and a small quantity of clothes, &c., they were obliged to keep till they went themselves. We brought away all their hogs; they wished them on account of their rooting the graves up.

The islanders' sentiments on seeing their belongings taken out to the *Morayshire* can only be conjectured. But there is a depth of feeling in George Hunn Nobbs's Register of those last days.

May 1ˢᵗ Thursday. This day assembled for the last time in our church, for Divine Service, it was a solemn time and the congregation was deeply affected.

May 2ⁿᵈ Breakfasted for the last time, on Pitcairns, and that too with heavy hearts. Previous to embarking, many went to the graves, & headstones, which has afforded us the melancholy, & soothing contemplation of the names & years, of those deposited beneath, but now we are about to leave those frail memorials which had become unspeakably dear to us, never to behold them again. These reflections caused our tears to fall, fast, & freely. We were all embarked, at Bounty Bay, & passing safely through the surf, commenced our Exodus. By four o,clock we were all safe on board the "Morayshire," & the ship made sail with a fair breeze. In the dusk of the evening Pitcairns Island receded from view. There were very few of its late Inhabitants who where not on deck, to take, "A long last lingering look" at that much loved & ever to be remembered spot.

They went westward, retracing the course their forebears had taken on board the *Bounty* to find Pitcairn Island.

The voyage was even more difficult than the departure from their home. The uprooted community was ill at ease at sea, and, although well cared for, cramped and uncomfortable. But the greatest discomfort was sea-sickness.

The moment the people got on board the sea-sickness began, and such terrible sea-sickness I never witnessed. The men and children got over it in a few days, but the women were more or less sick the whole passage. . . . During the whole of this night, the Rev. M^r. Nobbs & old Arthur Quintal, assisted occasionally by Lieut Gregorie, & the Captain of the ship, were attempting to relieve the sufferings of the sea sick. Those of the other men who were not sick, were nursing the infants It was a comfortless, and to most of our people a sleepless night. During the whole of the passage the community assembled on the birth [*sic*] deck, at the ringing of a bell. At 7 AM. when the Scriptures were read, & prayers offered to the Father of Mercies to implore his protection for the coming day. At 8, the mess tables were lowered & breakfast commenced, directly after which all the women & children who were able, went upon deck, while the men & lads gave the berth deck a thorough cleaning if the weather was fine, the beds & bedding were taken up for airing & the bed cabins, by an ingenious process, reduced to half their extreme size so that a snug dressing room was formed between berths & the sides of the ship, which was a great convenience. But notwithstanding the large size of the ship & the excellent arrangements, and numerous appliances to boot some of our women were sick during the whole passage and three or four were alarmingly ill, they required constant attendance night & day. But to continue the daily routine, at 1 P.M. dinner was served, at 3 P.M. the bell rang and Divine Service was performed, Lieut. Gregorie always attending with the community. After service all who were able went upon deck & generally remained there till six o'clock. At eight the bell again rang, and all assembled for prayer. The service concluded by all joining in the Evening hymn. Then whosoever choose, went to bed, some went on deck to sit for a while, while many spent a couple of hours, in singing hymns, in parts. Captain Mathers was most indefatigable in administering to the comfort of every one, but more especially to the sick. A more suitable person cannot in our opinion, have been sent to remove us. And Lieutenant Gregorie, although a very young man acted with much judgment and consideration.

In the margin of this copy of the Register is recorded the birth at sea of Reuben Denison Christian, son of Isaac and Miriam Christian, on 9th May. He was named in honour of Sir William Denison, who by this time was Governor of New South Wales.

On 6th June Norfolk Island was sighted from a distance, but in light winds progress was slow.

By the next day the *Morayshire* was about twenty-five miles from their new home.

On the seventh, Nobbs declared that "for picturesque beauty Norfolk Island is not to be compared with Pitcairn".

On the eighth they went ashore:

Cloudy weather. Close in with Norfolk Island, very much disappointed in its appearance from the present point of view, which is directly off the settlement, presents a succession of hillocks & shallow ravins covered with short brown grass, and scarcely a tree to be seen. Every one much disappointed having been accustomed to hear the place much extolled— No doubt other parts of the Island have a better appearance, but this side certainly loses in the comparison with our "Rock of the west." At 8 o'clock the anchor was let go, & preparations made for debarking. By one the whole community, assisted by the boats of HMS "Herald" were safely landed. During the whole of the debarkation Capt. Denham remained on the pier not withstanding the heavy rain and welcomed our people as they landed to their new home; & evinced the greatest anxiety for our comfort. Towards the close of this eventful day we all assembled in a large upper room in the Soldiers Barracks, when we solemnly & gratefully offered our thanks & praises, to our Triune God for His continued goodness & mercy, in thus bringing us to our future earthly home, & I trust we were sincere in imploring his watchful care that we swerve not to the right nor the left.

Six days after the landing at Norfolk Island Phoebe Adams died. She was buried on the island, and not at sea as had been feared by her grandfather.

Life was again to become an idyll for the Pitcairners. By 26th June the last of the convicts had departed, after instructing the new-comers on the use of tools and equipment they were leaving on the island, and the *Morayshire* had vanished over the southern horizon. The Pitcairners were alone on their new island.

"Now we are all alone, humanly speaking. Yet there is one in the midst of us who watcheth over us by night and by day," wrote Nobbs.

Captain Fremantle of H.M.S. *Juno*, which arrived at the island on 23rd June, was a more physical custodian. His principle task was to establish once and for all the island's sovereignty and the question of the new immigrants' land rights. Therefore he sent ashore a letter to the Chief Magistrate, Frederick Young.*

From the moment of their arrival on Norfolk, the Pitcairners believed they had sole right to the island. Fremantle, too, was of the same opinion in 1855, but the British Government would not permit such an arrangement.

His letter to the Chief Magistrate, then, written after discussions with the Governor, Sir William Denison, reads as follows:

To the Chief Magistrate of the Pitcairn Islanders now resident on Norfolk Island

All arrangements made by the community of Pitcairn Islanders as to the distribution of the land on Norfolk Island are to be subject to the approval of H.E. Sir W. T. Denison Governor Gen¹ of N.S.W.

The whole of the Coast line including the jetties, & the roads now made thro' out the Island are to be reserved as public property. The following buildings are also to be retained as belonging to H. M. Governt:

The gaol

The Chaplains House

Also 200 acres of cleared land at Long Ridge for a Glebe and 500 acres elsewhere.

The Islanders however are not debarred from making any temporary use of the above mentioned grounds & buildings. They are to understand that they are not allotted as property, to any individual.

This is communicated by direction of H.E. The Governor General.

(signed) STEPHEN G. FREMANTLE
Captain of H.M.S. Juno
Senior Officer in Australia

Norfolk Island
June 25, 1856

* Discovered among Bishop Selwyn's papers in the Auckland Museum by Mrs Merval Hoare of Norfolk Island in 1963, thereby settling a controversy that had lasted more than a century.

To dispose of the rest of the island, the Pitcairners cast lots for the houses. And although some of the buildings were bigger, or better, than others, there were no jealousies or discontent amongst the immigrants. Just as fraternally they set to farming their new lands; again, each one helping the others.

By mid July, school was commenced in the large barracks. Nobbs was in charge. As a minister, however, he was for a short period supplanted. Having for years languished on Pitcairn without an ordained clergyman to minister to their spiritual wants, the Pitcairners now found themselves with a bishop. Bishop Selwyn arrived at Norfolk Island on 4th July, aboard the missionary vessel *Southern Cross*.

It is through Bishop Selwyn that we learn of the Pitcairners' nostalgia for their old home, in letters written to him by some of his "flock". It was a restlessness perhaps as much for the past as anything else; a longing to go back to the comforting days of Fenua Maitai when the Good Land was as bountiful as it was beautiful.

More, it was the timeless urge in all simple people to go "home". Until a new generation of Pitcairners emerged on Norfolk Island, the old generation was pervaded with melancholy. There was almost a timorousness about them, bred of a permanent sense of insecurity at being removed for ever from Pitcairn Island.

Voicing a multitude of fears and confusion, John Quintal wrote to Bishop Selwyn on 13th December 1858:

I think you must remember the conversation I told you I have had with Mr Gregorie at Pitcairns Island when he came there to bring us away, how I told him that I did not wish to come if we are not to have a better school for our children. I told him also that we are coming in a strange place away from our home, and that our people will never be happy if we are not to have a pious and well educated clergyman to console, and drive away the thoughts of home from us. In this my dear Father I am not mistaken, for ever since we have been on this Island the people have been longing to be at home again. There is no diference in all, those that wish to come when we was in Pitcairn's Island is longing to go back as well as those that did not wish to come then, and I am sure it is because there is no such comforter to be had as I told Mr. Gregorie of when we was in Pitcairn's Island. There are two familys gone already and several more is looking out for and opportunity to go also, and my dear father knows that ever since his college is not allowed to sit up here, that is my determination also. And I beg you my dear father that we shall not be left under the teachings of a common sailor as we have been heretofore, but that you shall be the Bishop over us, and shall be looking out for our souls as you did while we are here on Norfolk Island.

As Quintal recorded, two families had gone already. There had been no news of them then, but few could not have thought of them daily—going back, back to the deserted houses, the fields and paths they all had known, and the same sea and sky that had once bounded their world at Pitcairn. Now mental images of their old homes were made all the more vivid with the thought of those two families back once more with well-remembered ghosts and fondly held memories on Pitcairn.

So much so, that

The talk of going back to Pitcairn is yet high among some of our people; but none has yet returned beside Mayhew and Moses [Young]. Capt. Swain of the Three Brothers was here about four months ago and promised to be back in the latter part of last month but he has not yet returned which if he do he said he will undoubtedly take somebody back.

So wrote Andrew Christian to Bishop Selwyn on 24th July 1861.

A month later, Charles Christian wrote to the Bishop in similar vein: "Great talking is still going on about going back to Pitcairn Island but it seems almost impossible for any one to go soon as we have not seen the Capt. they expected to take them in the month he promised to be here."

Those who had gone back were Moses and Albina Young with their five children, and William Mayhew Young, who had married the widow Margaret McCoy. With six of her children and a daughter from her second marriage to Mayhew, the group made a total of sixteen when they set out to return to Pitcairn.

Excitement and sadness attended their farewell, and a little envy as well. For, in addition to their nostalgia, the islanders felt they had a real grievance. From owning the whole of Pitcairn for whatever use they cared to put it, on Norfolk Island they had become in a way only tenants of the British Government. That the independently minded islanders felt this strongly is brought out in a letter from John Adams to Baron de Thierry on 21st January 1863, in which the grandson of the original John Adams of H.M.S. *Bounty* said:

Do not, I pray you, impute to me, the folly of those who dared to return to Pitcairn's Island again. I have done all I could to prevent such a wanton piece of folly but to no purpose. . . . It is an event I do deeply deplore, and will use my best endeavours to prevent the like from again happening. Still, I must confess that those who are dissatisfied have a reason, small though it may be, to be so. Have not the Government in deed, if not in words, broken their faith with us. Trace it from the beginning and if they have, in any one thing kept their word [*sic*]. Still I say the island itself is a most magnificent gift, and I for one appreciate it as such.

You must know, my dear friend, that when it was first proposed to us to remove here, we were told that the whole island and everything upon it were to be given unconditionally to us.

One feels, however, that if there had not been the question of land ownership, the Pitcairners would have found another source for their discontent. The unvarnished truth is that they were homesick.

On 18th December 1863 the second group of Pitcairners returned home, and in sufficient number—twenty-six—to repopulate Pitcairn Island once more. They went in the ship *St Kilda*.

On board were Thursday October Christian and his wife, Mary (or Polly as she was also called), their daughter Agnes, who married Samuel Warren of Rhode Island the day before they sailed, and their eight other children, John Mills's daughter, Elizabeth Young, who was to live to the age of about ninety-three, Robert Pitcairn Buffett and his wife, Lydia, and Simon and Mary Young and their eight children. The twenty-sixth member of the party was Hannah Adams.

As to the Pitcairners' bond with their homeland—and their families—there is perhaps no single item of evidence more revealing than Polly Christian's action when, on the voyage back, one of her children died. To all the islanders on board, burial at sea was out of the question, just as it had been for George Adams when his grandchild Phoebe had been ill on the voyage to Norfolk. Instead, the body of Polly's child was kept on board in a barrel, much to the distress of the crew. The distraught mother kept watch over her dead child for the rest of the voyage. The infant was buried on their arrival at Pitcairn.*

In a sense, it is hard not to see the burial of the child as symbolical of the natives' return to Pitcairn Island.

Thereafter, as the island community grew again, much of the old spirit waned. Although normal life was taken up again, something of Pitcairn's uniqueness seemed to depart. Somehow, the purposefulness of the people was less intense. The first task of the returning settlers, communally, had been to rebuild the church and schoolhouse. After that there was little

---

* Until recently, on both Norfolk and Pitcairn, there were few occasions more important or more dignified than a funeral. Even on Norfolk Island the whole community "closed down" as a mark of respect to the dead, even if the deceased only happened to be a visitor to the island.

zest for repairing the houses and replanting gardens. Still more of the island reverted to natural bush.

An irreconcilable sorrow pervaded their lives: the memories of the old days, the absence of so many of their fellows thousands of miles away on Norfolk.

In 1868 some of the Norfolk Island settlers, including old John Buffett, who was to live to the age of ninety-three, revisited Pitcairn and urged their kinsmen to rejoin the other families, most of them more prosperous than they ever were, on Norfolk Island. The Pitcairners declined.

And as the closing decades of the nineteenth century passed fewer and fewer ships called—perhaps a dozen in a year, where once there had been as many as forty. The world was beginning to forget Pitcairn. The story, and the people, that had so fascinated it had become a fleeting episode in mankind's hastening march to the twentieth century.

Chapter XIX

PITCAIRN ISLAND TODAY

Of the years remaining in the nineteenth century, there is little to record.

The one noteworthy event of the era was the conversion of the entire island, in 1887, to the Seventh Day Adventist faith, as the result of the visit of an American missionary of that persuasion. Otherwise, it is interesting to note that a form of parliamentary government, with seven members elected to an executive, was introduced in 1893. Yet this was a token of the changed society's needs, for the reports of the naval officers who visited Pitcairn towards the end of the nineteenth century all spoke of the community's deterioration, of lawlessness and lack of unity—even, in 1897, of murder!

The man who stemmed the tide of degeneration was James Russell McCoy, a great-grandson of the mutineer. The direction and purpose he gave the community, as Chief Magistrate and Chief Executive, on and off for thirty-seven years, earned the mutineer's great-grandson an honoured and secure place in Pitcairn's history.

In 1904 the British Consul at Tahiti, Mr R. T. Simons, visited Pitcairn and, abolishing the parliamentary system as too cumbersome for the tiny community, reintroduced the time-honoured office of Chief Magistrate, with two small committees to assist the appointees. The system, with some expansion and consolidation of judicial powers and definitions has existed until today.

By then, the only vessels calling at Pitcairn were the Seventh Day Adventist mission ship, *Pitcairn*, and an occasional merchantman.

Pitcairn was once more a forlorn and forgotten outpost in the Pacific, a curio of history, a small dot—two miles long and a mile wide—midway between New Zealand and Central America.

The sundering of Central America in 1914 by the Panama Canal, however, meant the end of isolation for Pitcairn. The opening of the canal placed Pitcairn on the direct shipping route to New Zealand, and brought a ship a week—many of them liners carrying hundreds of passengers.

Pitcairn was ushered back into the world, and the twentieth century.

In 1938 two Americans gave the island radio equipment, and for the first time the Pitcairn community was in direct and permanent contact with the outside world. (There had been other, but far less reliable radio equipment earlier on the island.) For many years Floyd McCoy, operating as a radio "ham", spoke to fellow amateurs, as well as official stations, all around the world. When he died in November 1963 the walls of his radio shack were covered with acknowledgment cards from his contacts, while his own cards had found pride of place in other radio "shacks" throughout the world. One of his contacts was a descendant of Captain Bligh, living in Nova Scotia.

The island received an official wireless station during World War II from the Royal New Zealand Navy.

The presence of the station probably saved Pitcairn from attack by the German raider *Komet* during the war. The *Komet's* commander, Rear Admiral Eyssen, feared that discovery of an attack on the island by his ship would jeopardize another operation he had in mind. One likes to imagine sentiment may also have influenced Eyssen, for about the time the *Komet* passed Pitcairn the film *Mutiny of the Bounty*, with Charles Laughton in his famous portrayal of Bligh, was screened on board.

Today life on Pitcairn Island is a logical extension of, and not much different from, the life lived in the first years after the death of the mutineers.

There is still no money used on the island, no taxation (though there is a small fee payable for gun licences), no stores, no price index, and little permanent work. The islanders work for themselves to keep themselves. Goods are exchanged on a barter system, or simply shared amongst themselves.

Apart from their whims and the weather, the Pitcairners' lives are regulated by the church bell. Three rings, repeated, means a public meeting is being held; five times, and the islanders know a ship is approaching. On Saturdays a slow continued ring calls the islanders to church. A repetition of two rings is the final call for church. A strike of three summons the able-bodied men to public work; four means a "share-out" in the Public Square in the main settlement, Adamstown.

One side of the Square is formed by the Court House, a single-storey timber building, one end of which serves as the museum and Chief Magistrate's office. Thirty yards across and opposite the courthouse is the church, outside which stands the bell. The third side consists of a new building housing a public dispensary, library, and post office. The fourth side is empty, except that facing the dispensary building is a long bench on which the Pitcairners can sit and wait for church or assembly, or just idle and gossip.

Apart from those in the Public Square, the only other official buildings on Pitcairn are the school and the teacher's residence, about three-quarters of a mile from the Square, and the radio station on the southern side of the island.

The Square is less than half a mile from The Edge, the point at which the mutineers reached flat ground after the difficult climb up from Bounty Bay, and where they laid out their first plantations.

When a vessel calls at Pitcairn each family donates a share of fruit for trading aboard the vessel. Bartering of the public fruit brings ashore flour, powdered milk, tinned meats and delicacies not obtainable on the island. These are then shared out among all the families.

It is at the time of a ship's visit that the island's only industry shows a return: curios and souvenirs sold to the ships' crews and passengers. The carvings, generally wooden flying-fish, tortoises, vases, and ship models, are personal property, and show a profit, either in barter goods or money, for the maker. The more skilled, or ambitious, of the islanders sometimes make walking-sticks and inlaid boxes. The women are especially skilled at weaving baskets and hats from pandanus leaves and painting shells. To boost their sales, Pitcairn had an exhibition at the 1965 New York World Fair—the smallest country to have an exhibition at the Fair.

As a general source of revenue, the island's greatest boon, perhaps, has been in postage stamps. First issued in 1940, Pitcairn Island stamps have been collected and prized by philatelists all over the world. One, inevitably, bore a drawing of H.M.S. *Bounty*. Other subjects illustrated on the stamps have included John Adams and the famous *Bounty* Bible, the island's original wheelbarrow, and scenes of island life. Even the school-teacher's house was featured on one stamp, as the island's quietness and limited variety of livelihood allows small scope for many more subjects. But so far, one not used is the Polynesian carvings at the bottom of Down Rope (originally known as "the Rope").

Early in 1964 these carvings were investigated, to see if their age and origin could be determined, by a party of scientists from the University of Otago in New Zealand. Thor Heyerdahl's archaeological expedition to the eastern Pacific in 1955 spent several days on Pitcairn, but the most the members found to interest them seemed to be the *Bounty's* remains, which some of the party's skin-divers explored. However, evidence of ancient occupation discovered by previous expeditions includes three religious sites. In the Otago Museum there is also a statue found on Pitcairn, regarded as similar in size and type to some found on Easter Island by Heyerdahl.

Whatever its antiquities, the islanders themselves are not terribly interested, although there is an abiding interest, sometimes shyly withheld from "strangers", in their notorious forebears and the early times on the island.

Their farm plots are still today based on the original division of the island by Fletcher Christian and his companions, and the land is held under a system of family ownership, and generally passes from hand to hand through marriage or inheritance. Typically, however, it is always possible for one Pitcairner to "borrow" farming land from another.

It is abundantly fertile land. Fruits, even with the trees untended, grow in profusion—lemons, oranges, limes, bananas, grapefruit, and pineapples. Sweet potatoes, called kumara in Polynesian dialect by the islanders, yams, arrowroot, and taro are plentiful; beans, sweet corn, tomatoes, and carrots can be grown easily.

On the other hand, the only useful animals on the island are fowls and goats, and they are not domesticated. The goats are occasionally hunted, sometimes eaten, and never milked. Egg-collecting is a haphazard adventure. The husbanding of the goats, or for that matter any other livestock, holds little appeal for the Pitcairners; hence the absence of cattle.

Their abiding interest is fishing. Their appetite for fish is as unfailing as the schools that abound in the waters round Pitcairn: rock cod, mullet, snapper, and mackerel. From June to August migratory whales cruise past the island. A few months later barracouta and tuna appear. Deep-sea or off-shore, the fishing is good at almost any season, and, no matter how small, a fish is never returned to the water. But a good day's catch can yield fifty to one hundred fish averaging between one and two pounds.*

The boats of Pitcairn are reputedly made in the pattern of a boat sent as a gift to the island by Queen Victoria. Thirty-six feet long and nine feet in beam, they row fourteen oars—twelve in pairs, with a sweep oar

---

* The same fondness of fish is to be observed on Norfolk Island. On a recent visit there, the author was sent back to mainland Australia laden with fresh-caught fish for islanders living on the mainland. To both donor and recipients there could hardly be a finer gift.

and one in the bow. They are as sturdy and solid as an English lifeboat. That they are as manoeuvrable as skiffs is a testimony to the Pitcairners' skill in handling the craft. It is one of the sights of Pitcairn, and a technique hardly changed since the Royal Navy visitor of last century marvelled at the islanders' adroitness.

The channel to Bounty Bay is narrow and rough and sweeps to the left to gain the pebbly beach. Two things could happen: if the turn of the channel is not negotiated, a jumble of sharp, surf-washed rock is seconds dead ahead of an erring boat; or, beforehand, a miscalculation in entering the channel could swamp the craft. In either case, there is no time for a second chance. Even on a calm day, a big surf runs; and on the calmest day the sea is a continual churning surge of rough water.

Wave follows wave, and a boat waiting to make an entry rises and falls, teeters forward and back. With little warning, the sweep oarsman picks the moment, and cries, "Pull ahead!" Twelve oars dip, the boat gathers speed, and the next moment is shooting in on the crest of a wave. Within seconds of entry into the channel, the sweep is heaving on his oar to swing the boat into the turn. Still carrying the initial momentum, the boat beaches gracefully. On really rough days it is an unnerving feat.

Facilities at Bounty Bay are little different from when the *Bounty* itself tied up there. Wharfage until 1960 was almost non-existent and facilities for boat-handling and unloading were very primitive. A small jetty has since been extended, however, and other improvements carried out under grants from Great Britain, the work of construction and maintenance being undertaken as a public duty in which everyone is expected to share.

To get goods up from the bay to The Edge and Adamstown, the job of carrying has for a number of years been simplified by a flying-fox. This is in marked contrast to the long period when there was no wheeled transport of any kind on Pitcairn, and the islanders' first essay at a wheelbarrow produced a curious and bulky structure as big as a donkey cart and seemingly owing much to the Old Testament in appearance.

Two customs both remarkable and peculiar to Pitcairn are the islanders' style of cricket, and their public feasts.

The cricket games are spontaneous affairs. Often the morning of the match has to be spent by the younger men in cutting and chopping undergrowth to clear the "pitch" and "outfield". Once the game is ready to start there is no limit to the number of players and no batting order. In a day, each side may bat up to seven times and by nightfall eight hundred runs will have been scored. In all probability a return match will be staged the next day, with a public dinner as the stake.

While not all may have played cricket, the whole island will be involved in preparing the feast. The Pitcairners' gusto for eating is hearty, not to say enormous. Held generally out of doors, the feast always begins with a simple grace, round a long table laden with dishes. Food cooked on open fires near by keeps the table constantly replenished; and the banqueters are generally equal to the challenge. Apart from conventional courses two island favourites are kumara, a sweet potato, and pillhai, compounded of baked bananas and coconut meat or pumpkin, with coconut milk, generally eaten cold. There is no single recipe for preparing pillhai, though all are similar. For beginners, it is usually something of an acquired taste.

The feast progresses to a quiet chorus of appreciative belching, as a complement to the hosts, while digestion is aided by steaming cups of cocoa and bran tea.

For all it is a lively and convivial time, none the less so for the absence of liquor. For Pitcairn has been dry almost since its conversion to Seventh Day Adventism.

When the guests have had their fill the party breaks up slowly. Acknowledgments are few. In such a close-knit community, much is taken for granted—in the best possible sense. " 'So long as you get enough' is the host's farewell and no Pitcairner would be so churlish as not to have eaten up to it."

The last remark is pure Pitcairnese—the island dialect which is spoken by all in a rapid, almost sing-song fashion. The idiom is a mixture of English and Tahitian. To visitors, the islanders speak English, softly and slightly slurred, but perfectly understandable. Among themselves, they generally speak the dialect. The same is true of Norfolk Island, where, despite the greater intrusion of outsiders in the community, the dialect has persisted, or been preserved.

In the dialect, one doesn't say, "Good day"; one says, "Wut-a-way you." "Good-bye" is "Toby". "I am pleased to meet you"—"I glaid fo see you." "How often do ships call?"—"Now-Humuch shep corl ya?" "What food grows on Pitcairn?"—"Wut wekle groos ana Pitkern?"

"Humuch sullun levan on Pitkern?" This last, "translated", means "How many people live on Pitcairn?"

In March 1964 there were eighty-five Pitcairners on the island, and ten "strangers".

Church and Schoolhouse, Pitcairn

Simon Young and his wife

There can be few groups anywhere in the world living as tranquilly as the Pitcairn Islanders (except possibly their cousins on Norfolk Island), but five years ago there were 150 souls on the island.

And this today seems to be the final point in the story of Pitcairn Island: the population is gradually declining.

The young men move off, principally to New Zealand; the older ones —grow older.

POSTSCRIPT

THE number of ships calling at Pitcairn Island is declining, not seriously, but sufficiently to worry the tiny population. In 1956 there were 65 calls; in 1957, 55; 1958, 58; 1959, 53; 1960, 47; 1961, 50; and in 1962, only 39.

Should the decline continue progressively, then the island, with its dependence upon shipping for supplies and revenue from the sale of souvenirs, could arrive at a crisis.

With this in mind, in late 1963, the island council reported its anxiety to the Governor of Fiji (who is also Governor of Pitcairn), while personal appeals were made to the United States and New Zealand for the maintenance of shipping services and for assistance. There was even one response in the United States—from a Congressman, John Bennet, who suggested that Pitcairn might qualify for a Peace Corps project!

However, the Commissioner of the South Pacific Office at Suva, Reid Cowell, spent January 1964 on the island, and reported that the outlook for Pitcairn need not be so gloomy. Assurances of support were forthcoming from three shipping companies, whatever the future held for the islanders. How justified Mr Cowell's hopes will be, remains to be seen.

The same problem exists on Norfolk Island, in different guise. There, communication with the outside world is only as far away as a twice-weekly air service operated by Qantas Empire Airways in conjunction with Air New Zealand. A Qantas DC4 flies from Sydney to Norfolk, and thence to Auckland as an ANZ flight. On Pitcairn, if the weather is particularly bad, people intending to land on the island may be delayed for weeks by being carried on to Panama or New Zealand, and then making another attempt. On Norfolk the weather occasionally closes the airport, built during World War II after the controversial destruction of many of the famous Norfolk pine-trees. The delay however, is usually only for a day or so.

About once a month a ship calls.

But in the pleasant somnolence and lassitude that turn life on Norfolk Island into one long, lazy afternoon, there is nothing for the younger generation to do. A job in the island Administration is prized, but vacancies are few. There is occasional stevedoring work when a ship has to be unloaded, but this is hardly a career. The whaling industry has closed down.

As a measure of the island's commerce, taxation, as on Pitcairn, is non-existent, except that once a year the residents are called on to pay five pounds into revenue, or work instead. One week's work on the roads, and an islander expunges his tax debt. It is not unusual for less able-bodied, or less willing, islanders, to pay someone else to work the tax out for them.

The Norfolk Islanders, too, speak the dialect heard on Pitcairn, though with an influx of permanent residents from New Zealand, mainland Australia, and even the United Kingdom, the descendants of the *Bounty* settlers constitute little more than fifty per cent of the island's population.

But all have been infected by the same spirit. Rarely is anything locked up on the island, there is no real main street, no public lighting. One policeman has little to do. Tourists are enchanted by the peaceful, lacka-daisical air on the island. The friendliness evident on Pitcairn is also evident on Norfolk. A passing motorist—there are about five hundred vehicles on the island, which has a population of about one thousand—always gives a friendly wave on passing a pedestrian, be he islander or a mainlander.

The old convict buildings are now in ruins, but preserved and cared for by the island authorities. With only one or two funerals a year, the cemetery is equally a tourist attraction, lying as it does overlooking the sea.

But even if the mortality rate is low, it only serves to accentuate the problems of the island's youth. Their only outlet for permanent employment is mainland Australia or New Zealand.

Very slowly the youthful population of the island is being eroded, as the young people leave. Often their surnames are lost on Australians and New Zealanders: Adams, Christian, McCoy, Quintal, and Young*—the mutineers perpetuated for ever, a fate they perhaps never dreamed of when first they sailed from Spithead on H.M.S. *Bounty*.

---

* The only *Bounty* names remaining on Pitcairn are Christian and Young.

LIST OF THE INHABITANTS OF PITCAIRN ISLAND 1790-1856

From the Arrival of the *Bounty* to the Departure of the *Morayshire*

Containing, where possible, date of birth, name, date of death, names of parents, and date of marriage and name of marriage partner.

NOTE. Numbers in brackets refer the reader to the sequence number prefacing each person listed in this appendix.

★ Returned to Pitcairn in 1858.

+ Returned to Pitcairn in 1863.

1. b. 4th November 1763	John Adams (Alexander Smith)	d. 5th March 1829
	m. (i) 1788, Teehuteatuaonoa (21)	
	(ii) 1789, Obuarei (19)	
	(iii) c. 1803 & 17th December 1825, Teio (22)	
2. b. c. 1761	William Brown	d. c. 1793
	m. 1789, Teatuahitea (20)	
3. b. 23rd September 1764	Fletcher Christian	d. c. 1793
	Charles Christian & Anne Dixon	
	m. 1788, Mauatua (18)	
4. b. c. 1763	William McCoy (Mickoy)	d. c. 1798
	m. 1789, Teio (22)	
5. b. c. 1758	Isaac Martin	d. c. 1793
	m. 1789, Teehuteatuaonoa (21)	
6. b. c. 1748	John Mills	d. c. 1793
	m. 1789, Vahineatua (27)	
7. b. c. 1767	Matthew Quintal	d. c. 1799
	m. 1789, Tevarua (24)	
8. b. c. 1763	John Williams	d. c. 1793
	m. (i) 1789, Faahotu (16)	
	(ii) 1791, Toofaiti (26)	
9. b. c. 1762	Edward Young	d. c. 1800
	George Young & ——	
	m. 1789, Teraura (23)	

10. Minarii (Menalee)   d. c. 1793
    m. Mareva (17)
11. Teimua   d. c. 1793
    + Mareva (17)
12. Niau   d. c. 1793
    + Mareva (17)
13. Tetahiti (Taroamiva)   d. c. 1793
    Tahuhuatama & ——
    m. Tinafornea (25)
14. Ohoo   d. c. 1791
    + Tinafornea (25)
15. Tararo (Talaloo)   d. c. 1791
    m. Toofaiti (26)
16. Faahotu   d. c. 1790
    m. 1789, John Williams (8)
17. Mareva   d. ?
    m. Minarii (10)
    + Niau (12)
    + Teimua (11)
18. Mauatua (Maimiti, Isabella)   d. 19th September 1841
    m. 1788, Fletcher Christian (3)
19. Obuarei (Balhadi)   d. 1793-1799
    m. 1789, Alexander Smith (1)
20. Teatuahitea   d. 1808-14
    m. 1789, William Brown (2)
21. Teehuteatuaonoa (Jenny)   Left by *Sultan*, 1817
    m. (i) 1788, Alexander Smith (1)
       (ii) 1789, Isaac Martin (5)
22. Teio (Mary—"Sore Mummy")   d. 14th March 1829
    m. (i) 1789, William McCoy (4)
       (ii) c. 1803 & 17th December 1825, John Adams (1)
23. b. c. 1775 Teraura (Susannah)   d. 15th July 1850
    m. (i) 1789, Edward Young (9)
       (ii) c. 1805, Thursday October Christian (29)

24. Tevarua (Sarah, "Big Sullee")
m. 1789, Matthew Quintal (7) — d. c. 1799

25. Tinafornea
m. Tetahiti (13)
+ Ohoo (14) — d. 1808-14

26. Toofaiti (Nancy)
m. (i) Tararo (Talaloo) (15)
(ii) 1791, John Williams (8) — d. 9th June 1831

27. Vahineatua (Prudence)
m. 1789, John Mills (6) — d. 29th April 1831

28. b. c. November 1789. Sarah (Sully)
—— & Teio (22)
m. c. 1810, Charles Christian I (33) — d. 7th March 1826

29. b. October 1790. Thursday October Christian
Fletcher Christian (3) & Mauatua (18)
m. c. 1805, Teraura (23) — d. 21st April 1831

30. b. 1791. Matthew Quintal II
Matthew Quintal (7) & Tevarua (24)
m. c. 1811, Elizabeth Mills (32) — d. September 1814

31. b. 1791-2. Daniel McCoy I
William McCoy (4) & Teio (22)
m. c. 1811, Sarah Quintal (37) — d. 26th December 1832

32. b. 1791-2. Elizabeth (Betsy) Mills
John Mills (6) & Vahineatua (27)
m. (i) c. 1811, Matthew Quintal II (30)
(ii) c. 1823, William Young (43) — d. 14th January 1842

33. b. 1791-2. Charles Christian I
Fletcher Christian (3) & Mauatua (18)
m. c. 1810, Sully (28) — d. 2nd January 1866

34. b. 1793. Mary Ann Christian
Fletcher Christian (3) & Mauatua (18)
never married

35. b. 1793. John Mills II
John Mills (6) & Vahineatua (27)
never married — d. 1814

36. b. 1794-9	John Quintal (?) Matthew Quintal (7) & —— never married	d. aged one week
37. b. 1794-9	Sarah (Seldarb) Quintal Matthew Quintal (7) & Tevarua (24) m. (i) c. 1811, Daniel McCoy (31) (ii) 6th October 1844, George Adams (52)	d. 27th November 1851
38. b. 1794-7	Dinah Adams John Adams (1) & Vahineatua (27) m. 4th March 1819, Edward Quintal I (49)	d. 18th January 1864
39. b. 1794-9	Polly Young Edward Young (9) & Toofaiti (26) m. 1st April 1827, George Adams (52)	d. 17th December 1843
40. b. 1794-9	Robert Young Edward Young (9) & Toofaiti (26) never married	d. 18th August 1831
41. b. 1794-9	Arthur Quintal I Matthew Quintal (7) & Tevarua (24) m. (i) c. 1816, Catherine McCoy (50) (ii) 3rd May 1835, Mary Christian (71)	d. 19th November 1873
42. b. 1794-9	George Young Edward Young (9) & Toofaiti (26) m. c. 1821, Hannah Adams (51)	d. 4th May 1831
43. b. 1794-9	William Young Edward Young (9) & Toofaiti (26) m. c. 1823, Elizabeth (Mills) Quintal (32)	d. 6th February 1839
44. b. 1794-9	Edward Young II Edward Young (9) & Mauatua (18) m. c. 1829, Polly Christian (60)	d. 6th November 1831
45. b. 1794-9	Dorothy (Dolly) Young Edward Young (9) & Mauatua (18) m. 10th February 1824, John Buffett (82)	d. 24th April 1863
46. b. 1794-9	Jane Quintal Matthew Quintal (7) & Tevarua (24) m. Local chief of Rurutu, after leaving Pitcairn 19th December 1826	

47. b. 1794-9
Rachel (Rebecca) Adams
John Adams (1) & Vahineatua (27)
m. 26th November 1824, John Evans (83)
d. 7th September 1876

48. b. 1799
James Young
Edward Young (9) & ——
never married
d. 1806

49. b. 1800
Edward Quintal I
Matthew Quintal (7) & Teraura (23)
m. 4th March 1819, Dinah Adams (38)
d. 8th September 1841

50. b. 1800
Catherine McCoy
William McCoy (4) & Teio (22)
m. c. 1816, Arthur Quintal I (41)
d. 8th June 1831

51. b. 1800
Hannah Adams
John Adams (1) & Vahineatua (27)
m. c. 1821, George Young (42)
d. 27th August 1864

52. b. 6th June 1804
George Adams
John Adams (1) & Teio (22)
m. (i) 1st April 1827, Polly Young (39)
(ii) 6th October 1844, Sarah (Quintal) McCoy (37)
d. 29th October 1873

53. b. 1806
Joseph Christian
Thursday October Christian (29) & Tevarua (24)
never married
d. 24th November 1831

54. b. January 1808
Charles Christian II
Thursday October Christian (29) & Tevarua (24)
m. 18th October 1829, Maria Christian (67)
d. 25th June 1831

55. b. c. 1810
Sarah (Big Salah) Christian
Charles Christian I (33) & Sully (28)
m. 18th October 1829, George Hunn Nobbs (102)
d. 5th December 1899

56. b. c. 1811
Mary (Big Melly) Christian
Thursday October Christian (29) & Tevarua (24)
never married
d. 25th October 1852

57. b. c. 1812
Fletcher Christian II
Charles Christian I (33) & Sully (28)
m. 17th January 1833, Peggy (Christian) McCoy (64)
d. 5th April 1852

58. b. c. 1812   William McCoy II   d. 17th February 1849
Daniel McCoy I (31) & Sarah Quintal (37)
never married

59. b. c. 1812   John Quintal I   d. 14th November 1838
Matthew Quintal II (30) & Elizabeth Mills (32)
m. 17th January 1833, Maria (Christian) Christian (67)

60. b. c. 1814   Polly Christian   d. 16th May 1831
Thursday October Christian (29) & Teraura (23)
m. c. 1829, Edward Young II (44)

61. b. c. 1814   Daniel McCoy II   d. 27th June 1831
Daniel McCoy I (31) & Sarah Quintal (37)
m. 18th October 1829, Peggy Christian (64)

62. b. c. 1814   Matthew Quintal III   d. 8th December 1865
Matthew Quintal II (30) & Elizabeth Mills (32)
never married

63. b. c. 1815   Edward Christian   d. 3rd June 1831
Charles Christian I (33) & Sully (28)
never married (died at Marutea or Lord Hood's Island)

64. b. c. 1815   Peggy Christian   d. 12th May 1884
Thursday October Christian (29) & Tevarua (24)
m.   (i) 18th October 1829, Daniel McCoy II (61)
     (ii) 17th January 1833, Fletcher Christian II (57)

65. b. 1816   Hugh McCoy   d. 27th June 1831
Daniel McCoy I (31) & Sarah Quintal (37)
never married

66. b. 1816   Arthur Quintal II   d. 20th August 1902
Arthur Quintal I (41) & Catherine McCoy (50)
m. 22nd October 1837, Martha Quintal (77)

67. b. 1816   Maria Christian   d. 12th January 1889
Charles Christian I (33) & Sully (28)
m.   (i) 18th October 1829, Charles Christian II (54)
     (ii) 17th January 1833, John Quintal I (59)
     (iii) 7th June 1840, William Quintal (68)

68. b. 1817	William Quintal Edward Quintal I (49) & Dinah Adams (38) m. 7th June 1840, Maria (Christian) Quintal (67)		d. 6th July 1905
69. b. 1818	Charles (Little Charlie) Christian III Charles Christian I (33) & Sully (28) m. 30th October 1836, Charlotte Quintal (78)		d. 22nd May 1886
70. b. 1818	Catherine (Kitty) Quintal Arthur Quintal I (41) & Catherine McCoy (50) never married		d. 15th May 1831
71. b. 1819	Mary Christian Charles Christian I (33) & Sully (28) m. 3rd May 1835, Arthur Quintal I (41)		d. 25th April 1843
72. b. 1819	Matthew McCoy Daniel McCoy I (31) & Sarah Quintal (37) m. 30th October 1836, Margaret Christian (75)		d. 31st January 1853
73. b. 1820	John Quintal II Arthur Quintal I (41) & Catherine McCoy (50) m. 5th November 1837, Dinah Young (87)		d. 2nd November 1910
74. b. 1820	Thursday October (Doctor) Christian II Thursday October Christian (29) & Teraura (23) m. 24th March 1839, Polly Young (89)		
75. b. 1822	Margaret Christian Charles Christian I (33) & Sully (28) m. (i) 30th October 1836, Matthew McCoy (72) (ii) 17th January 1858, William Mayhew Young (98)		d. 30th November 1874
76. b. 1822	George Martin Frederick Young George Young (42) & Hannah Adams (51) m. 25th December 1849, Mary Evans (126)		d. 25th September 1899
77. b. 1822	Martha Quintal Edward Quintal I (49) & Dinah Adams (38) m. 22nd October 1837, Arthur Quintal II (66)		d. 25th December 1893
78. b. 1822	Charlotte Quintal Arthur Quintal I (41) & Catherine McCoy (50) m. 30th October 1836, Charles Christian III (69)		d. 16th August 1883

79.	b. 1822	Jane McCoy Daniel McCoy (31) & Sarah Quintal (37) never married	d. 4th June 1831
80.	b. 1823	Simon Young George Young (42) & Hannah Adams (51) m. 31st July 1845, Mary Buffett Christian (100)	d. September 1893
81.	b. 1823	Mayhew Young William Young (43) & Elizabeth Mills (32) died aged 9 months	d. 1823
82.	b. 16th July 1797	John Buffett m. 10th February 1824, Dorothy Young (45) arrived Pitcairn 10th December 1823	d. 5th May 1891
83.	b. c. 1804	John Evans m. 26th November 1824, Rachel Adams (47) arrived Pitcairn 10th December 1823	d. 30th December 1891
84.	b. 25th April 1824	Phoebe Quintal Arthur Quintal I (41) & Catherine McCoy (50) m. 9th April 1848, Jonathan Adams (104)	d. 1900
85.	b. 23rd July 1824	Sarah McCoy Daniel McCoy I (31) & Sarah Quintal (37) never married	d. 9th May 1833
86.	b. 31st October 1824	Edward Quintal II Edward Quintal I (49) & Dinah Adams (38) never married	d. 5th January 1856
87.	b. 16th November 1824	Dinah Young George Young (42) & Hannah Adams (51) m. 5th November 1837, John Quintal II (73)	d. 9th May 1881
88.	b. 3rd January 1825	Thomas Buffett John Buffett (82) & Dorothy Young (45) m. (i) 20th June 1853, Louisa Quintal (106) (ii) 25th May 1875, Dorcas Young (122)	d. 18th October 1900
89.	b. 28th January 1825	Mary (Polly) Young William Young (43) & Elizabeth Mills (32) m. 24th March 1839, Thursday October Christian II (74)	

90. b. 26th April 1825	Isaac Christian Charles Christian I (33) & Sully (28) m. 31st July 1844, Miriam Young (108)	d. 31st October 1877
91. b. 9th July 1825	James Quintal Arthur Quintal I (41) & Catherine McCoy (50) m. 22nd July 1855, Priscilla Christian (132)	d. 7th September 1898
92. b. 21st July 1826	John Buffett II John Buffett (82) & Dorothy Young (45) m. 12th October 1845, Elizabeth Young (93)	d. 23rd June 1906
93. b. 8th September 1826	Elizabeth (Betsy) Young George Young (42) & Hannah Adams (51) m. 12th October 1845, John Buffett II (92)	d. 10th October 1863
94. b. 23rd October 1826	Samuel McCoy Daniel McCoy (31) & Sarah Quintal (37) m.　(i) 19th September 1858, Ruth Quintal (107) 　　(ii) 1st February 1863, Polly Christian (139)	d. 7th September 1876
95. b. 31st January 1827	Abraham Blatchly Quintal Edward Quintal I (49) & Dinah Adams (38) m. 25th December 1848, Esther Maria Nobbs (121)	d. 20th September 1910
96. b. 21st July 1827	Caroline Quintal Arthur Quintal I (41) & Catherine McCoy (50) m. 16th April 1843, John Adams II (97)	d. 13th June 1869
97. b. 10th November 1827	John Adams II George Adams (52) & Polly Young (39) m. 16th April 1843, Caroline Quintal (96)	d. 29th May 1897
98. b. 4th December 1827+	William Mayhew Young William Young (43) & Elizabeth Mills (32) m. 17th January 1858, Margaret (Christian) McCoy (75)	d. 1877
99. b. 27th May 1828	David Buffett John Buffett (82) & Dorothy Young (45) m.　(i) 28th January 1851, Martha Young (110) 　　(ii) 20th July 1881 Maria Elizabeth (Quintal) Christian (151)	d. 7th August 1924
100. b. 1st October 1828	Mary Buffett Christian John Buffett (82) & Mary Christian (56) m. 31st July 1845, Simon Young (80)	

101. b. 31st October 1828 — Jemima Young
George Young (42) & Hannah Adams (51)
never married — d. 5th May 1868

102. b. 1799 — George Hunn Nobbs
Francis Rawdon-Hastings & Jemima Ffrench
m. 18th October 1829, Sarah Christian (55)
arrived Pitcairn 5th November 1828 — d. 6th November 1884

103. b. 11th November 1828+ — Albina McCoy
Daniel McCoy I (31) & Sarah Quintal (37)
m. 9th July 1848, Moses Young (109)

104. b. 3rd January 1829 — Jonathan Adams
George Adams (52) & Polly Young (39)
m. 9th April 1848, Phoebe Quintal (84) — d. 23rd May 1906

105. b. 12th January 1829 — John Valentine Mansell Evans
John Evans (83) & Rachel Adams (47)
never married — d. before 1892 in New Zealand

106. b. 7th March 1829 — Louisa Quintal
Edward Quintal I (49) & Dinah Adams (38)
m. 20th June 1853, Thomas Buffett (88) — d. 5th February 1873

107. b. 8th May 1829 — Ruth Quintal
Arthur Quintal I (41) & Catherine McCoy (50)
m. 19th September 1858, Samuel McCoy (94) — d. 29th September 1862

108. b. 30th August 1829 — Miriam Young
William Young (43) & Elizabeth Mills (32)
m. 31st July 1844, Isaac Christian (90) — d. 25th November 1911

109. b. 30th September 1829+ — Moses Young
Edward Young II (44) & Polly Christian (60)
m. 9th July 1848, Albina McCoy (103)

110. b. 19th January 1830 — Martha Young
George Young (42) & Hannah Adams (51)
m. 28th January 1851, David Buffett (99) — d. 30th January 1872

111. b. 26th March 1830 — Robert Pitcairn Buffett
John Buffett (82) & Dorothy Young (45)
m. 7th December 1862, Lydia Young (123)

112. b. 7th April 1830	Rebecca (Pot) Christian Charles Christian II (54) & Maria Christian (67) m. 22nd January 1854, William Evans (114)	d. 2nd March 1871
113. b. 19th June 1830	Josiah Chester Adams George Adams (52) & Polly Young (39) m. 19th September 1858, Dinah McCoy (150)	d. 2nd February 1907
114. b. 8th August 1830	William Evans John Evans (83) & Rachel Adams (47) m. 22nd January 1854, Rebecca Christian (112)	d. 3rd March 1873
115. b. 18th August 1830	Phillip McCoy Daniel McCoy II (61) & Peggy Christian (64) m. (i) 25th December 1851, Sarah Quintal (131) (ii) 17th October 1869, Lucy Anne Hagar Christian (220)	d. 28th July 1913
116. b. 19th September 1830	Reuben Elias Nobbs George Hunn Nobbs (102) & Sarah Christian (55) never married	d. 2nd March 1855
117. b. 7th–23rd March 1831	Lucy Anne Quintal Arthur Quintal I (41) & Catherine McCoy (50) born aboard the *Lucy Anne* on the way to Tahiti	d. 25th April 1831
118. b. 6th June 1831	Nancy Quintal Edward Quintal I (49) & Dinah Adams (38) m. 10th August 1851, Jacob Christian (129)	d. 24th December 1853
119. b. 7th August 1831	Charles Driver Christian Charles Christian II (54) & Maria Christian (67) m. 5th July 1855, Maria Lucy Christian (147)	d. 22nd October 1906
120. b. 30th May 1832	Benjamin Claudius Christian John Buffett (82) & Mary Christian (56) m. 25th December 1851, Eliza Quintal (127)	d. 4th August 1897
121. b. 30th August 1832	Esther Maria Nobbs George Hunn Nobbs (102) & Sarah Christian (55) m. 25th December 1848, Abraham Blatchly Quintal (95)	d. 23rd July 1910
122. b. 16th September 1832	Dorcas Young William Young (43) & Elizabeth Mills (32) m. 25th May 1875, Thomas Buffett (88)	d. 3rd December 1917

123. b. 16th September 1832	Lydia Young William Young (43) & Elizabeth Mills (32) m. (i) 24th March 1850, Daniel McCoy III (125) (ii) 7th December 1862, Robert Pitcairn Buffett (111)	
124. b. 15th April 1773	Joshua Hill arrived 28th October 1832, aboard the *Maria* from Tahiti departed 8th December 1837, aboard H.M.S. *Imogene* for Val- paraiso	
125. b. 28th December 1832	Daniel McCoy III Daniel McCoy I (31) & Sarah Quintal (37) m. 24th March 1850, Lydia Young (123)	d. 7th April 1855
126. b. 17th January 1833	Mary Evans John Evans (83) & Rachel Adams (47) m. 25th December 1849, George Martin Frederick Young (76)	d. 1st June 1909
127. b. 11th June 1833	Eliza Quintal John Quintal I (59) & Maria Christian (67) m. 25th December 1851, Benjamin Claudius Christian (120)	d. 16th May 1906
128. b. 1st September 1833	Fletcher Christian Nobbs George Hunn Nobbs (102) & Sarah Christian (55) m. 20th June 1853, Susan Quintal (130)	d. 3rd March 1912
129. b. 24th September 1833	Jacob Christian Fletcher Christian II (57) & Peggy Christian (64) m. (i) 10th August 1851, Nancy Quintal (118) (ii) 14th October 1855, Maria Elizabeth Quintal (151)	d. 16th October 1877
130. b. 5th November 1833	Susan Quintal Edward Quintal I (49) & Dinah Adams (38) m. 20th June 1853, Fletcher Christian Nobbs (128)	d. 18th February 1917
131. b. 5th April 1835	Sarah Quintal John Quintal I (59) & Maria Christian (67) m. 25th December 1851, Phillip McCoy (115)	d. 28th July 1868
132. b. 11th August 1835	Priscilla Christian Fletcher Christian II (57) & Peggy Christian (64) m. 22nd July 1855, James Quintal (91)	d. 21st November 1906

133. b. 7th September 1835	Francis Mason Nobbs George Hunn Nobbs (102) & Sarah Christian (55) m. 25th December 1856, Harriet Augusta Quintal (161)	d. 15th June 1909
134. b. 27th November 1835	Edward Buffett John Buffett (82) & Dorothy Young (45) m. 3rd October 1858, Louisa Victoria Rose Quintal (160)	d. 28th November 1911
135. b. 23rd December 1835	George Francis Mason Evans John Evans (82) & Rachel Adams (47) m. 3rd October 1858, Catherine Christian (156)	d. 6th May 1910
136. b. 17th January 1836	Henry Joshua Quintal Edward Quintal I (49) & Dinah Adams (38) m. 21st March 1858, Jane McCoy (142)	d. 16th July 1873
137. b. 17th June 1836	Absolom Quintal Arthur Quintal I (41) & Mary Christian (71) never married	d. 14th June 1868
138. b. 6th October 1836	Jane Agnes Nobbs George Hunn Nobbs (102) & Sarah Christian (55) m. 25th August 1861, John Quintal IV (164)	d. 21st April 1926
139. b. 10th November 1836	Polly Christian Fletcher Christian II (57) & Peggy Christian (64) m. 1st February 1863, Samuel McCoy (94)	d. 30th April 1892
140. b. 4th February 1837	Ellen Quintal John Quintal I (59) & Maria Christian (67) m. 24th November 1861, Stephen Christian (178)	d. 7th November 1910
141. b. 19th June 1837	Robert Young William Young (43) & Elizabeth Mills (32) never married	d. 18th November 1837
142. b. 10th July 1837	Jane McCoy Matthew McCoy (72) & Margaret Christian (75) m. 21st March 1858, Henry Joshua Quintal (136)	d. 19th January 1917
143. b. 6th August 1837	Dinah Evans John Evans (83) & Rachel Adams (47) m. 25th December 1856, John Quintal III (152)	d. 11th June 1870

144. b. 5th September 1837
Caleb Quintal
Edward Quintal I (49) & Dinah Adams (38)
m. 25th December 1857, Ann Naomi Nobbs (148)
d. 7th May 1873

145. b. 7th November 1837
Nathaniel Quintal
Arthur Quintal I (41) & Mary Christian (71)
m. 1st March 1863, Abby Louisa Taber Quintal (193)
d. 1st May 1895

146. b. 16th December 1837
Andrew Christian
Charles Christian III (69) & Charlotte Quintal (78)
never married
d. 24th December 1837

147. b. 13th June 1838
Maria Lucy (Ory) Christian
Fletcher Christian II (57) & Peggy Christian (64)
m. 5th July 1855, Charles Driver Christian (119)
d. 13th October 1904

148. b. 4th July 1838
Ann Naomi Nobbs
George Hunn Nobbs (102) & Sarah Christian (55)
m. 25th December 1857, Caleb Quintal (144)
d. 27th September 1931

149. b. 31st July 1838
Edmund Johnston Quintal
Arthur Quintal II (66) & Martha Quintal (77)
never married
d. 1st September 1839

150. b. 11th August 1838
Diana (Dinah) McCoy
Matthew McCoy (72) & Margaret Christian (75)
m. 19th September 1858, Josiah Chester Adams (113)
d. 8th September 1929

151. b. 14th November 1838
Maria Elizabeth Quintal
John Quintal I (59) & Maria Christian (67)
m. (i) 14th October 1855, Jacob Christian (129)
   (ii) 20th July 1881, David Buffett (99)
d. 28th April 1900

152. b. 23rd December 1838
John Quintal III
John Quintal II (73) & Dinah Young (87)
m. 25th December 1856, Dinah Evans (143)
d. 1st March 1868

153. b. 5th July, 1839
Joseph Quintal
Arthur Quintal I (41) & Mary Christian (71)
m. (i) 21st March 1858, Martha Evans (154)
   (ii) 26th June 1878, Emily Lucy Christian (born on Norfolk Island)
d. 26th May 1912

154. b. 12th July 1839	Martha Evans John Evans (83) & Rachel Adams (47) m. 21st March 1858, Joseph Quintal (153)		d. 17th September 1876
155. b. 22nd September 1839	James Wingate Johnstone Nobbs George Hunn Nobbs (102) & Sarah Christian (55) m. 21st March 1858, Isabella Emily Christian (159)		d. 26th March 1909
156. b. 3rd November 1839	Catherine Christian Charles Christian III (69) & Charlotte Quintal (78) m. 3rd October 1858, George Francis Mason Evans (135)		d. 3rd September 1894
157. b. 3rd December 1839	Unnamed male child (McCoy) Matthew McCoy (72) & Margaret Christian (75) died shortly after birth		d. 3rd December 1839
158. b. 7th December 1839	Joseph Napoleon Quintal Edward Quintal I (49) & Dinah Adams (38) never married		d. 2nd October 1841
159. b. 13th December 1839	Isabella Emily Christian Fletcher Christian II (57) & Peggy Christian (64) m. 21st March 1858, James Wingate Johnstone Nobbs (155)		d. 10th February 1895
160. b. 30th December 1839	Louisa Victoria Rose Quintal Arthur Quintal II (66) & Martha Quintal (77) m. 3rd October 1858, Edward Buffett (134)		d. 27th August 1892
161. b. 30th April 1840	Harriet Augusta Quintal John Quintal II (73) & Dinah Young (87) m. 25th December 1857, Francis Mason Nobbs (133)		d. 21st November 1897
162. b. 23rd July 1840	Julia Christian Thursday October Christian II (74) & Mary Young (89) never married		d. 15th June 1850
163. b. 13th December 1840	Unnamed female child (McCoy) Matthew McCoy (72) & Margaret Christian (75) died within two hours of birth		d. 13th December 1840
164. b. 4th January 1841	John Quintal IV William Quintal (68) & Maria Christian (67) m. 25th August 1861, Jane Agnes Nobbs (138)		d. 29th April 1907

165. b. 17th June 1841	Cornelius Quintal Arthur Quintal I (41) & Mary Christian (71) m. 13th June 1870, Ellen Amelia Moore (of New Zealand)	d. 10th February 1934
166. b. 4th July 1841	Andrew Christian Charles Christian III (69) & Charlotte Quintal (78) never married	d. 26th May 1862
167. b. 9th September 1841	Stephen Christian Fletcher Christian II (57) & Peggy Christian (64) never married	d. 10th December 1842
168. b. 6th October 1841*	Agnes Christian Thursday October Christian II (74) & Mary Young (89) m. 6th December 1863, Samuel R. Warren* (of Providence, Rhode Island)	
169. b. 11th October 1841	Mary McCoy Matthew McCoy (72) & Margaret Christian (75) m. 19th July 1868, Pardon Snell (of Little Compton, Connecticut)	d. 22nd January 1930
170. b. 17th October 1841	Matilda Quintal John Quintal II (73) & Dinah Young (87) never married	d. 17th January 1866
171. b. 22nd July 1842	Rhoda Quintal Arthur Quintal II (66) & Martha Quintal (77) never married	d. 29th November 1857
172. b. 10th October 1842	Oliver Macy Quintal William Quintal (68) & Maria Christian (67) m. c. 1880 (in New Zealand), Jemima Buffett (born on Norfolk Island)	d. 23rd February 1922
173. b. 8th December 1842	Adeline Sophia Christian Charles Christian III (69) & Charlotte Quintal (78) m. 3rd May 1869, Sydney Herbert Nobbs (208)	d. 2nd April 1870
174. b. 31st March 1843	Albert Christian Thursday October Christian II (74) & Mary Young (89) never married	d. 19th January 1861
175. b. 16th April 1843	Mary Quintal Arthur Quintal I (41) & Mary Christian (71) m. 18th December 1864, Pardon Snell	d. 5th April 1868

176.	b. 5th May 1843	George Edwin Coffin Nobbs George Hunn Nobbs (102) & Sarah Christian (55) never married	d. 5th September 1864
177.	b. 21st May 1843	Kezia Quintal John Quintal II (73) & Dinah Young (87) never married	d. 26th March 1868
178.	b. 5th October 1843	Stephen Christian Fletcher Christian II (57) & Peggy Christian (64) m. 24th November 1861, Ellen Quintal (140)	d. 16th May 1918
179.	b. 16th November 1843 +	Sarah McCoy Matthew McCoy (72) & Margaret Christian (75) m. Alphonse Downs Christian (195)	
180.	b. 16th May 1844	Polly (Pauline) Adams John Adams II (97) & Caroline Quintal (96) m. 6th March 1864, Ephraim Christian (186)	d. 5th May 1920
181.	b. 2nd June 1844	Edward Quintal III William Quintal (68) & Maria Christian (67, never married	d. 24th March 1855
182.	b. 18th July 1844	Edward Quintal IV Arthur Quintal II (66) & Martha Quintal (77) m. (i) 8th January 1865, Cordelia Ruth Christian (206) (ii) 16th January 1873, Angeline Ophelia McCoy (257)	d. 4th January 1901
183.	b. 9th September 1844	Gilbert Edwin Christian Charles Christian III (69) & Charlotte Quintal (78) m. 19th June 1864, Jemima Sarah Nobbs (187)	d. 10th January 1866
184.	b. 10th October 1844	Levi Ward Quintal John Quintal II (73) & Dinah Young (87) never married	d. 30th August 1846
185.	b. 7th January 1845	Elias Christian Thursday October Christian II (74) & Mary Young (89)	
186.	b. 15th February 1845	Ephraim Christian John Buffett (82) & Mary Christian (56) m. 6th March 1864, Polly Adams (180)	d. 20th May 1920

187. b. 13th May 1845

Jemima Sarah Nobbs
George Hunn Nobbs (102) & Sarah Christian (55)
m. 19th June 1864, Gilbert Edwin Christian (183)

d. 14th January 1920

188. b. 26th June 1845

Nathan Christian
Fletcher Christian II (57) & Peggy Christian (64)
never married

d. 28th October 1860

189. b. 4th September 1845

James Russell McCoy
Matthew McCoy (72) & Margaret Christian (75)

190. b. 28th October 1845

Henry Samuel Hunt Christian
Isaac Christian (90) & Miriam Young (108)
m. (i) 23rd December 1866, Eleanor Clotilda Christian (194)
(ii) 26th November 1874, Alice Maude Christian (born on Norfolk Island)

d. 8th June 1905

191. b. 28th November 1845

Gilbert Warren Fysh Adams
John Adams II (97) & Caroline Quintal (96)
m. 28th November 1867, Francis Adelaide Quintal (227)

d. 10th February 1875

192. b. 27th January 1846

Frederick Lorenzo Fisher Young
Simon Young (80) & Mary Buffett Christian (100)
never married

d. 26th August 1864

193. b. 27th May 1846

Abby Louisa Taber Quintal
William Quintal (68) & Maria Christian (67)
m. 1st March 1863, Nathaniel Quintal (145)

d. 1st September 1929

194. b. 19th July 1846

Eleanor Clotilda Christian
Charles Christian III (69) & Charlotte Quintal (78)
m. 23rd December 1866, Henry Samuel Hunt Christian (190)

d. 26th March 1868

195. b. 3rd August 1846*

Alphonso Downs Christian
Thursday October Christian II (74) & Mary Young (89)
m. (i) , Sarah McCoy (179)
(ii) , Alice H. Christian

196. b. 18th September 1846

Emma Young (or Quintal)
Granddaughter of Dinah (Adams) Quintal (38)
m. 15th August 1875, Forrescue Moresby Buffett (246)

d. 12th August 1916

197. b. 11th November 1846

Edmund Joseph Napoleon Quintal
Arthur Quintal II (66) & Martha Quintal (77)
m. , Elizabeth Snell

d. in Australia

198. b. 27th November 1846 — Alfred Augustine Nobbs
George Hunn Nobbs (102) & Sarah Christian (55)
m. 23rd August 1868, Mary Emily Christian (242) — d. 28th September 1906

199. b. 3rd May 1847+ — Harriet Melissa McCoy
Matthew McCoy (71) & Margaret Christian (75)
m. May 1871, Daniel Christian (270)

200. b. 7th May 1847 — Henry Seymour Buffett
John Buffett II (92) & Elizabeth Young (93)
m. 27th November 1873, Marianne Scelina Buffett (274) — d. 1st May 1931

201. b. 24th May 1847 — William B. Swain Christian
Fletcher Christian II (57) & Peggy Christian (64)
never married — d. 1st July 1868

202. b. 1st October 1847 — Byron Stanley Mitchell Adams
John Adams II (97) & Caroline Quintal (96)
m. 12th February 1871, Maria Edith McCoy (241) — d. 9th September 1902

203. b. 2nd November 1847* — Eliza Coffin Palmer Young
Simon Young (80) & Mary Buffett Christian (100)

204. b. 24th December 1847 — Almira Emeline Christian
Isaac Christian (90) & Miriam Young (108)
m. 21st May 1867, John McLiver (of Auckland, New Zealand) — d. in New Zealand

205. b. 7th February 1848 — Helen Amelia Quintal
William Quintal (68) & Maria Christian (67)
m. 1882, Charles Frederick Yager — d. 17th November 1921

206. b. 30th March 1848 — Cordelia Ruth Christian
Charles Christian III (69) & Charlotte Quintal (78)
m. 8th January 1865, Edward Quintal IV (182) — d. 26th November 1868

207. b. 29th April 1848 — William Wilburn Quintal
John Quintal II (73) & Dinah Young (87)
never married — d. 31st October 1852

208. b. 27th May 1848 — Sydney Herbert Nobbs (changed name to Sydney Nobbs Rawdon and died in England)
George Hunn Nobbs (102) & Sarah Christian (55)
m. (i) 3rd May 1869, Adeline Sophia Christian (173)
(ii) In England, Dora —— (of Canada)

209. b. 8th July 1848 +	Alice Sophia McCoy Matthew McCoy (72) & Margaret Christian (75) m. 23rd August 1871, Robert Young III (222)	d. 30th March 1851
210. b. 31st July 1848	Anna Rose Christian Thursday October Christian II (74) & Mary Young (89) never married	
211. b. 15th November 1848	George Calvin Clifton Adams Jonathan Adams (104) & Phoebe Quintal (84) never married	d. 14th September 1862
212. b. 16th January 1849	Mary Elizabeth Young Moses Young (109) & Albina McCoy (103)	d. 22nd August 1934
213. b. 24th March 1849	Rachel Hope Quintal Arthur Quintal II (66) & Martha Quintal (77) m. 21st December 1874, James Taylor (of England)	d. 18th July 1911
214. b. 19th April 1849	George Webb Adams John Adams II (97) & Caroline Quintal (96) m. (i) 1868, Abigail Leah Christian (219) (ii) 17th August 1881, Martha Coffin Quintal (born on Norfolk Island)	
215. b. 23rd July 1849	Eveline Helen Buffett John Buffett II (92) & Elizabeth Young (93) never married	d. 28th February 1929
216. b. 28th July 1849	Isaac Godfrey Christian Isaac Christian (90) & Miriam Young (108) m. 2nd July 1884, Frances Elizabeth Edwards	d. in New Zealand
217. b. 4th September 1849	Unnamed male child (Quintal) William Quintal (68) & Maria Christian (67) died one week after birth	d. 12th September 1849
218. b. 3rd October 1849	Hannah Quintal John Quintal II (73) & Dinah Young (87) m. 12th June 1865, Isaac Robinson	d. 24th August 1914
219. b. 21st October 1849	Abigail Leah Christian Fletcher Christian II (57) & Peggy Christian (64) m. 1868, George Webb Adams (214)	d. 12th December 1874

220. b. 28th October 1849	Lucy Ann Hagar Christian	d. 4th June 1909
221. b. 20th December 1849	Charles Christian III (69) & Charlotte Quintal (78) m. 17th October 1866, Phillip McCoy (115)	d. 15th November 1911
222. b. 6th January 1850	Eliza Sabia (Seabury) Adams Jonathan Adams (104) & Phoebe Quintal (84) m. 4th May 1878, Albert Victor Bataille (of Belgium)	d. 26th March 1872
223. b. 20th April 1850 +	Robert Young III Simon Young (80) & Mary Buffett Christian (100) m. 23rd August 1871, Alice Sophia McCoy (209)	d. 31st May 1941
	Charles Carleton Vieder Young Moses Young (109) & Albina McCoy (103)	d. 2nd May 1860
224. b. 18th September 1850	Robert Charles Grant Young George Martin Frederick Young (76) & Mary Evans (126) never married	
225. b. 24th December 1850	Charles William Grant Charles A. Grant Captain Grant left his wife on Pitcairn on 3rd July 1850 and picked her up again on 14th February 1851	
226. b. 8th January 1851	Mary Ann McCoy Matthew McCoy (72) & Margaret Christian (75) never married	
227. b. 21st January 1851	Francis (Fanny) Adelaide Quintal William Quintal (68) & Maria Christian (67) m. 28th November 1865, Gilbert Warren Fysh Adams (191)	d. 28th June 1912
228. b. 27th April 1851	Mary Isabel Adams Jonathan Adams (104) & Phoebe Quintal (84) m. 13th October 1875, Charles Richard Holmes Christian (261)	d. 27th August 1929
229. b. 13th July 1851	Fairfax Moresby Mitchell Quintal Abraham Blatchly Quintal (95) & Esther Maria Nobbs (121) m. 26th September 1895, Sarah Harriet Selwyn Quintal (born on Norfolk Island)	
230. b. 5th August 1851	Joseph Allen McCleave Buffett John Buffett II (92) & Elizabeth Young (93) m. 27th November 1873, Kathleen Laura Nobbs (262)	d. 19th January 1921

231.	b. 5th September 1851	Thomas Austin Buffett David Buffett (99) & Martha Young (110) never married	d. 10th February 1874
232.	b. 15th September 1851	Julia Etheline Quintal Arthur Quintal II (66) & Martha Quintal (77) never married	d. 16th November 1869
233.	b. 17th October 1851	Leonard Elliott Wood Christian Isaac Christian (90) & Miriam Young (108) m. (i) 18th August 1874, Mary Ellen Olivia Buffett (256) (ii) 12th July 1908, Eleanor Jane Sophia Nobbs (born on Norfolk Island)	d. 19th November 1926
234.	b. 28th October 1851	William Ward Dillon Adams John Adams II (97) & Caroline Quintal (96) m. 26th February 1874, Sarah Eliza Christian (born on Norfolk Island)	d. 19th December 1912
235.	b. 5th November 1851	Sarah Clara Quintal John Quintal II (73) & Dinah Young (87) m. 14th May 1873, William Champion	d. 31st December 1894
236.	b. 9th November 1851	Julia Anna Rose Christian Thursday October Christian II (74) & Mary Young (89)	
237.	b. 13th December 1851*	Benjamin Stanley Young Simon Young (80) & Mary Buffett Christian (100)	
238.	b. 30th January 1852	Emily Wellesley Christian Charles Christian III (69) & Charlotte Quintal (78) m. 6th January 1875, George Bailey	d. 11th January 1922
239.	b. 7th March 1852	David Richard Barker Young Moses Young (109) & Albina McCoy (103)	d. 14th March 1852
240.	b. 13th June 1852	John Forrester Young George Martin Frederick Young (76) & Mary Evans (126) m. 19th April 1876, Eliza Louisa (Lil) Nobbs (born on Norfolk Island)	d. 17th November 1913
241.	b. 26th August 1852	Maria Edith McCoy Phillip McCoy (115) & Sarah Quintal (131) m. 12th February 1871, Byron Stanley Mitchell Adams (202) the one-hundredth descendant of Fletcher Christian of H.M.S. *Bounty*	d. 28th September 1930

242. b. 3rd October 1852 — Mary Emily Christian
Benjamin Claudius Christian (120) & Eliza Quintal (127)

243. b. 19th January 1853 — Alice Maud Quintal   d. 22nd November 1856
m. 23rd August 1868, Alfred Augustine Nobbs (198)
William Quintal (68) & Maria Christian (67)
never married

244. b. 27th January 1853 — Augusta Ross Adams   d. 21st August 1899
Jonathan Adams (104) & Phoebe Quintal (84)
m. 3rd March 1874, George Henry Parkin Christian (254)

245. b. 5th April 1853 — Rebecca Holman Ascension McCoy   d. 28th May 1868
Matthew McCoy (72) & Margaret Christian (75)
never married

246. b. 12th May 1853 — Fortescue Moresby Buffett   d. 30th October 1927
David Buffett (99) & Martha Young (110)
m. 15th August 1875, Emma Quintal (196)

247. b. 20th May 1853 — Henry Chads Christian   drowned in Tasmania 1878
Jacob Christian (129) & Nancy Quintal (118)
never married

248. b. 31st May 1853 — Elizabeth Holman Adams   d. 2nd December 1868
John Adams II (97) & Caroline Quintal (96)
never married

249. b. 28th June 1853 — John Moresby Acland Quintal
Abraham Blatchly Quintal (95) & Esther Maria Nobbs (121)
m. Harriet Cawthray

250. b. 14th July 1853 — Emily Evangeline Buffett   d. 6th October 1899
John Buffett II (92) & Elizabeth Young (93)
m. 11th April 1883, George Rowland St. Clair Evans (born on
Norfolk Island)

251. b. 9th August 1853 — William Henry Holman Christian   d. 28th May 1868
Charles Christian III (69) & Charlotte Quintal (78)
never married

252. b. 13th August 1853 — Rosalind Amelia Young
Simon Young (80) & Mary Buffett Christian (100)
m. 27th November 1907, Rev. David Nield

253. b. 5th October 1853	Ernest Heywood Christian Thursday October Christian II (74) & Mary Young (89) m. Florence Buffett	d. 28th August 1940
254. b. 16th October 1853	George Henry Parkin Christian Isaac Christian (90) & Miriam Young (108) m. 3rd March 1874, Augusta Ross Adams (244)	d. 7th (14th ?) November 1853
255. b. 7th November 1853	Jacob Dyas Nobbs Fletcher Christian Nobbs (128) & Susan Quintal (130) died within a week of birth	d. 11th October 1895
256. b. 31st January 1854	Mary Ellen Olivia Buffett Thomas Buffett (88) & Louisa Quintal (106) m. 18th August 1874, Leonard Elliott Wood Christian (233)	d. 31st October 1914
257. b. 3rd July 1854	Angeline Ophelia McCoy Phillip McCoy (115) & Sarah Quintal (131) m. 16th January 1873, Edward Quintal IV (182)	d. 25th May 1855
258. b. 9th August 1854	Nancy Alice Prudence Quintal John Quintal II (73) & Dinah Young (87) never married	d. in New Zealand
259. b. 24th August 1854	Jonathan Lorenzo Adams Jonathan Adams (104) & Phoebe Quintal (84) never married	d. 24th January 1888
260. b. 2nd September 1854	Laura Agnes Evans William Evans (114) & Rebecca Christian (112) never married	drowned at Norfolk Island
261. b. 31st October 1854	Charles Richard Holmes Christian Benjamin Claudius Christian (120) & Eliza Quintal (127) m. 13th October 1875, Mary Isabel Adams (228)	d. 1st June 1930
262. b. 20th December 1854	Kathleen Laura Nobbs Fletcher Christian Nobbs (128) & Susan Quintal (130) m. 27th November 1873, Joseph Allen McCleave Buffett (230)	d. 27th July 1930
263. b. 26th December 1854	Emily Rachel Young George Martin Frederick Young (76) & Mary Evans (126) never married	

264. b. 5th January 1855	Caroline Augusta Adams John Adams II (97) & Charlotte Quintal (78) never married	d. 21st April 1855
265. b. 25th March 1855	Charles Allen Christian Charles Christian III (69) & Charlotte Quintal (78) m. 29th August 1877, Norah Leonora Nobbs (born on Norfolk Island)	d. 8th December 1910
266. b. 29th April 1855	Amelia Rosamond Quintal William Quintal (68) & Maria Christian (67) never married	d. 11th February 1868
267. b. 29th April 1855	Mary Louisa Quintal William Quintal (68) & Maria Christian (67) m. 15th December 1874, John Matthew Pattison Quintal (born on Norfolk Island)	d. in New Zealand
268. b. 3rd May 1855	Colin William Lyndsay Buffett John Buffett II (92) & Elizabeth Young (93) m. Annie Taylor (of England)	d. 8th September 1921
269. b. 5th June 1855	Mary Ann Young Simon Young (80) & Mary Buffett Christian (100) never married	
270. b. 27th July 1855	Daniel Christian Thursday October Christian II (74) & Mary Young (89) m. May 1871, Harriet Melissa McCoy (199)	
271. b. 24th September 1855	Nancy Alice Quintal John Quintal II (73) & Dinah Young (87) m. 1st August 1877, Henry Stephen Fremantle Quintal (276)	d. 5th March 1928
272. b. 29th October 1855	William Henry Hodgson Evans William Evans (114) & Rebecca Christian (112) m. 17th October 1883, Rachel Quintal (born on Norfolk Island)	d. 19th April 1926
273. b. 25th January 1856	Phoebe Cleaveline Adams Jonathan Adams (104) & Phoebe Quintal (84) never married	d. 15th June 1856
274. b. 4th February 1856	Marianne Scelina Buffett Thomas Buffett (88) & Louisa Quintal (106) m. 27th November 1873, Henry Seymour Buffett (200)	d. 1st March 1943

275. b. 9th February 1856 +
Sarah Grace Young
Moses Young (109) & Albina McCoy (103)
m. 24th May 1877, George Edwin Selwyn Young (born on Norfolk Island)
d. 1907

276. b. 5th March 1856
Henry Stephen Fremantle Quintal
Abraham Blatchly Quintal (95) & Esther Maria Nobbs (121)
m. 1st August 1877, Nancy Alice Quintal (271)

277. b. 19th April 1856
Priscilla Pitcairn Quintal
James Quintal (91) & Priscilla Christian (132)
never married
d. 5th April 1868

278. b. 9th May 1856
Reuben Denison Christian
Isaac Christian (90) & Miriam Young (108)
never married
born on *Morayshire* on the way to Norfolk Island
d. 24th April 1868

LIST OF PITCAIRNERS WHO LANDED AT TAHITI
IN 1831

Name	Age	Name	Age
George Adams	26	Dinah Quintal (*née* Adams)	32-37
Polly Adams (*née* Young)	32-37	William	14
John II	3.4	Martha	9
Jonathan	2.2	Edward II	6.5
Josiah Chester	0.9	Abraham Blatchly	4.2
Charles Christian I	c. 40	Louise	2.0
Fletcher II	c. 19	Edward Young II	32-37
Edward	16	Polly Young (*née* Christian)	17
Charles III	13	Moses	1.6
Mary	12	George Young	32-37
Margaret	9	Hannah Young (*née* Adams)	31
Isaac	5.11	George Martin Frederick	9
Charles Christian II	20	Simon	8
Maria Christian (*née* Christian)	15	Dinah	6.4
Rebecca	0.11	Elizabeth (Betsy)	4.6
Thursday October Christian I	40	Jemima	2.5
Teraura (Susannah)	c. 56	Martha	1.2
Joseph	25	William Young	32-37
Mary	c. 20	Elizabeth (Quintal) Young (*née*	
Mary Buffett Christian	2.6	Mills)	c. 40
Thursday October II	11	John (Quintal) I	c. 19
Daniel McCoy II	17	Matthew (Quintal) III	c. 17
Peggy McCoy (*née* Christian)	16	Mary (Polly)	6.2
Phillip	0.7	William Mayhew	3.3
Daniel McCoy I	c. 40	Miriam	1.7
Sarah McCoy (*née* Quintal)	32-37	John Buffett	33.7
William	c. 19	Dorothy (Dolly) Buffett (*née*	
Hugh	15	Young)	32-37
Matthew	12	Thomas	6.2
Jane	9	John II	4.8
Sarah	6.8	David	2.11
Samuel	4.5	Robert Pitcairn	1.0
Albina	2.5	John Evans	c. 27
Arthur Quintal I	32-37	Rachel Evans (*née* Adams)	32-37
Catherine Quintal (*née* McCoy)	31	John Valentine Mansell	2.2
Arthur II	15	William	0.7
Catherine	13	George Hunn Nobbs	32
John II	11	Sarah Nobbs (*née* Christian)	21
Charlotte	9	Reuben Elias	0.6
Phoebe	6.11	Mauatua (Maimiti—Isabella)	
James	5.8	Mary Ann Christian	38
Caroline	3.8	Toofaiti (Nancy)	
Ruth	1.11	Robert Young	32-37
Lucy Ann	newly born	Vahineatua (Prudence)	
Edward Quintal I	31		

APPENDIX III

LIST OF CHIEF MAGISTRATES ON PITCAIRN ISLAND 1838-1966

Year	Magistrate		Year	Magistrate	
1838	Edward Quintal		1855	George Martin Frederick Young	(Norfolk Island)
1839	Edward Quintal		1856	George Martin Frederick Young	(Norfolk Island)
1840	Arthur Quintal I		1857	George Martin Frederick Young	(Norfolk Island)
1841	Arthur Quintal I		1858	Isaac Christian	(Norfolk Island)
1842	Fletcher Christian II		1859	George Martin Frederick Young	(Norfolk Island)
1843	Matthew McCoy		1860	Thomas Buffett	(Norfolk Island)
1844	Thursday October Christian II		1861	Thomas Buffett	(Norfolk Island)
1845	Arthur Quintal II		1862	Arthur Quintal II	(Norfolk Island)
1846	Arthur Quintal II		1863	Arthur Quintal II	(Norfolk Island)
1847	Charles Christian III		1864	Arthur Quintal II	(Norfolk Island)
1848	George Adams		1864	Thursday October Christian II	(Pitcairn Island)
1849	Simon Young		1865	Moses Young	
1850	Arthur Quintal II		1866	Moses Young	
1851	Thursday October Christian II		1867	Thursday October Christian II	
1852	Abraham Blatchly Quintal		1868	Robert Pitcairn Buffett	
1853	Matthew McCoy		1869	Moses Young	
1854	Arthur Quintal II		1870	James Russell McCoy	

Chief Magistrates

1871	James Russell McCoy
1872	James Russell McCoy
1873	Thursday October Christian II
1874	Not Recorded
1875	Moses Young
1876	Thursday October Christian II
1877	Not Recorded
1878	James Russell McCoy
1879	James Russell McCoy
1880	Thursday October Christian II
1881	Moses Young
1882	Thursday October Christian II
1883	James Russell McCoy
1884	Benjamin Stanley Young
1885	Benjamin Stanley Young
1886	James Russell McCoy
1887	James Russell McCoy
1888	James Russell McCoy
1889	James Russell McCoy
1890	Charles Carleton Vieder Young
1891	Charles Carleton Vieder Young
1892	Benjamin Stanley Young
1905–06	James Russell McCoy
1907	Arthur Herbert Young
1908	William Alfred Young
1909	Edmund McCoy
1910–19	Gerard Bromley Christian
1920	Charles R. Parkin Christian
1921	Fred Christian
1922	Charles R. Parkin Christian
1923–24	Edgar Allen Christian
1925	Charles R. Parkin Christian
1926–29	Edgar Allen Christian
1930–31	Arthur Herbert Young
1932	Edgar Allen Christian
1933–34	Charles R. Parkin Christian
1935–39	Edgar Allen Christian
1940	Andrew David S. Young
1941	Frederick Martin Christian
1942	Charles R. Parkin Christian
1943	Frederick Martin Christian
1944	Charles R. Parkin Christian
1945–48	Henry Norris Young
1949	Charles R. Parkin Christian
1950–51	Warren C. Christian
1952–54	John Lorenzo Christian
1955–57	Charles R. Parkin Christian
1958–60	Warren C. Christian
1961–66	John Lorenzo Christian

Presidents of the Council

1893–96	James Russell McCoy
1897–	William Alfred Young
1898–04	James Russell McCoy
1904	William Alfred Young

BIBLIOGRAPHY

Books and Pamphlets

Alexander, J. H., *The Islands of the Pacific: From the Old to the New*. 1908.
Anonymous, *An Account of the Mutinous Seizure of the Bounty, with the Succeeding Hardships of the Crew*. (n.d.)
Anonymous, *Description of Pitcairn's Island and its Inhabitants*. 1839.
Anonymous, *Interesting Narratives and Discoveries*. 1813.
Anonymous, *Story of Bounty*. 1878.
Anonymous, *The Transformed Island: a Story of the South Seas*. 1854.
Anonymous, *Voyage Through the Islands of the Pacific Ocean*. 1824.
Anthony, I., *Saga of the Bounty, Its Strange History as Related by the Participants Themselves*. 1935.
Archer, F., *Recollections of a Rambling Life*. 1897.
Armstrong, Warren, *Mutiny Afloat*. 1956.
Australia, Department of Territories, *Norfolk Island Centenary Celebrations 1856-1956*.
Baarslag, Karl, *Island of Adventure*. 1944.
Bancroft, H. H., *New Pacific*. 1912.
Barnard, C. G., *Narrative of the Adventures . . . 1812-1816*. 1829.
Barrow, Sir John, *Eventful History of the Mutiny and Piratical Seizure of H.M.S. Bounty*. 1831. Also 1914 ed.
Bechervaise, J., *Thirty-six Years of a Seafaring Life, by an Old Quarter-Master*. 1839.
Becke, Louis, and Jeffery, Walter, *The Mutineer: A Romance of Pitcairn Island*. 1898.
Beechey, F. W., *Narrative of a Voyage to the Pacific . . .* , vol. i. 1831.
Belcher, Lady, *Mutineers of the Bounty*. 1870.
Bligh, William, *An Answer to Certain Assertions . . . 1794*. (In *Australiana Facsimiles*, vol. ii, published for the Australiana Society. 1952.)
Bligh, William, *Dangerous Voyage*. 1817.
Bligh, William, *A Narrative of the Mutiny on Board His Majesty's Ship Bounty*. 1790. (In *Australiana Facsimiles*, vol. ii. 1952.)
Brodie, Walter, *Pitcairn's Island and the Islanders in 1850*. 1851.
Brown, J. M., *Peoples and Problems of the Pacific*, vol. i. 1927.
Buck, P. H., *Vikings of the Sunrise*. 1938.
Burrows, M., *Pitcairn's Island*. 1853.
Campbell, J., *Maritime Discovery and Christian Missions*. 1840.
Campbell, J., *Norfolk Island and Its Inhabitants*. 1879.
"Captain, The", *The Mutiny of the Bounty, with History of the Survivors. . . .* 1936.
Carteret, Philip, "Voyage Round the World, 1766-9", in *Hawkesworth's Voyages*, vol. ii, 1823.
Carteret, Philip, "Passage from Masasuero to Queen Charlotte's Islands, 1767", in *Hawkesworth's Voyages*, vol. ii. 1823.
Casey, R. J., *Easter Island*. 1932.
Chauvel, C., *In the Wake of the Bounty*. 1933.
Chisholm, A. S. M., *Independence of Chile*.
Choyce, J., *The Log of a Jack Tar*.
Christian, Edward, *A Short Reply to Captain William Bligh's Answer*. 1795. (In *Australiana Facsimiles*, vol. ii, published for the Australiana Society. 1952.)
Christensen, A. H., *Heirs of Exile*. 1955.
Clark, C., *My Yarns of Sea-Foam and Gold-Dust*. 1897.
Clarke, W. K. L., *A History of the S.P.C.K.* 1959.
Coman, Katherine, *History of Contract Labor in the Hawaiian Islands*.
Cooper, Gordon, *Isles of Romance and Mystery*. 1949.
Danielsson, Bengt, *What Happened on the Bounty*. 1962.
Delano, A., *Narrative of Voyages and Travels in the Northern and Southern Hemispheres*. 1817.
Delano, A., *Pitcairn's Island*. 1819.

Dick, W. H., *Mutiny of the Bounty*. 1882.
Dundonald and Bourne, *Life of Thomas, Lord Cochrane*, vol. i, 1869.
Francis, B., *Isles of the Pacific*. 1882.
Fullerton, W. Y., *Romance of Pitcairn Island*. 1923.
Gessler, C., *The Leaning Wind*. 1943.
Hale, E. E., *Stories of the Sea*. 1880.
Hall, James Norman, *Shipwreck*. 1935.
Hawkesworth, John, *An Account of the Voyages . . . for making Discoveries in the Southern Hemisphere*. 1773.
Herbert, D., *Great Historical Mutinies*. 1876.
Heyerdahl, Thor, *Aku-Aku: The Secret of Easter Island*. 1958.
Hill, Joshua, *Memorandum* (signed copy in Dixson Library). 1841.
Hood, T. H., *Cruise in the Western Pacific*. 1863.
Howe, H., *Life and Death on the Ocean*. 1865.
Hurd, E. T., *The Wreck of the Wild Wave*. 1942.
Jackson, G. G., *Romance of Exploration*. 1930.
Johnson, Irving & Electra, *Western Bound in the Schooner Yankee*. 1936.
Johnson, Irving & Electra, and Edes, Lydia, *Yankee's People and Places*. 1956.
Jore, L., *Un Belge au Service de la France*. 1944.
Kotzebue, Otto von, *A New Voyage Round the World*, vol. i. 1830.
Lucas, Sir C., *The Pitcairn Island Register Book*. 1929.
McFarland, A., *Mutiny in the Bounty*. 1884.
Langdon, Robert, *Island of Love*. 1959.
Mackaness, George, *Life of Vice-Admiral William Bligh*. 1951.
Massachusetts Sabbath School Society, *Aleck and the Mutineers of the Bounty*. 1855.
Minutes of the Proceedings of the Court-martial . . . on ten persons charged with mutiny. . . . 1794. (In *Australiana Facsimiles*, vol. ii, published for the Australiana Society. 1952.)
Moerenhout, J.-A., *Voyages aux Iles du Grand Ocean*. 1837.
Murray, Hugh, *Adventures of British Seamen*. 1827.
Murray, Rev. Thomas, *Pitcairn, the Island, the People and the Pastor*. 1853.
Neill, J. S., *Ten Years in Tonga*. 1955.
Nicoll, M. J., *Three Voyages of a Naturalist*. 1908.
O'Brien, F., *Atolls of the Sun*. 1923.
Orlebar, J., *Midshipman's Journal During 1830*.
Parkinson, Sydney, *Journal of a Voyage to the South Seas*. 1773.
Pilling, H. G., *Report on a Visit to Pitcairn Island . . . 1929*. 1930.
"Poor Member of Christ, A", *Friday Christian: or the First-Born on Pitcairn's Island*. 1849.
Ross, A. S. C., *The Pitcairnese Language*. 1964.
Rowe, Newton A., *Voyage to the Amorous Island*. 1955.
Routledge, K., *Mystery of Easter Island*. 1919.
Rutter, C., *True Story of the Mutiny of the Bounty*. 1936.
Shapiro, Harry L., *Descendants of the Mutineers of the Bounty*. 1929.
Shapiro, Harry L., *Heritage of the Bounty*. 1936.
Shapiro, Harry L., *Robinson Crusoe's Children*. 1928.
Shillibeer, J., *Narrative of the Briton's Voyage to Pitcairn's Island*. 1817.
Shipley, C., *Sketches in the Pacific*. 1851.
Shoberl, F., *South Sea Islands*, vol. ii. (n.d.)
South Pacific Commission, *A Guide to Pitcairn*. 1963.
Stackpole, Edouard A., *The Sea Hunters*. 1953.
Staines, Sir T., & Pipon, P., *Interesting Report on the Only Remaining Mutineers of His Majesty's Ship Bounty, Resident on Pitcairn's Island in the Pacific Ocean*. (n.d.)
Suttor, H. M., *Australian Milestones*, vol. ii. 1925.
Vidil, Charles, *Histoire des Mutins de la Bounty et de l'Ile Pitcairn, 1789-1930*. 1932.
Ward, F. P. & M. L., *Come Ashore*. (n.d.)
Warren, Samuel, *The Paradise in the Pacific (Works of Samuel Warren*, vol. v). 1855.
Warren, T. Robinson, *Dust and Foam*. 1859.
Whipple, A. B. C., *Yankee Whalers in the South Seas*. 1954.
Wilkinson, C. S., *Wake of the Bounty*. 1953.
Wilks, Mark, *Tahiti*. 1844.
Williams, John, *Narrative of Missionary Enterprise in the South Sea Islands*. 1837.
Wilson, James, *Missionary Voyage to the Southern Ocean*. 1799.
Young, Rosalind, *Mutineers of the Bounty*. 1924.
Young, Rosalind, *Mutineers of the Bounty, the Pitcairn Islanders from 1859-80*. 1881.
Young, Rosalind, *Mutineers of the Bounty and Story of Pitcairn Island, 1790-1894*. 1924.

PERIODICALS

Bechervaise, E., "Mutiny of the Bounty", *Victorian Geographic Journal*, 1920.

Bladen, F. M., "Settlement of the Pitcairn Islanders on Norfolk Island", *Australian Historical Society Journal and Proceedings*, March 1906.

Brazier, Rev. B. F., "Norfolk Island", *Historical Society of Queensland Journal*, vol. ii, February 1920.

Bruce, H. W., "Voyage of H.M.S. Imogene", *Nautical Magazine*, November 1910.

Buffett, John, "Narrative of 20 Years Residence of Pitcairn's Island", *The Friend*, vol. iv, 1846.

Clark, R. P., "School on Pitcairn", *Atlantic Monthly*, April 1937.

Dorsenne, Jean, "Les Saints Mutins de Pitcairn", *Mercure de France*, vol. lxxiv, July-August 1908.

Eliott, L. S., "Romance of Pitcairn Island", *The Trident*, vol. i, no. 3, 1939.

Emory, K. P., "Stone Implements of Pitcairn Island", *Polynesian Society Journal*, vol. xxxvii, 1928.

Gerbault, A., "Les Peuplements de Mangareva, de Pitcairn, et de l'île de Pacques", *Société des Etudes Oceaniennes*, Bulletin 13, 1926.

Green, Marc T., "Lonely Isle", *Asia*, vol. xlv, December 1945.

Jones, Maude, "Pitcairn Islanders: An Attempt to Bring Them to Hawaii", *Hawaiian Annual for 1936*.

Keith, A., "Physical Characteristics of Two Pitcairn Islanders", *Man*, August 1917.

King, Henry, "Extract from the Journal of Captain Henry King of the Elizabeth", *Edinburgh Philosophical Journal*, vol. iii, 1820.

Macdonald, A., "Pitcairn Today", *Walkabout*, December 1938.

Macdonald, A. C., "Discovery of Pitcairn Island", *Australian Association for the Advancement of Science Report*, 1911.

Maddox, K., "Touching at Pitcairn", *Sydney University Medical Journal*, vol. xxix, August 1935.

Maude, H. E., "Tahitian Interlude", *Journal of the Polynesian Society*, vol. lxviii, no. 2, June 1959.

Maude, H. E., "In Search of a Home", *Journal of the Polynesian Society*, vol. lxvii, no. 2, June 1958.

Pipon, P., "The Descendants of the Bounty's Crew", *United Service Journal*, no. 63, 1834. (An abridgment of Pipon's MS. narrative, which is in the Mitchell Library.)

Raine, Thomas, "Visit to Pitcairn's Island in the Ship Surry, 1821", *Australian Magazine*, 1821.

Samuel, E., "Life on Pitcairn Island", *Man Junior*, March-May 1940.

Selwyn, Mrs S., "Visit to Norfolk Island in the Winter of 1856", *New Zealand Quarterly Review*, vol. i, no. 3, July 1857.

Shillibeer, J., "Pitcairn's Island", *Naval Chronicle*, 1817.

Trood, T., "Pitcairn and Norfolk Islands", *Sydney Quarterly Magazine*, 1892.

Waldegrave, W., "Recent Accounts of the Pitcairn Islanders", *Royal Geographical Society Journal*, vol. iii, 1833.

Were, Eric, "Ten Weeks on Pitcairn Island", *Australian Women's Weekly*, 27th November 1963.

Wiltshire, A. R. L., "Local Dialects of Norfolk and Pitcairn Islands", *Royal Australian Historical Society Journal*, vol. xxv, 1939.

Unsigned Articles

"Pitcairn Islanders in 1849", *Chambers Edinburgh Journal*, 1850.

"Present Condition of the Pitcairn Islanders", *Chambers Edinburgh Journal*, 1864.

"Christmas on Pitcairn Island", *Crown Colonist*, December 1936.

"Life on Pitcairn Island Today", *Crown Colonist*, December 1938.

"Tahiti and Pitcairn Islanders", *Evangelical Magazine and Missionary Chronicle*, vol. ii, March 1832.

"Account of the Mutinous Seizure of the Bounty", *General Magazine*, 1790.

"Pitcairn's Island", *The Mirror*, 1831.

"Pitcairn's Island", *The Mission Field*, 1856.

"Voyage of Her Majesty's Ship Actaeon, Captain the Rt. Hon. Lord Edward Russell, Valparaiso to the Marquesas, Sandwich, Tahiti and Pitcairn Islands", *Nautical Magazine*, vol. vii, 1838.

"Account of the Descendants of Christian and Other Mutineers of the Bounty", *Naval Chronicle*, January-June 1815.

"Another Account of the Descendants of the Mutineers of the Bounty", *Naval Chronicle*, January-June 1815.
"Mutineers of the Bounty", *Naval Chronicle*, January-June 1809.
"Mutineers of the Bounty", *Naval Chronicle*, January-June 1816.
"Pitcairn Island", *New Nation Magazine*, December 1930.
"A Virtuous Colony", *Once a Week*, 1865.
"Pitcairn: New Angles on the Old Story of the Bounty", *Pacific Islands Monthly*, January 1942.
"The Rev. G. H. Nobbs and the Pitcairn Islanders", Parish Annual, vol. viii, 1866.
"Recent Account of the Pitcairn Islanders", *Royal Geographical Society of London Journal*, vol. iii, 1833.
Analysis of List of Pitcairn Islanders landed in Tahiti, 23rd March, 1831: from a Letter of Capt. Sandilands, *Royal Geographical Society of London Proceedings*, vol. i, 1855-6, 1856-7.
"Narrative of a Voyage from Valparaiso to the South Sea Islands in Her Majesty's Ship Actaeon towards the end of the Year 1836", *United Service Journal*, 1838, part 1.
"Pitcairn Island, the Bounty's Crew", *Bengal Hurkaru*, 2nd October 1826 (reprinted in the *United Service Journal*, 1829, part 2).

General

Asiatic Journal, October 1822.
Gentleman's Magazine, vol. lxxxviii, July and December 1818.
National Geographic Magazine, January 1946, January 1949, December 1957.
Nautical Magazine, vol. ix, 1840.
Norfolk Island News (news sheets), 1958-65.
Norfolk Island Pioneer (newspaper), 1885-6.
Pacific Islands Monthly.
Pitcairn Miscellany (news sheet), 1959.
Quarterly Journal of Science and Art, vol. i, 1819.
Royal Australian Historical Society Journal.
South Pacific Commission Bulletins.

Cuttings

Letter from H. Carleton on the Offer of Land on Huahine to the Pitcairners, *The Shipping Gazette and Sydney General Trade List*, 19th October 1850.
"An Arcadia of the Pacific", Newspaper Cuttings, vol. 52, Mitchell Library.
"Old Story Retold, the Mutineer on Pitcairn", Newspaper Cuttings, vol. 136, Mitchell Library.
"South Sea Islands", Newspaper Cuttings, Mitchell Library.
"Ship Crusader touched at Pitcairn Island", *The Australian*, 13th October 1840.
Letter from William Quintal, 10th November 1839, *Journal of Commerce*, 10th September 1840 (reprinted in *The Australian*, 21st January 1841).
"Pitcairn's Island", *Illustrated London News*, 6th November 1852.
"Almost Certainly the Anchor of the Bounty . . . a Relic Raised from the Sea-bed after 150 Years", *Illustrated London News*, 26th August 1939.
"Account of Bounty Mutineers", *Sydney Gazette*, 27th October 1810.
"Account of Mutineers of the Bounty and their Descendants at Pitcairn Island", *Sydney Gazette*, 17th July 1819.
"Pitcairn Island Touched at by the Surry", *Sydney Gazette*, 2nd June 1821.
"Latest Account of Pitcairn's Island", *Sydney Morning Herald*, November 1844 (reprinted from *Friend of Temperance*).

MANUSCRIPTS

Adams, John, Autographed MS. narrative of the mutiny of the Bounty, given to Captain Beechey in December, 1825. Mitchell Library.
Anonymous, Journal of a voyage from London to New South Wales and V.D.'s Land 1820-1821—Visit of the Surry to Pitcairn Island, April 11, 1821. Mitchell Library.
Anonymous, Diary on Pitcairn Island 1851-53 (possibly that of Moses Young). Mitchell Library.
Bligh, William, Log of the Proceedings of His Majesty's Ship Bounty, Lieut. Mr. Bligh Commander from Otaheite towards Jamaica, vol. 2. Mitchell Library MS.
Bonwick Transcripts, series I, box 80. Mitchell Library.
Calder, J. E., Papers, Miscellaneous: Narrative of the wreck of the Essex. Mitchell Library.

Carteret, Philip, A voyage round the Globe in the Years 1766, 67, 68, & 69, by Philip Carteret, Commander of His Majesty's Sloop the Swallow. Dixson Library.
Dashwood, Y. F., View in Pitcairn's Island, January 1833, Drawing Book No. 2. Mitchell Library.
Folger, Mayhew, Log of the Topaz 1807-1809. Nantucket Whaling Museum.
Howard, Frederic, Letter to his sister Emily, 1856. Mitchell Library.
London Missionary Society, South Seas Letters. Mitchell Library.
Morrison, James, Journal. Mitchell Library.
Nobbs, G. H., Pitcairn Island Recorder, 1838. Mitchell Library.
Nobbs, G. H., Pitcairn Island Register 1790 to 1856-7. Dixson Library.
Nobbs, G. H., Nobbs Papers. Mitchell Library.
Quintal, William, List of original settlers. List of present inhabitants according to their seniority, May 13, 1853. Mitchell Library.
Ramsay, Dr, Scrap book of the log of the ship Surry. MS. in the possession of E. C. R. Raine, of Edgecliff, Sydney.
Ryder, Sir A. P., Remarks on places visited 1837-8. Mitchell Library.
Selwyn, Bishop, Papers. Auckland Museum and Library.

OFFICIAL RECORDS AND PAPERS

Colonial Office, Correspondence on the subject of the removal of the inhabitants of Pitcairn's Island to Norfolk Island, 1857.
Colonial Office, Further Paper, 1857.
Colonial Office, Correspondence with the Government of New South Wales re Pitcairn Islanders settled in Norfolk Island, 1863.
Colonial Office, Further Correspondence re condition of Pitcairn Island, 1901.
Rodwell, Sir C. H., Report on a Visit to Pitcairn Island, Great Britain and Ireland Colonial Reports Miscellaneous, No. 93, 1921.
Western Pacific High Commissioner for Pitcairn, Henderson, Ducie and Oeno Islands, Pitcairn Island Ordinances.
Discovery of Pitcairn Islanders: photostat and typescript copies of original letters in the Public Records Office, London. Mitchell Library.
Consular Dispatches and Papers relating to Pitcairn Islands, 1822-1827, 1837-39, Great Britain and Ireland, Foreign Office Consular Dispatches and Papers relating to the Pacific, 1822-1844, vols 1 & 4 (P.R.O. photostats from F.O.58). Mitchell Library.
Admiralty 1/5630-Y9, Moresby on Pitcairn, 31st December 1853.
Admiralty 1/6454, Reports on Pitcairn.
Admiralty 1/6489-Y161, Report of H.M.S. *Opal* on Pitcairn, with photograph of inhabitants.
1853 Dispatch 90, 3rd September, Consul Toup Nicolas, Petition of Inhabitants of Pitcairn Island to be removed to some other islands.
1853 Dispatch 42, Consul Nicolas, 16th December, answer to 90. Norfolk Island will be available for Pitcairn Islanders.
1854 Dispatch 14, Admiralty, 15th February, Moresby's letter with copy of one from Pitcairn Islanders to the Queen.
Historical Records of Australia, series I, Governors' Dispatches (for R. Darling's Dispatches, 1831-2, see vol. xvi).
United States Senate, Hearings Before the Committee on Immigration. 1921.

INDEX

INDEX